100 TRAILS of the

BIG SOUTH FORK

TENNESSEE & KENTUCKY

BIG SOUTH FORK

TENNESSEE & KENTUCKY

Hiking • Mountain Biking • Horseback Riding

Fourth Edition

RUSS MANNING

Published by
The Mountaineers
1001 SW Klickitat Way, Suite 201
Seattle, WA 98134

© 2000 by Russ Manning

First edition © 1989 as *The Best of the Big South Fork*. Second edition © 1990. Third edition © 1995 as *Trails of the Big South Fork National River and Recreation Area* by Russ Manning and Sondra Jamieson.

Published simultaneously in Great Britain by Cordee, 3a DeMontfort Street, Leicester, England, LE1 7HD

Manufactured in the United States of America

Project Editor: Christine Ummel Hosler
Editor: Carol Peschke
Maps by Ken Smith, Dana Peick
All photographs by Russ Manning, unless otherwise noted
Series cover and book design by Jennifer LaRock Shontz
Layout by Alice C. Merrill

Cover photograph: *The Cumberland River runs through the dense forest of the Big South Fork National River and Recreation Area in Tennessee.* © 1991 www.corbis.com/Pat O'Hara
Frontispiece: *Angel Falls Overlook*

Library of Congress Cataloging-in-Publication Data
Manning, Russ.
    100 trails of the Big South Fork : Tennessee and Kentucky / by Russ Manning.—
4th ed.
       p. cm.
    Rev. ed. of: Trails of the Big South Fork National River and Recreation Area. 3rd ed.
c1995.
    Includes bibliographical references and index.
    ISBN 0-89886-638-3 (pbk.)
    1. Hiking—Big South Fork National River and Recreation Area (Tenn. and Ky.)—
Guidebooks. 2. Trails—Big South Fork National River and Recreation Area (Tenn. and
Ky.)—Guidebooks. 3. Big South Fork National River and Recreation Area (Tenn. and
Ky.)—Guidebooks. I. Title: One hundred trails of the Big South Fork. II. Title: Trails of the
Big South Fork. III. Manning, Russ. Trails of the Big South Fork National River and Recre-
ation Area. IV. Title.
    GV199.42.B55 M36 1999
    796.51'0976871—dc21
                                                99-050715
                                                CIP

CONTENTS

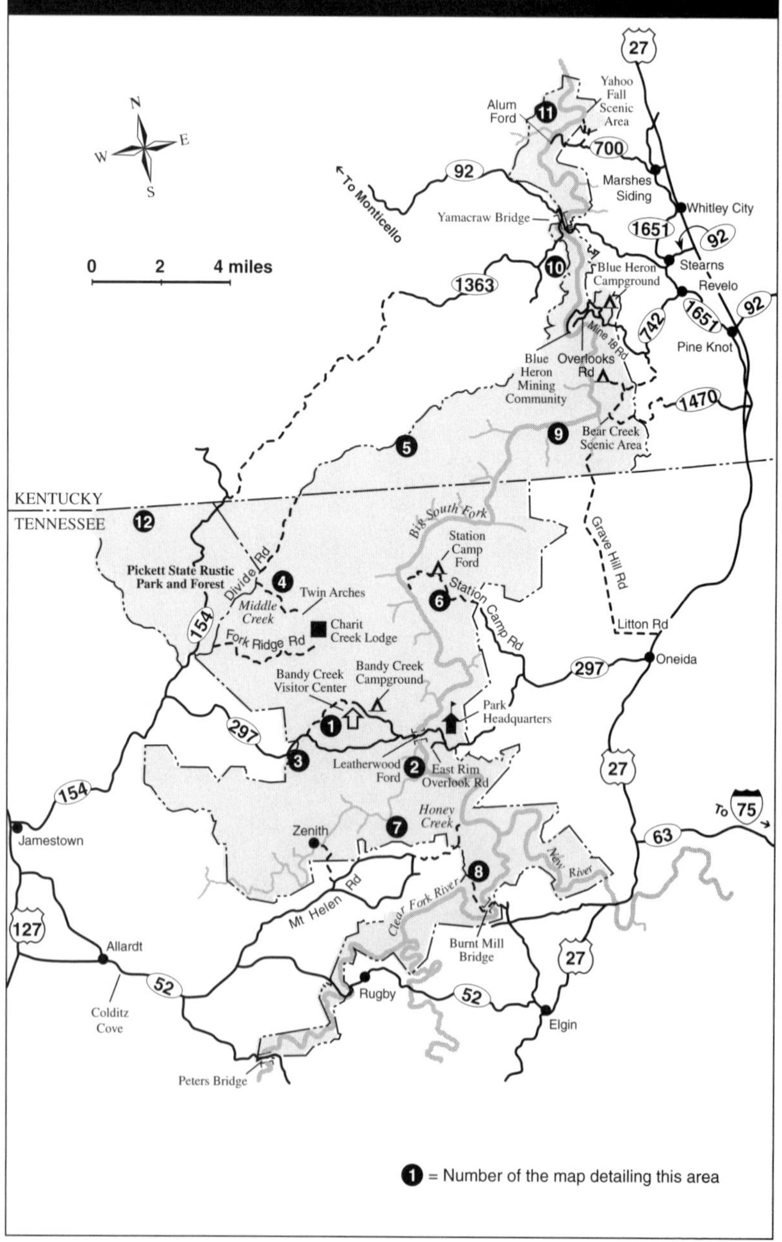

Big South Fork National River and Recreation Area
N
W E
S
0 2 4 miles
27
Yahoo Fall Scenic Area
Alum Ford
11
700
92
To Monticello
Marshes Siding
Whitley City
Yamacraw Bridge
1651
92
1363
10
Blue Heron Campground
Stearns
Revelo
Mine 18 Rd
742
1651
92
Blue Heron Mining Community
Overlooks Rd
Pine Knot
1470
KENTUCKY
TENNESSEE
12
5
Bear Creek Scenic Area
9
Big South Fork
Station Camp Ford
Grave Hill Rd
Pickett State Rustic Park and Forest
Divide Rd
4
Twin Arches
Middle Creek
6
Station Camp Rd
Litton Rd
154
Fork Ridge Rd
Charit Creek Lodge
297
Oneida
Bandy Creek Visitor Center
Bandy Creek Campground
1
Park Headquarters
297
3
Leatherwood Ford
2
East Rim Overlook Rd
27
154
To 75
Honey Creek
Jamestown
7
New River
Zenith
63
Mt Helen Rd
8
Clear Fork River
127
Allardt
Burnt Mill Bridge
27
52
Rugby
52
Colditz Cove
Elgin
Peters Bridge
1 = Number of the map detailing this area

ACKNOWLEDGMENTS

I am grateful to the National Park Service staff at the Big South Fork National River and Recreation Area for their support in the preparation of this book. Park ranger interpreter Howard Ray Duncan, National Park Service archeologist Tom Des Jean, and chief of interpretation Steven Seven provided valuable information about the park and the history of the region. I appreciate the support of former park ranger management assistant Ron Wilson.

Former chief of maintenance Fred Kelley, trail crew leader Wally Linder, roads and trails supervisor Palace Anderson, and former forestry technician Jeanne Richardson provided trail information.

I also thank Jeanne Richardson, Howard Ray Duncan, Wally Linder, Ron Wilson, and Fred Kelley for reviewing all or part of the early draft manuscript. Wally Linder provided valuable information on trails for this new edition.

I thank former Pickett State Rustic Park manager Billy G. Smith for reviewing the section on Pickett State Park and Forest.

KEY TO MAP SYMBOLS

———————	Paved Road	⬚ (dotted)	Gorge
———————	Secondary Road	■	Building (farm, stables, park office)
– – – – – –	Unpaved Road	⬤	Overlook
- - - - - - -	Trail	⬆	Ranger Station
86	Trail Number	⬆	Visitor Center
JMT	John Muir Trail	▲	Campground
———··———	Boundary (park or state)	Ⓢ	Trailhead (start)
∼∼∼∼	River or Stream	][	Bridge
●	City	⚊	Picnic Area

PREFACE

On the Cumberland Plateau in Tennessee, the Big South Fork of the Cumberland River flows north into Kentucky, draining some of the most primitive and isolated lands in the eastern United States.

Before there was a national river and recreation area, local people who loved the outdoors spent many seasons wandering the forests and exploring the gorges of the watershed. In those days, the Big South Fork was Tennessee's and Kentucky's best kept secret.

My first encounter was along the road from Oneida that crossed the river at Leatherwood Ford, now TN 297. Then, it was a gravel road that dipped precariously into the gorge and crossed the old wooden bridge that still spans the river. From Leatherwood Ford, I explored along the river one afternoon looking for Angel Falls. I expected a waterfall, but found instead a huge rapids where the water rushed downriver.

Later, I hiked to Twin Arches at a time when most people thought the idea of such a phenomenal geologic structure existing in Tennessee was preposterous, but it wasn't a tall tale, just hard to find. In the Kentucky portion of the watershed, I wandered through the site of the abandoned Blue Heron Mining Community; only the old rusting tipple, used to separate the coal, remained.

The threat of eventual development of this isolated area convinced many that the Big South Fork needed protection before its wilderness character was lost forever. This brought about the establishment of the Big South Fork National River and Recreation Area. Now tagged with a federal abbreviation (BSFNRRA), the Big South Fork is still a land of isolated river gorge, natural stone arches, numerous rock shelters, slender waterfalls, and old homesites linked by 300 miles of trails and many more miles of old roads. In this guide, I describe these routes for hiking, horseback riding, and mountain biking in the Big South Fork and surrounding area.

View from the Devils Jump Overlook

INTRODUCTION

The upper Cumberland Plateau area that encompasses the Big South Fork was originally occupied by a succession of Native American peoples, from the Paleo-Indians, through the Archaic and Woodland cultures, to the Mississippian tradition.

These early inhabitants were originally big-game hunters. By 1000 B.C., they had developed pottery and led a more refined existence, catching fish in the rivers and streams and gathering nuts and berries. Around A.D. 900, they began to grow some of their food and, by A.D. 1000, were experienced farmers, growing primarily corn and squash. This led the people to move to the broad, fertile river valleys away from the plateau country, which because of the topography and the marginal soil was not very good for growing crops.

By the time European settlers encountered the Native Americans of the southeastern United States, they had coalesced into the historic tribes. The Cherokees and Shawnees dominated the region. They did not live on the plateau but often hunted the area, using the caves and natural rock shelters as campsites.

The Native Americans lost their claim to the Southeast region, including the Cumberland Plateau, in several treaties forced on them in the late 1700s and early 1800s. Before and during this period, the descendants of the Europeans who had settled the eastern United States began to filter westward. Hunters were among the first to penetrate the plateau region. They and their descendants eventually settled the Big South Fork country, taking up subsistence farming.

When the first settlers arrived, they lived in the rock shelters the Native Americans had frequented, closing them off with leaning poles. They soon built pole cabins with dirt floors. Eventually, the homes became log cabins with split-log flooring, a loft or second story, and a stone chimney. The people lived by raising crops and livestock and by hunting.

During the period from 1812 to 1865, much saltpeter mining occurred in the rock shelters and caves of the plateau country. An ingredient in gunpowder, saltpeter was a precious commodity during the War of 1812 and the Civil War.

Coal mining and lumbering gradually became important economic activities, contributing to a steady increase in population. The last group of immigrants were the managers and workers who ran the railroads, coal mines, and lumbering operations of a large industrial development that occurred between 1900 and 1920. The largest operation in the Big South Fork region was the Stearns Coal and Lumber Company, founded in 1902 and eventually commanding many thousands of acres of land. In its peak year, the Stearns Company produced 1 million tons of coal and 18 million board feet of lumber.

With the Depression of the 1930s, the economic prospects of the region declined, never to recover. The coal company towns, lumber mills, and rail lines were abandoned. Stearns opened its Blue Heron Mine in 1938, and although the mine continued operation until 1962, the economic boom had already ended.

The camps and settlements eventually were abandoned. Only a few isolated farmsteads and homesites remained. Some coal mining continued, along with oil and gas exploration. But for the most part, the forest and river gorge were left in silence to heal.

A National River and Recreation Area Is Created

Federal involvement with the Big South Fork dates from 1881, when the Army Corps of Engineers conducted a study for improving navigation on the river. No action was taken.

Then in 1933, the Corps proposed a dam at Devils Jump, a rapids in a narrow part of the river gorge in Kentucky. The dam was originally projected to cost $200 million and would have been the highest dam in the East. Although proposed for Kentucky, the dam would have flooded the river gorge in Tennessee.

During the 1950s and 1960s, the Devils Jump Dam was authorized several times in the U.S. Senate but never passed the U.S. House of Representatives. Over the years, other studies recommended flood control lakes, dams at other sites, and pump storage facilities.

In 1966, a local conservation group, Tennessee Citizens for Wilderness Planning (TCWP), set out to find permanent protection for the Big South Fork and to put to rest the dam and lake proposals that kept being resurrected. TCWP first tried to get the Big South Fork included in the Tennessee Scenic Rivers Bill that was soon to pass the state legislature. But when the bill passed in 1968, the Big South Fork was excluded from the list of rivers.

Then TCWP turned its attention to an impending national bill. An early study by the now-defunct Bureau of Outdoor Recreation had designated the Big South Fork as worthy of being included in a National Wild and Scenic Rivers Bill. But when the national bill was passed, also in 1968, the Big South Fork was again excluded.

Because of the public interest generated by TCWP, Congress requested new studies on the Big South Fork. One was to examine new dam proposals and a second was to study alternatives. The Corps of Engineers, the Bureau of Outdoor Recreation, the U.S. Forest Service, and the National Park Service (NPS) were to be involved in the studies.

TCWP acted as an advisory group for the alternatives study, which presented several suggestions for how to preserve the Big South Fork, including national recreation area, national forest, national park, and scenic river. With the public sentiment apparently behind saving the river, the decision was made not to publish a dam study.

During this time, TCWP gained strength by forming the Big South Fork Coalition, a union of various conservation groups. The group was headed by Liane Russell, a research geneticist living in Oak Ridge who, along with her husband, Bill Russell, also a research geneticist, helped found TCWP.

The coalition worked with then-Senator Howard Baker, Jr., to draft a bill calling for a combination of national river and national recreation area. Introduced in 1972 as part of a water resources bill, the legislation would have automatically given the Army Corps of Engineers authority over the proposed new area. The bill was pocket-vetoed by President Richard Nixon for reasons having nothing to do with the Big South Fork.

The Big South Fork Coalition took advantage of this delay by rewriting the bill so that management of the area would be turned over to the NPS after establishment by the Corps of Engineers. The coalition thought the NPS would bring more experience in preservation and conservation to the task of managing the proposed new national river and recreation area.

The legislation was reintroduced as part of the 1974 Water Resources Development Act. Passed and then signed into law on March 7, this act authorized the Big South Fork National River and Recreation Area (BSFNRRA), encompassing 123,000 acres.

By the time the national river and recreation area was authorized, only about forty households of year-round residents still lived within the proposed boundaries. Their lands were purchased for the establishment of the park.

These last inhabitants of the Big South Fork watershed had been living primarily on subsistence farms. Growing crops, raising livestock, gathering nuts and berries, hunting, trapping, fishing, and building their own homes were all part of their lifestyle. The farms occasionally included a fenced-off rock shelter as a holding area for livestock.

In the intervening years, the Army Corps of Engineers also laid out trails and built visitor facilities as funding became available. The NPS took over management on an interim basis as pieces were completed.

In November 1990, the U.S. Congress passed legislation authorizing the official transfer of the park to the NPS. The transfer from the Corps of Engineers to the NPS was officially recognized on August 25, 1991, at the dedication of the new park headquarters building. The ceremony was also a symbolic dedication of the BSFNRRA.

GETTING THERE

The BSFNRRA lies atop the Cumberland Plateau west of I-75 between Lexington, Kentucky, to the north and Knoxville, Tennessee, to the south.

From the north on I-75, approach the Kentucky portion of the BSFNRRA by exiting at Mount Vernon and taking KY 461 and then KY 80 southwest to Somerset and turning south on US 27. You'll eventually reach a west turn on KY 92 toward the community of Stearns. The Big South Fork Kentucky Visitor Center lies off to your right soon after the turn. In Stearns, take KY 1651 south to Revelo and turn right on KY 742, which becomes

Getting to the Big South Fork

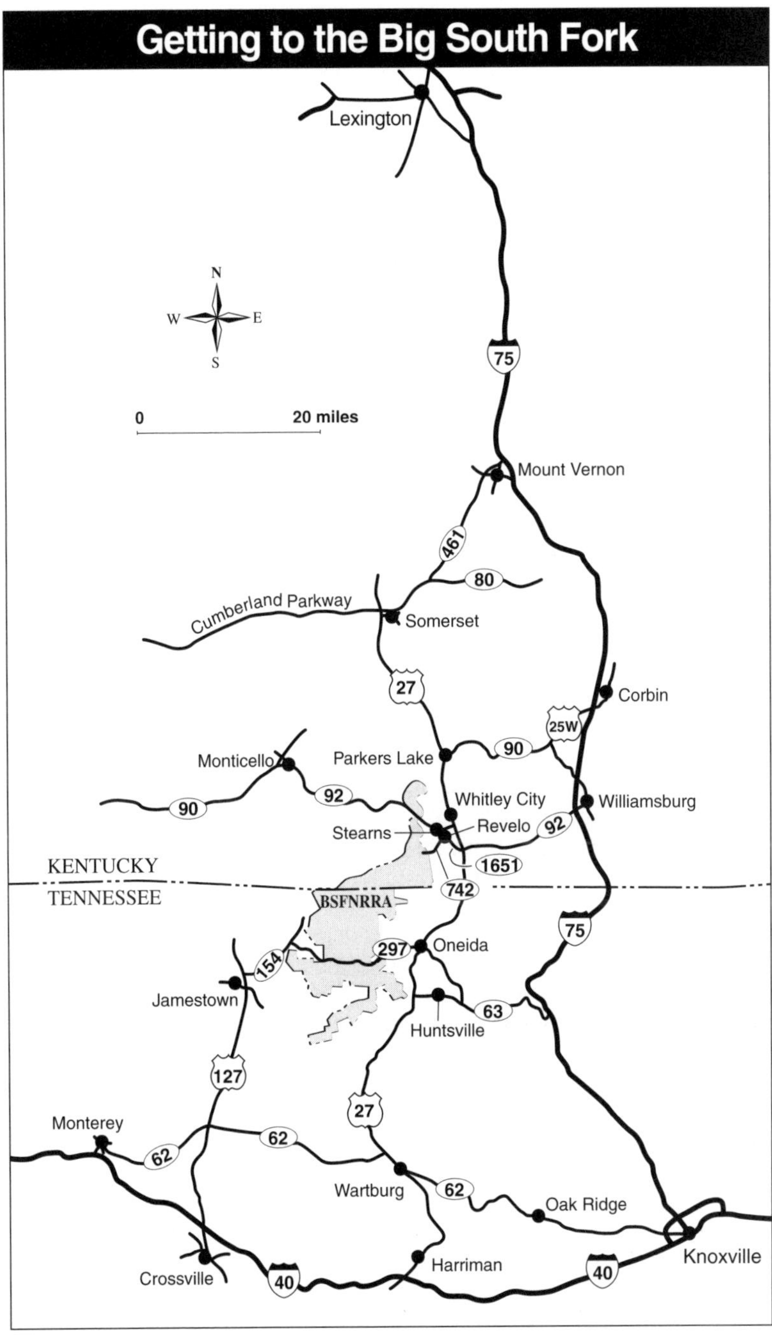

Mine 18 Road, to get to the Blue Heron Mining Community. You can also reach the park from the north on I-75 by exiting onto US 25W near Corbin and heading southwest to a turn west on KY 90 to US 27 and then turning south toward Stearns.

Traveling from the west in Kentucky, go east on the Cumberland Parkway to Somerset and then south on US 27 toward Stearns. Or you can take KY 90 east and then, in Monticello, pick up KY 92, which eventually crosses the Yamacraw Bridge over the Big South Fork and leads into Stearns.

To approach the Tennessee portion of the park from the north or the south, take TN 63 west from the I-75 exit for Huntsville and Oneida. Pass through Huntsville and reach US 27, then turn north to Oneida, where you'll pick up TN 297, which to the west enters the park, crosses the Big South Fork River at Leatherwood Ford, and goes by a turn to the Bandy Creek Visitor Center.

If you are traveling from the west in Tennessee on I-40, get off at the Monterey exit, pick up TN 62, and continue east to a junction with US 127. Turn north to Jamestown; continue north and turn northeast on TN 154. At TN 297, turn east to reach the Bandy Creek Visitor Center. Farther east on I-40, pick up US 127 headed north at the Crossville exit; even more to the east, you can reach Oneida and the east side of the park by taking US 27 north from the Harriman exit. From the Oak Ridge area, take TN 62 northwest to Wartburg, then pick up US 27 headed north.

GEOLOGY OF THE BIG SOUTH FORK

At one time, a sea covered portions of what are now Tennessee and Kentucky. Great deltas formed where rivers flowing from Appalachian highlands to the east met this sea along a shoreline in the area that would become the Cumberland Plateau.

About 300 million years ago, a final episode of Appalachian mountain building began. The new mountains that formed in the east eroded quickly, depositing a layer of sand and gravel more than 100 feet thick over the entire delta system of what was to be the plateau region. Later, the shoreline settled and the sea reinvaded, dropping its silt. This cycle of mountain building to the east, followed by erosion and deposition of sediment, repeated in several pulses over millions of years during a time geologists call the Pennsylvanian Period.

Under the increasing weight, these piled-up layers consolidated into rock. The thick sand and gravel layer first laid down eventually became erosion-resistant Pennsylvanian sandstone.

Later, the land rose high above sea level in three intervals of secondary uplift as less dense rock below was forced upward by surrounding dense rock. Erosion immediately began lowering these new mountains but slowed when the resistant Pennsylvanian sandstone was encountered. So after millions of years of erosion, a plateau still stands 2,000 feet above sea level. Called the Cumberland Plateau in Tennessee and Kentucky, it is part

Cracks-in-the-Rocks

of the Appalachian Plateaus Province that stretches from the southern border of New York to central Alabama.

Waters gather on the surface of the plateau to form streams, creeks, and rivers. The Clear Fork and New Rivers converge to create the Big South Fork, which then flows north across the Cumberland Plateau to join the Cumberland River in Kentucky. The river system carves a deep gorge, exposing the resistant sandstone layers in the bare rock walls that line the rim. Side streams flow over breaks in the sandstone to form waterfalls. In exposed hillsides and ridges, erosion sweeps away soft layers under the hard sandstone, creating numerous rock shelters and natural sandstone arches. These geologic features make the Big South Fork one of the most interesting areas for outdoor recreation in the eastern United States.

The rock shelters of the region played a primary role in the human history of the Big South Fork area, being used for everything from hunting camps and livestock pens to schools and out-of-the-way meeting places for union organizers during the times of mining and lumbering. When you pass through these areas, leave them undisturbed. Digging and rummaging around in the shelters diminishes their value as an archaeological record.

FLORA AND FAUNA

Nearly all the forests of the Cumberland Plateau have been altered by fire, logging, coal mining, and agriculture. But in many places, such as the Big South Fork, second-growth timber has reclaimed the disturbed land, and small pockets of old-growth forest remain in secluded coves and ravines.

The plateau forest of today consists of two distinct communities. The uplands forest inhabits the tableland area, including mountainous regions where overlying beds of soil and stone have yet to erode down to the capstone rock. In these mountains, pine and oak grow on shallow, sandy soils along dry ridgetops, and on the more moist slopes the mixed pine and oak forest also contains occasional sugar maple, basswood, buckeye, poplar, and beech. The tableland area is dominated by a mixed oak forest. Along streams and marshy areas, the oaks are interspersed with poplar, red maple, black gum, and sourwood.

Whereas the uplands forest is fairly uniform, the plateau gorges are occupied by a more varied ravine forest in which several tree species are dominant. The Big South Fork flows through such a complex forest. Distinct climax communities (stable communities of plants that are able to perpetuate themselves) have developed because of differences in elevation, slope exposure, and moisture.

From the edge of the river gorge, thickets of pine, chestnut oak, sourwood, and various shrubs begin the progression of forest communities. The forest on the rim is patrolled by white-tailed deer. The pine warbler and red-breasted nuthatch forage for conifer seeds and insects. Hawks and crows nest in the trees. Hairy woodpeckers, common flickers, and pileated woodpeckers search the trees for insects. The pine seeds are food for the red crossbill, evening grosbeak, bobwhite, turkey, gray squirrel, eastern chipmunk, and white-footed mouse. The eastern cottontail romps in bushy areas.

The massive walls of the gorge stand bare except for a few irregularities in the rock surface that provide footholds for alum root, a few ferns, and small wind-swept pines. Vultures, eastern phoebes, and swallows nest in precarious crevices in the cliff face; an occasional bat clings to the underside of a rock overhang. The red-tailed hawk surveys the gorge from a perch, and the timber rattlesnake and northern copperhead bask in the bright sun.

From the base of the walls, the south-facing slopes descend, clothed in mixed oak communities where turkey, gray squirrel, and opossum are attracted to the mast and thick undergrowth. The wood thrush, hooded warbler, and downy woodpecker frequent the understory, and the red-eyed vireo, scarlet tanager, and tufted titmouse feed in the canopy.

Indian Rock House

In the heads of gorges and shaded coves of the north-facing slopes, where understory and groundcover are inhibited, hemlock and rhododendron live in virtual solitude except for a passing deer, bobcat, or fox. Pine and black-poll warblers and the golden-crowned kinglet search for seeds and insects in the canopy.

A forest of sugar maple, beech, poplar, basswood, ash, and buckeye on the low moist slopes provides refuge for gray fox, skunk, and raccoon. The barred owl and red-shouldered hawk search for the smoky shrew, eastern mole, eastern wood rat, white-footed mouse, and eastern chipmunk.

Along the floor of the gorge persists an alluvial forest of sycamore and river birch with wild oats and dense stands of cane; beaver and muskrat, maybe even mink and otter, live along the river. The Louisiana waterthrush, spotted sandpiper, and American woodcock explore the wet sand. Recent floods have left debris hanging in the limbs of shrubs and trees along the riverbank.

A gravel and rubble zone possessing a few shrubs edges the river. The strip is inhabited by the bullfrog, southern leopard frog, pickerel frog, water snake, and midland painted turtle. Deer and other large species come to the stream for water as wood ducks paddle by. In the water, riverweed grows on rocks with diatoms and algae in association. These support the zooplankton and aquatic insects that are food for the bluebreast darter, rainbow trout, longear sunfish, and smallmouth bass. Belted kingfishers skim the surface, and green herons lunge for fish and amphibians. Rough-winged swallows, eastern phoebes, and bats feed on the congregating insects.

These plant and animal communities overlap and intermingle to form a single rejuvenated forest.

TRAILS OF THE BIG SOUTH FORK

There are 300 miles of trails in the national river and recreation area. Some are for hiking only. Horse trails may also be used by hikers and mountain bikers. A few designated bike trails may be used only by mountain bikers and hikers.

The hiking trails in the Big South Fork are marked with a red arrowhead in a white blaze, with the exceptions of the John Muir Trail (JMT), which has a blue silhouette of Muir on a white blaze; the Sheltowee Trace, which has a white or sometimes blue turtle and white diamonds; the Yahoo Falls trails, which have yellow, green, and blue arrowheads in a white blaze; and occasionally a connector trail that has an arrowhead blaze of blue or gray.

Horse trails have the yellow or orange silhouette of a horse's head on a white blaze. Mountain bike trails are blazed with orange arrows on posts or white arrows on brown metal signs or bicycle images on small wooden signs; these trails are blazed one-way for safety. Horse riders and mountain bikers should not ride off trail.

Once at the trailhead, you should be able to find your way by following the trail descriptions and reading the signs at most trail junctions. Always let someone know where you are going. If you get lost, do not leave the trail.

Some of the routes described in this book cover old roads and paths that are proposed trails. These have no blazes and no signs, so there is always a chance of getting lost. I have included a few of these trails for experienced hikers and explorers. Please do not attempt these trails if you are new to outdoor recreation. If you travel these trails, pay attention to where you are going so you can at least retrace your steps to get back out if you lose your way. *You are expected to assume full responsibility for knowing where you are going and for not getting lost.*

Short Walks

Found throughout the national river and recreation area, short walks provide quick and usually easy access to various attractions. If you have only a brief time to spend in the park or are a beginner to hiking, you'll get a taste of what's waiting for you by taking one or two of these short walks.

The 0.4-mile **Riverwalk** at Leatherwood Ford on TN 297 leads along the shore of the river. Start at the information gazebo and take the path and steps down toward the old Leatherwood Ford Bridge and turn right on the paved walkway. The trail includes boardwalks, benches, and bridges scattered among patches of sand, river rock, and alluvial forest. The boardwalks and platforms are built so low that they are often submerged when the river is at flood stage; at high water, use caution walking along the river.

The 0.1-mile **East Rim Overlook Trail,** from the end of the East Rim Overlook Road across from the park headquarters on TN 297, goes down a paved walkway to a platform view of the Big South Fork Gorge.

The 0.4-mile **Yamacraw Loop** drops beside a tumbling stream and passes along the river shore. From Stearns, take KY 92 west to the crossing of the Big South Fork and turn right into the Yamacraw Day Use Area just before the Yamacraw Bridge. The loop first follows the Sheltowee Trace north but soon turns left off the trace to drop to the edge of the river; the turn is not signed. Along the river, the trail parallels an old dirt road that circles back under the highway bridge and ascends to meet the other end of the parking area; most hikers use the road, so the trail has become overgrown.

The 0.1-mile **Devils Jump Overlook Trail** leads to a broad platform at the gorge rim and a view of the Devils Jump Rapids in the river far below. Turn west on the Overlooks Road off the Mine 18 Road on the way to the Blue Heron Mining Community. At 1.1 miles, you'll see the parking area for the overlook on the left.

At the end of the Overlooks Road, 0.3 mile beyond the Devils Jump Overlook, you'll find a turnaround loop and parking for the 0.2-mile **Blue Heron Overlook Trail** that leads to a panoramic overlook of the gorge. Just before reaching the overlook, you'll see a trail to the right that has a blue arrowhead blaze. This trail descends the bluff in a series of stairs to connect with the Blue Heron Loop in 0.1 mile.

At the Blue Heron Mining Community, you can walk the **Blue Heron Exhibit Trail** from the depot/museum. The 0.2-mile Loop A of the trail begins across the road from the depot and leads by exhibits and then crosses the road to loop back to the depot. On the 0.3-mile Loop B to the right of the depot, you'll pass several interpretive buildings, the Mine 18 entrance, and the east end of the tipple bridge; a side trail blazed with a gray arrow leads 0.2 mile along the old tramroad to the former powder magazine, where the mining company stored explosives.

To get to the 0.2-mile **Bear Creek Overlook Trail,** turn south off the Mine 18 Road that leads down to the Blue Heron Mining Community at a sign directing you to the Bear Creek Scenic Area, and follow additional signs 3.6 miles to the scenic area. From the parking area, the trail leads through

School replica at Blue Heron

an abandoned field and then the woods to a platform overlook offering a sweeping view of the Big South Fork Gorge.

VISITING THE BIG SOUTH FORK

Your trip to the Big South Fork will be safer and more enjoyable if you come well prepared. Even if you are out for only a short time, wear walking shoes or boots. Always bring water, a lunch or snacks, and rain gear. The Mountaineers recommends that you take the "Ten Essentials" with you on every hike: extra clothing, extra food, sunglasses with UV protection, a knife, a first-aid kit, matches in a waterproof container, some firestarter (candle or chemical fuel), a flashlight, a map, and a compass. In this part of the country, raingear is also essential. A plastic sheet or emergency blanket may also come in handy.

If you are camping, you'll need everything for surviving in the open overnight and for as many days as you plan to be out. If you are inexperienced, the park rangers or your local outfitters can advise you on the equipment needed. Pets are allowed but must be on a leash at all times; consider leaving them at home.

Check the topographical maps that cover your area. The maps in this book are designed to help you with the general route and trail connections; they do not provide detailed navigating. At the minimum, you should bring a trail map that gives you an overall view of the park and the trail connections, available at the visitor centers.

Precautions

Be especially careful climbing on rocks, hiking or riding along the edge of bluffs, crossing streams, and passing near the river. Do not climb on waterfalls. *You are expected to take full responsibility for your own safety, keeping in mind that being in a wilderness setting far from medical attention is an inherently hazardous activity.* It is best to travel with someone; if one of you is hurt, the other can care for the injured and then go for help.

The northern copperhead and the timber rattler live here; always watch where you put your feet and hands, and give snakes a wide berth. On warm spring and summer days, the gnats, black flies, and mosquitoes can be a bother, so carry along insect repellent. Before starting a hike, spray your shoetops, socks, legs, and pants with repellent to discourage ticks; one type, the deer tick, can transmit a spirochete that causes Lyme disease. Remember to check yourself after a hike.

Stream crossings can be easy or difficult. After a heavy rain, some streams can become swollen with rushing water. Do not attempt to cross such a stream unless you are sure you can make it. If you cannot see the bottom, you probably should not try to ford.

In cold and wet weather, you face the danger of hypothermia. The symptoms are uncontrollable shivering, slurred speech, memory lapse, stumbling, fumbling hands, and drowsiness. If you are wet and cold, get under some shelter, change into dry clothes, and drink warm fluids. Get in a sleeping bag, if one is available. To prevent hypothermia, stay dry, eat even if you are not hungry, and drink water even if you are not thirsty.

Finally, hunting is allowed in the park, subject to the regulations of the states of Kentucky and Tennessee. Check at the visitor centers or with any ranger to determine whether hunting is going on; always wear bright clothing during hunting seasons.

Camping

The Bandy Creek Campground is located in the Tennessee portion of the park near the Bandy Creek Visitor Center, north of TN 297 on the west side of the river; reservations may be made (see Appendix for phone number and website address). The smaller Blue Heron Campground is in the Kentucky portion of the park, north of Mine 18 Road on the way to the Blue Heron Mining Community on the east side of the river. New equestrian camps are located at Station Camp East on the Station Camp Road in Tennessee and at the Bear Creek Scenic Area off KY 742 in Kentucky; reservations may be made for the equestrian camps (see Big South Fork Horse Camps in Appendix). These are all fee campgrounds.

Kentucky View

There's also primitive camping at Alum Ford at the end of KY 700 at the northern end of the park.

If you plan to camp in the backcountry, let a ranger know your plans, even though registration is not required. You may camp virtually anywhere, but set up at least 25 feet from trails, gravel and dirt roads, rock shelters, the gorge rim, and major geologic and historic features; at least 100 feet from streams and paved roads; and at least 200 feet from trailheads, parking lots, and cemeteries. Leave flowers, rocks, and other natural features undisturbed. Select campsites for minimal impact.

You may use only dead and down timber from outside the camp area for campfires. Keep fires small, and use only existing fire rings; build fires only where safe and legally permitted. Consider using a stove even where wood fires are permitted. Hang your food at night to keep it away from animals (4 feet from the tree trunk and 10 feet off the ground).

Boil all water in the backcountry at least 1 minute before drinking it to destroy bacteria and other microorganisms, including *Giardia lamblia*, a flagellate protozoan causing an intestinal disorder called giardiasis. Filters and water-purifying tablets can be used, but ask your supplier for ones that remove *Giardia*.

There are no backcountry toilets. Bury your waste at least 6 inches deep and at least 200 feet away from trails, water sources, and campsites. Pack out all trash and litter, including toilet paper.

HOW TO USE THIS BOOK

The trail descriptions in this book begin with those near the Bandy Creek Visitor Center, which is the first destination for most visitors new to the park. The trail descriptions then spread out from this central location and are grouped by access point. The accompanying maps are designed to help you find the access points and the trailheads. The trail numbers correspond to the numbers on the maps.

Each trail name is accompanied by an icon representing its intended use: ⫘ for hiking only; ⬳ for mountain biking and hiking; and ∩ for horseback-riding, mountain-biking, and hiking.

For each trail description, the distance is given, indicating one-way whenever the trail is not a loop. For those who prefer short outings, the distance is also provided to an attraction part way that can be a closer destination.

There is also a rating of easy, moderate, or strenuous. This difficulty rating is based on a subjective judgment of the strenuousness of the trail. Although a 10-mile trail would be difficult for anyone not used to hiking, it might be rated easy if it is fairly level, has no creek crossings, and is easy walking. So look not only at the degree of difficulty, but also at the distance.

The elevation gain or loss for a trail indicates the difference in elevation between the trail's highest and lowest points, usually at the beginning or end of the hike. But there could be several ups and downs along the way. *Elevation change* indicates the difference between the lowest and highest points on a loop trail, because if you are covering a loop, you will gain and lose the same elevation. *Elevation change* is also used when the hike is one-way but a high or low point is along the trail rather than at one end.

Cautions are listed about obstacles you might encounter on the trail, such as creek crossings, rocky footing, mudholes, and steep climbs and descents. Trail connections are included so you may combine several trails for longer outings.

After briefly mentioning the trail's attractions and giving directions to the trailhead, the description tells what you'll encounter along the trail. The mileages given in the descriptions are almost always cumulative. If you want to hike or ride a trail in the reverse direction from the description, it probably will be helpful to calculate the reverse mileages.

A NOTE ABOUT SAFETY

Safety is an important concern in all outdoor activities. No guidebook can alert you to every hazard or anticipate the limitations of every reader. Therefore, the descriptions of roads, trails, routes, and natural features in this book are not representations that a particular place or excursion will be safe for your party. When you follow any of the routes described in this book, you assume responsibility for your own safety. Under normal conditions, such excursions require the usual attention to traffic, road and trail conditions, weather, terrain, the capabilities of your party, and other factors. Because many of the lands in this book are subject to development and/or change of ownership, conditions may have changed since this book was written that make your use of some of these routes unwise. Always check for current conditions, obey posted private property signs, and avoid confrontations with property owners or managers. Keeping informed on current conditions and exercising common sense are the keys to a safe, enjoyable outing.

—*The Mountaineers*

Map 1. Bandy Creek

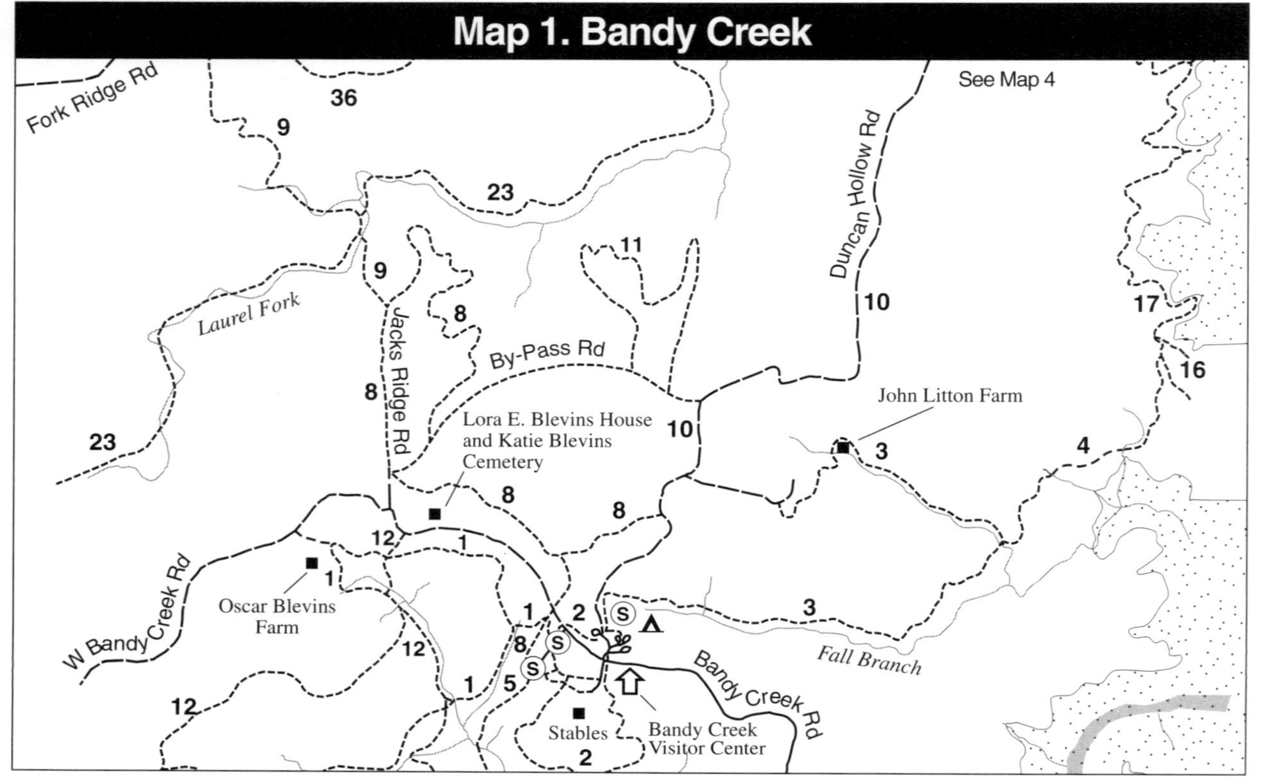

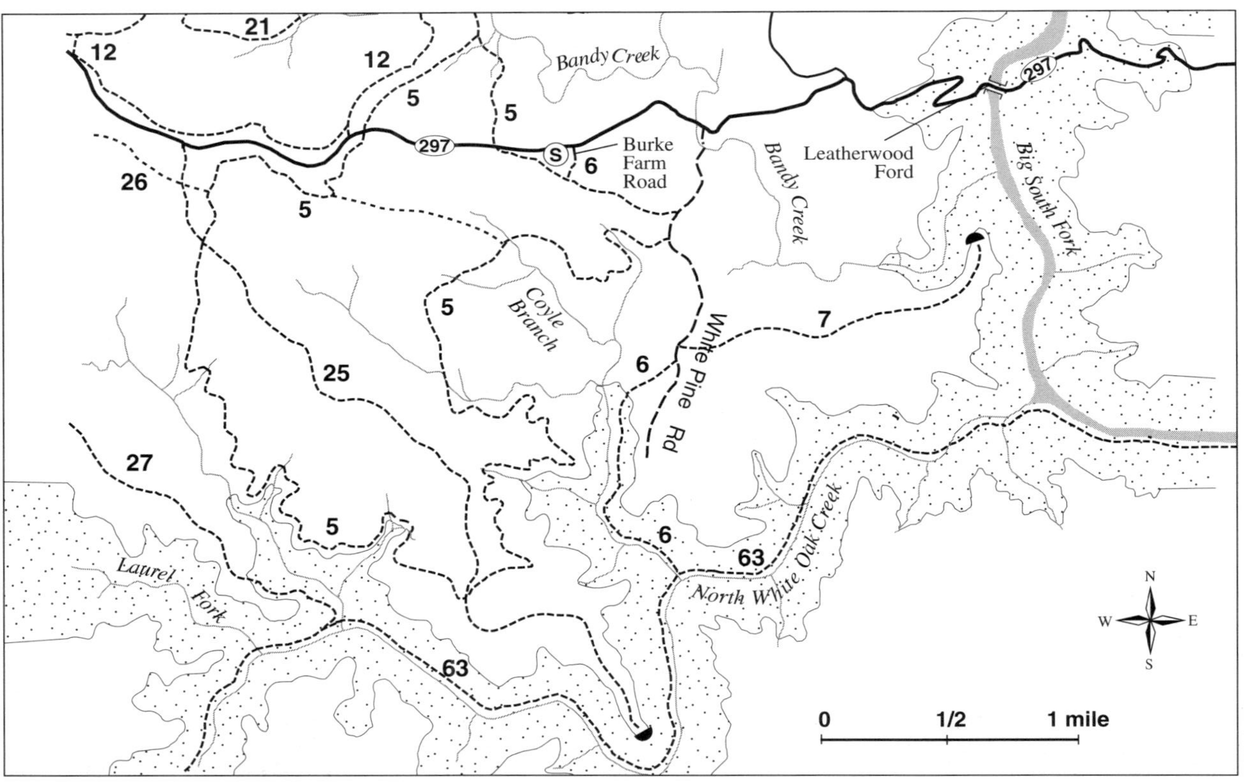

21
12
12
Bandy Creek
5
5
297
S
6
Burke Farm Road
26
Leatherwood Ford
Bandy Creek
Big South Fork
297
5
5
Coyle Branch
7
White Pine Rd
25
6
27
6
5
63
North White Oak Creek
Laurel Fork
63
N
E
S
W
0   1/2   1 mile

The name *Bandy Creek* is derived from an early homestead that was abandoned in the area; the word *abandoned* was shortened to *banded*, which was then corrupted to *bandy.*

If you're visiting the BSFNRRA for the first time, you'll probably want to start at the Bandy Creek Visitor Center. The Bandy Creek complex includes horse stables, a campground, and a swimming pool. Hiking trails lead to old homesites, horse trails head northwest to Charit Creek Lodge and turn south to North White Oak Creek, and specially developed mountain bike trails offer riding opportunities.

To get to the visitor center in the Tennessee portion of the park, turn north on Bandy Creek Road off TN 297 on the west side of the Big South Fork River. If you are coming from the west, the turn is just before the road drops into the river gorge. Coming from the east, descend into the gorge, cross the river on the bridge at Leatherwood Ford, and travel up the other side to get to the turnoff. After making the turn, go 1.8 miles then turn left to reach the visitor center; beyond are the horse stables. Turn right at the junction to reach the campground. At 0.2 mile farther up Bandy Creek Road, turn left to find parking for the Bandy Creek Trailhead on the right and the Bandy Creek Equestrian Trailhead straight ahead at the end of the road. The North Bandy Creek Trail leads from the stables to the Bandy Creek Equestrian Trailhead.

1 | OSCAR BLEVINS FARM LOOP 🚶

Distance: 3.6 miles
Difficulty: Easy
Elevation change: 180 ft
Cautions: Creek crossings, stairs
Connections: Bandy Creek Campground Loop 🚶, North Bandy Creek Trail ⋂, West Entrance Trail 🚶, Collier Ridge Loop 🚲

Attractions: Stands of tall laurel and rhododendron line the trail along Bandy Creek on the way to the Oscar Blevins Farm, a historic farmsite that includes a large barn flanked by a hog shed, chicken coop, corn crib, and a log house built in 1879 by John B. Blevins, a great-uncle of Oscar Blevins. Oscar and Ermon Blevins lived here starting in 1940. They later moved into the newer woodframe house where they lived until 1979, when their land was purchased for the park.

The 1879 farmhouse

Trailhead: Start at the Bandy Creek Trailhead. The Oscar Blevins Farm Loop heads straight into the woods and the Bandy Creek Campground Loop crosses the path at the trailhead. The Blevins Loop begins as a gravel path with a small footbridge over a low area. Numbered posts correspond to a printed guide you can get at the visitor center.

Description: At 0.1 mile, cross the North Bandy Creek Trail, a horse route. Then a footbridge near the West Bandy Creek Road takes you over a small creek just before the actual loop at 0.2 mile. The best approach is to hike the loop clockwise, to the left.

The trail descends gradually, following the small creek, a tributary of Bandy Creek that may be dry at times. Enter a miniature gorge with the creek cascading down the rock bluff and spilling over a ledge just at a wooden platform, where you must step down a wooden stairway. Soon after, cross the boundary into Scott State Forest, an inholding still owned by the state of Tennessee. The trail then passes through stands of laurel and at 0.5 mile crosses a footbridge over a wet area.

At 0.7 mile, a side trail up to the right leads to Muleshoe Rockshelter, where old mule shoes have been found. At 1.0 mile, cross the north branch of Bandy Creek on a bridge. On the other side of the creek is a junction with the West Entrance Trail on the left. Stay straight.

You'll soon merge with a roadbed that is part of the Collier Ridge Bike Loop. Pass the site of the old farmstead of Billie Blevins; fields, an old chicken coop, and the foundation of a house remain. The trail crosses King Branch and soon parallels Bandy Creek. At 1.6 miles, a trail up to the left is the other side of the bike loop. The bike trail also continues straight with the hiking trail, which is the access to the loop for bikers. Soon after the junction on the bike loop, the hiking trail bears left, leaving the bike trail, and follows another old road to cross Bandy Creek again on a bridge at 1.7 miles.

As you approach the site of the Oscar Blevins farm, pass the remains of a split-rail fence. Where you cross a footbridge, an abandoned root cellar sits on the left. At 2.0 miles, you'll stand in front of the frame house that was the home of Oscar and Ermon Blevins. The older structures are behind the house.

In front of the house, a road leads out to West Bandy Creek Road. Turn right on a footpath to continue the hiking loop. After a couple of bridges, cross the upper end of the Collier Ridge Loop at 2.5 miles. Cross another footbridge; at 2.8 miles you'll reach the location of interpretive post 20. An overgrown side path here leads 50 yards up to the West Bandy Creek Road across from the Lora E. Blevins Farmstead and the Katie Blevins Cemetery. Oscar Blevins is buried there.

Crossing three boardwalks over drainages and swinging through the head of a hollow, close the loop at 3.4 miles. Then return along the connector to the trailhead.

2 ⌐ BANDY CREEK CAMPGROUND LOOP 👣

Distance: 2.3 miles
Difficulty: Easy
Elevation change: 80 ft
Cautions: Footbridges slippery in wet weather
Connections: Oscar Blevins Farm Loop 👣, Duncan Hollow Trail ∩, John Litton Farm Loop 👣, North Bandy Creek Trail ∩

Attractions: This loop introduces you to the facilities at Bandy Creek and to the uplands forest of the Cumberland Plateau.

Bandy Creek Visitor Center

Trailhead: Start at the Bandy Creek Trailhead. You may also begin the loop at the visitor center.

Description: From the trailhead, take the path to the right. Cross a boardwalk over a low area, pass under a powerline, and at 0.1 mile cross the Bandy Creek Road where the pavement gives way to gravel; the gravel section to the left is called the West Bandy Creek Road. The trail curves to the right below campsites to pass behind the volleyball court and swimming pool and cross Duncan Hollow Road at 0.4 mile. At the trailhead for the John Litton Farm Loop on the other side, walk a few feet up that trail to turn right and pass behind the campfire circle. Emerge on a road within the campground. Bear right along roads toward the campground entrance. Behind the check-in kiosk, take a path to the left that crosses the Bandy Creek Road and enters the visitor center parking area at 0.7 mile.

Head straight into the woods to walk through an uplands forest of mixed pine and oak as the trail circles the horse stables. At 1.9 miles, on the other side of the stables, the path crosses the North Bandy Creek Trail leading from the stables to the Bandy Creek Equestrian Trailhead. Emerge to pass a pond and turn left toward the visitor center amphitheater, then turn right on a path. Cross a couple of boardwalks and reach a junction with a path to the equestrian trailhead to the left. Staying straight, cross the trailhead road and circle right to arrive back at the Bandy Creek Trailhead at 2.3 miles.

3 | JOHN LITTON FARM LOOP 🚶

Distance: 5.9 miles
Difficulty: Easy to moderate
Elevation change: 300 ft
Cautions: Ladders, footbridges, stairway
Connections: Bandy Creek Campground Loop 🚶, Fall Branch Trail 🚶, Duncan Hollow Trail ⋂, Duncan Hollow Loop 🚲, Katie Trail ⋂

Attractions: This loop takes you by terraced rock bluffs and Fall Branch Falls en route to the John Litton Farm historic site. The Litton Farm is also called the General Slaven Farm, for the Slaven family that lived there in later years (General was his name, not a title). The Slaven family added a frame addition and porches to the original log cabin built by John Litton around 1900.

Fall Branch Falls

Trailhead: Across from the Bandy Creek Visitor Center, drive into the campground and bear left to park at the swimming pool; you'll see the trailhead for the John Litton Farm Loop just as Duncan Hollow Road enters the woods. You may also take the Bandy Creek Campground Loop 0.4 mile to the right from the Bandy Creek Trailhead to reach the beginning of the John Litton Farm Loop. Turn right into the woods to hike the loop counterclockwise, the best approach; the return route will be along Duncan Hollow Road.

Description: The trail begins as a gravel path that passes a path to the right leading to the campground campfire circle. The trail then parallels Duncan Hollow Road to the left but soon swings right and crosses a couple of plank bridges over small drainages at 0.1 mile before leading into a fragrant pine and laurel forest.

Soon you'll hear Fall Branch as the trail switches back and drops toward the creek on your right. Skirt sandstone shelves on your left with hemlocks balanced at the edge. Two wooden platforms with ladders at 0.3 mile drop the trail into the small gorge of Fall Branch. The path then takes you past dripping rock overhangs and with switchbacks gradually descends into a carpet of ferns beside the creek. In this hollow, you'll see debris from a 1998 snowstorm that broke limbs and uprooted trees.

The trail passes rock bluffs and makes several side stream crossings over footbridges. Cross the Scott State Forest boundary and then pass under a power line. At 1.9 miles the trail arrives at Fall Branch Falls. The creek pours off a rock shelf and drops 10 feet into a green pool—a perfect spot for lunch, relaxing, or maybe a dip in the pool.

From here the trail climbs away from Fall Branch through a young pine grove. Along the way, watch for climbing fern, so thick at one location on both sides of the trail it resembles miniature kudzu. At 2.8 miles, take a bridge across the North Fork of Fall Branch to a junction with the Fall Branch Trail to the right. To stay with the John Litton Farm Loop, turn left. Cross several small side streams; some have footbridges, others you just step over. The trail eventually merges with an old roadbed leading to the farm at 3.7 miles. The John Litton Farm sits in a cove, with the John Litton cabin to the left.

The trail curves left over an earthen dam holding back blackberry bushes and a stream-fed pond still alive with fish. Cross a footbridge over the spillway for the pond and then descend to a junction with an old road that has come down from the Duncan Hollow Road. To the left sits a side-opening English barn built by John Litton. The trail turns to the left beside the barn on another old roadway. Cross a bridge over the North Fork and then turn right to climb away from the farm. The ascent includes several switchbacks and a set of stairs.

Back on the plateau top, the trail joins a roadbed that reaches a clearing at 4.5 miles. Turn right to stay along the edge of the woods. Pass an old farmsite up to the left and bear right through a corner of the woods. The trail then crosses a footbridge over a drainage to merge with an old road to the right. Up the road at 4.8 miles is a junction with the gravel road that leads to the farm; it's gated farther down to prevent vehicle access. Turn left on the gravel road to complete the loop. A proposed rerouting will eventually take the hiking trail off this road to loop back through the woods.

Along the road, cross the meandering boundary of Scott State Forest. At 5.0 miles is a junction with the Duncan Hollow Road. The Duncan Hollow Trail and the Duncan Hollow Loop follow this road to the right. Turn left. Pass under a powerline. At 5.4 miles, the road passes an American Chestnut Field Laboratory on the left, where efforts are being made to grow blight-resistant trees. Soon after, pass a field of white pines on the right.

At 5.6 miles the Katie Trail turns west to connect with the North Bandy Creek Trail, which leads to the Bandy Creek Equestrian Trailhead. Stay straight on the road to cross the state forest boundary once more and complete the loop at 5.9 miles.

4 | FALL BRANCH TRAIL

Distance: 1.9 miles one-way
Difficulty: Easy
Elevation gain: 150 ft
Cautions: None
Connections: John Litton Farm Loop, John Muir Trail

Attractions: This trail connects the John Litton Farm Loop with the JMT while passing by a large rock shelter and several isolated streams. Such shelters were used as hunting camps by the Cherokees and Shawnees and were later used as shelter by the white people who first settled the plateau country.

Trailhead: Across from the Bandy Creek Visitor Center, drive into the campground and bear left to park at the swimming pool; you'll see the trailhead for the John Litton Farm Loop. Follow the John Litton Farm Loop 2.8 miles counterclockwise to the Fall Branch Trail.

Description: From the junction with the John Litton Farm Loop, the Fall Branch Trail heads downstream along the North Fork of Fall Branch. At 0.1 mile, the trail threads a rock passageway, curves left, and crosses a footbridge over a small drainage to pass in front of a deep rock shelter, a large opening in the sandstone bluff. Beyond the shelter, climb steps along the rock wall and pass a smaller hole in the wall before making switchbacks left and right to climb above the rock shelter.

The trail continues to climb with other switchbacks, eventually joining an old roadbed. At 0.3 mile, cross the boundary of Scott State Forest, leaving the forest. Then drop through a cove and pass an old roadway up to the left. At 0.8 mile, cross a small footbridge at an old roadway going downhill to the right.

The trail curves left up a cove and drops to a bridge over the upper end of the cove at 1.2 miles. Turn right after the bridge and begin an ascent with switchbacks left and right. After swinging through a couple more coves, watch for a left turn at 1.5 miles. Then watch for a right turn as you descend to a bridge over a tributary of Fall Branch at 1.8 miles; this is the last source of water before the top of the plateau.

After the bridge, the trail turns left and begins an ascent with several switchbacks to connect with the JMT at 1.9 miles.

5 | SOUTH BANDY CREEK TRAIL / NORTH WHITE OAK LOOP ∩

Distance: 17.5 miles
Difficulty: Moderate
Elevation change: 200 ft
Cautions: Creek crossings, sandy patches
Connections: North Bandy Creek Trail ∩, Leatherwood Overlook Trail ∩, Coyle Branch Trail ∩, Gar Blevins Trail ∩, Groom Branch Trail ∩

Attractions: This popular horse trail circles through the uplands forest of the plateau tableland and provides access to the Leatherwood Overlook and the North White Oak Overlook.

Trailhead: Begin this trail from the Bandy Creek Equestrian Trailhead that is just beyond the hiking trailhead on the side road off Bandy Creek Road. A corral is there for day use only. If you're walking or biking and want to avoid some horse traffic, there's also access off TN 297. Head west on TN 297 from the junction of the Bandy Creek Road. The highway dips to cross Bandy Creek. At 1.2 miles turn left onto Burke Farm Road, which is paved for the first few yards; park here so you do not block the road. Follow the dirt road into the woods and connect with the loop trail in 0.1 mile.

Description: At the Bandy Creek Equestrian Trailhead, the North Bandy Creek Trail leads left 0.3 mile to the stables; this short section of trail is closed to mountain bikes because of the frequent horse traffic from the stables. (The North Bandy Creek Trail also heads to the right to connect with horse trails to the north.) Head straight into the woods on the South Bandy Creek Trail.

At 0.1 mile the gravel trail crosses the boundary into Scott State Forest. Descend to a ford of Bandy Creek at 0.5 mile. At 0.7 mile, the trail reaches a junction with the North White Oak Loop. To cover the trail clockwise, stay left.

The trail crosses a streambed on a bridge and then switchbacks left down to cross a small creek on a bridge at 1.0 mile. Ascend to a crossing of TN 297 at 1.8 miles. On the other side, turn left to parallel the highway. At 2.0 miles, emerge into an open area where there is additional access off TN 297. Stay with the road straight ahead. At 2.2 miles, a side road right leads down to a pond. You'll reach a junction at 2.3 miles, where it's 0.1 mile left up to the alternative parking for hikers and mountain bikers on TN 297. If you begin and end there, you'll trim about 3 miles from the route.

Continue straight on the old road. Pass open fields on the right and then the left. The road is mostly hard-packed gravel.

At 2.9 miles, connect with the old White Pine Road and bear right; to the left, the old roadway leads out to TN 297 after fording Bandy Creek. At 3.0 miles is a junction. The North White Oak Loop turns right off the road and the White Pine Road continues straight ahead as the Coyle Branch Trail, with access to the Leatherwood Overlook Trail. Making the right turn, drop off the road through a wet area and ascend to pass through a pine woods with large patches of ground cedar, following the trace of an old road. Now that the trail is off the road, mountain bikers should watch for patches of sand.

Cross a small stream at 3.4 miles, part of the headwaters of Coyle Branch of North White Oak Creek, and soon after cross the boundary into Scott State Forest. As the trail meanders through the woods, it crosses and re-crosses the forest boundary several times.

At 4.5 miles, cross an earth-filled causeway that traverses a wet area that's also part of the headwaters of Coyle Branch. The trail passes through posts that limit vehicle access at 5.3 miles; soon after, pass an old road coming down from the right and pass through posts on the other side. The trail then crosses a shallow tributary of Coyle Branch and bears left. At 5.8 miles, another trail comes in from the right, following an old roadbed. Here you can turn right to cut across this upper end of the loop to the other side in 0.3 mile, part of the Cumberland Valley Loop. Stay straight.

Ford the West Fork of Coyle Branch at 6.3 miles, where the stream undercuts a low rock bluff to the right. The trail then heads downstream along the creek's drainage, swinging right frequently to cross the drainages of side streams. Watch for a small waterfall on one of these at 7.2 miles.

The trail crosses an old road at 8.5 miles and then reaches a junction at 8.7 miles. To the right the Gar Blevins Trail cuts through the middle of the loop to emerge on TN 297 in 2.3 miles. To the left the North White Oak Overlook Trail leads 1.6 miles out to an overlook of North White Oak Creek, which you may want to see before going on. Stay straight to continue the loop.

At 10.3 miles, cross an old road that is a fork off the Gar Blevins Trail up to the right. To the left, the old road is overgrown. Continuing on the loop trail, pass large rocks up to the right and at 11.3 miles cross a footbridge over a bottom area thick with cinnamon fern. The trail soon crosses a bridge over a creekbed with more fern.

At 12.3 miles, cross a shallow creek that flows across the path and then cross the main creek on a bridge and soon another footbridge over a small stream. At 13.0 miles, the path crosses another creek on a bridge; again notice the stands of cinnamon fern downstream. You'll soon cross a footbridge over a low area.

At 14.1 miles the trail once again crosses the Gar Blevins Trail (TN 297 lies 0.3 mile to the left); stay straight. At 14.4 miles is a junction with the Groom Branch Trail to the left (which crosses the Gar Blevins Trail in 70 yards and heads west to the Cumberland Valley Trailhead in 2.4 miles); again, stay straight. At 15.2 miles, pass an old road to the left and cross the Scott State Forest boundary. At 15.5 miles the trail crosses an old road; a trail follows the roadbed to the right for 0.3 mile to cut across the upper part of the North White Oak Loop. To continue clockwise around the loop, you would turn here to avoid a ride or walk along the road; this is the route of the Cumberland Valley Loop.

To complete the North White Oak Loop, stay straight across this old road and emerge on TN 297 at 15.9 miles. If you started at the Bandy Creek Equestrian Trailhead, cross the road and continue on the trail. Descend to close the loop at 16.8 miles. Turning left, ascend back to the trailhead at 17.5 miles, fording Bandy Creek again along the way.

If you started the loop at the parking area on TN 297, turn right at the highway and walk or bike down the road 0.5 mile to pick up the horse trail again, turning right off the road and proceeding another 0.5 mile to the junction with the road up to the parking area for a loop total of 14.6 miles.

6   COYLE BRANCH TRAIL ∩

Distance: 2.1 miles one-way
Difficulty: Strenuous
Elevation loss: 550 ft
Cautions: Sandy patches; steep, rocky descent
Connections: North White Oak Loop ∩, Leatherwood
    Overlook Trail ∩, O&W Railbed ∩

Attractions: This trail provides access to North White Oak Creek and the Oneida & Western (O&W) Railbed from the Bandy Creek area.

Trailhead: The Coyle Branch trail is accessed off the North White Oak Loop; from the Bandy Creek Equestrian Trailhead, head straight into the woods on the South Bandy Creek Trail. At 0.1 mile the gravel trail crosses the boundary into Scott State Forest. Descend to a ford of Bandy Creek at 0.5 mile. At 0.7 mile, the trail reaches a junction with the North White Oak Loop; turn left. Ascend to cross TN 297 at 1.8 miles and stay with the North White Oak Loop. For alternative parking, continue west from the turnoff for the Bandy Creek Visitor Center on TN 297. At 0.6 mile, just past the White Pine United Baptist Church and just before TN 297 crosses Bandy Creek, pass White Pine Road on the left that provides unofficial access to the Coyle Branch Trail (at this writing blocked by down trees). Continue west on TN 297 another 0.6 mile and turn left onto Burke Farm Road and park so you do not block the road. This is the alternative access for hikers and mountain bike riders described for the North White Oak Loop (with a horse trailer, you may want to begin at the Bandy Creek Equestrian Trailhead or the Bandy Creek Stables). At 0.1 mile down this road, connect with the North White Oak Loop and turn left to a junction with the old White Pine Road at 0.6 mile. From this junction, stay with the North White Oak Loop to the right until the loop turns off to the right at 0.8 mile from the alternative parking, or 3.0 miles from the Bandy Creek Trailhead.

Description: Stay straight on the Coyle Branch Trail following the old roadbed from where the North White Oak Loop turns down to the right. Pass another old road to the left and at 0.4 mile reach a junction with a road to the left that takes you to the Leatherwood Overlook. Stay straight to continue on the Coyle Branch Trail.

At 0.5 mile is a fork with the Coyle Branch Road right and the White Pine Road continuing left. Here you can take a side excursion of 0.7 mile on the White Pine Road, which is graveled until it emerges into the long Duvall Fields, an agricultural lease area. At the far end of the fields, you can walk a path that leads down through the woods to a view of the Coyle Branch Gorge.

Back at the fork, bear right off the White Pine Road onto the Coyle Branch Road. You'll soon reach the end of the access for motorized vehicles and begin a steep, rocky descent along the old roadbed. At 0.8 mile, pass the trace of an old road up to the left and, soon after, drop below the rock bluff to an overhang; below to your right you'll see or hear Coyle Branch. Now parallel the creek downstream.

After a level stretch, round a rock bluff to the left and descend again to cross a small drainage and thread a rock passageway at 1.0 mile. At 1.3 miles, drop down a 2-foot rock ledge and continue your descent, passing mudholes along the way if there have been recent rains.

At 2.1 miles, the trail reaches a junction with the old O&W Railbed; just to the right, Coyle Branch joins North White Oak Creek. At this writing, the old railbed is open to motorized vehicles, but at some time it may be converted to a bicycle and horse trail. You can turn left on the railbed to get to a ford of North White Oak Creek and the O&W Bridge beyond. Turning right, you can connect with the Gernt Trail or continue on to the Zenith area. Or retrace your route back to TN 297.

7   LEATHERWOOD OVERLOOK TRAIL ∩

Distance: 1.9 miles one-way
Difficulty: Easy
Elevation change: Mostly level
Cautions: None
Connections: Coyle Branch Trail ∩

Attractions: This side trail leads to an overlook of Leatherwood Ford. You'll have a view of the river and the Leatherwood Ford Bridge; to the left lies the Bandy Creek Gorge.

Trailhead: Access this trail from the North White Oak Loop. From the Bandy Creek Equestrian Trailhead, head straight into the woods on the South Bandy Creek Trail. At 0.1 mile the gravel trail crosses into Scott State Forest. Descend to a ford of Bandy Creek at 0.5 mile. At 0.7 mile, the trail reaches a junction with the North White Oak Loop. Turn left and cross TN 297 at 1.8 miles. At 3.0 miles along the North White Oak Loop, continue straight on the old White Pine Road as the loop turns off right. In another 0.4 mile, turn left on the Leatherwood Overlook Trail as the Coyle Branch Trail continues straight.

Description: Turning left on the Leatherwood Overlook Trail, pass old roads to the right and left and then pass through the Terry/Thompson Fields, an agricultural lease area. You'll see a pond to your right in the field. At 1.3 miles is the woodline at a junction; the road continues to the right while the trail to the overlook goes straight. If you were to stay on the road, you'd reach the end of vehicle access in 0.3 mile.

Continuing toward the overlook from the junction at the end of the field, travel along the trail on old roadway. Descend to hitching rails at 1.8 miles and walk out to the overlook at 1.9 miles.

Leatherwood Overlook

8 | NORTH BANDY CREEK TRAIL / KATIE TRAIL / JACKS RIDGE LOOP ∩

Distance: 8.2-mile loop
Difficulty: Easy
Elevation change: 200 ft
Cautions: None
Connections: South Bandy Creek Trail ∩, North White Oak Loop ∩, By-Pass Road ∩, Black House Branch Trail ∩

Attractions: You'll have a pleasant horse ride with sandy tread on the Jacks Ridge Loop, with a view of Laurel Fork Gorge and blooming mountain laurel in May and June.

Trailhead: Begin at the Bandy Creek Equestrian Trailhead.

Description: Head north (right) on the North Bandy Creek Trail from the trailhead. (To the left this trail leads from the trailhead to the stables, where you may also begin the ride. Straight ahead is the South Bandy Creek Trail, with access to the North White Oak Loop.)

At 0.3 mile, cross the Oscar Blevins Farm Loop hiking trail, which begins at the hiking trailhead. Then at 0.4 mile cross the gravel West Bandy Creek Road and reach a junction with the Katie Trail at 0.6 mile. Right on this trail takes you to the Duncan Hollow Road in 0.4 mile. Turn left.

Pass through an open area; stay with the wide main trail where paths lead off to the right that connect with By-Pass Road. At 1.3 miles, cross a low area on a short causeway and then emerge into another open area that's at a distance behind the Lora E. Blevins Farmstead and the Katie Blevins Cemetery.

At 1.5 miles, step over a small creek as the trail turns left to pass through another open area. You'll then reach a junction with the Jacks Ridge Loop at 2.0 miles. Stay straight. Just beyond, cross By-Pass Road, which comes down from Jacks Ridge Road to the left (to the right, By-Pass Road connects with the Duncan Hollow Road to the east in 2.3 miles).

Beyond this crossing of By-Pass Road, the trail joins Jacks Ridge Road. Back to the left, you can reach West Bandy Creek Road in 0.1 mile, where you can also access the Jacks Ridge Loop; there's parking at the road junction for one vehicle.

As you continue down the Jacks Ridge Road, pass a couple of old roads to the right and reach a junction at 2.7 miles. To the left the Black House Branch Trail follows an old road down to a ford of Laurel Fork and then heads north toward Charit Creek Lodge. Stay straight at this junction to continue the loop.

You'll soon bear left off the old roadbed, where the road ends for motorized vehicles. The trail now follows a path through the woods, dotted with

Horseback riding on North Bandy Creek Trail

blooming mountain laurel in May and early June. At 3.3 miles, pass under a powerline and turn left up the cleared area to a distant view of the Laurel Fork Gorge before turning to the right back into the woods.

After the trail meanders through the woods, it passes back under the powerline at 4.0 miles. At 4.6 miles, cross a bridge over a small creek and then a couple of short causeways and emerge onto the end of an old road at 5.2 miles. Turn right to connect with another road and turn right. The trail veers left off this road at 5.5 miles.

At 6.1 miles, the trail connects with By-Pass Road. This is a designated horse route. Turn right to close the loop at 6.2 miles. It's then 2.0 miles back along the Katie Trail and the North Bandy Creek Trail to the Bandy Creek Equestrian Trailhead.

9 | BLACK HOUSE BRANCH TRAIL ∩

Distance: 2.0 miles one-way
Difficulty: Moderate
Elevation change: 360 ft
Cautions: Creek fords, steep descent and ascent
Connections: Jacks Ridge Loop ∩, Laurel Fork Creek Trail ⋊⋉,
Fork Ridge Trail ∩, Charit Creek Lodge Trail ∩

Attractions: This horse trail provides access from the Bandy Creek area to the Middle Creek area and Charit Creek Lodge to the northwest, with a descent into Laurel Fork Gorge.

Trailhead: From the Bandy Creek Equestrian Trailhead, go north along the North Bandy Creek Trail and then follow the Katie Trail and the Jacks Ridge Loop to the junction with the Black House Branch Trail at 2.7 miles. This junction can also be accessed along the Jacks Ridge Road, which can be reached by continuing north on the West Bandy Creek Road 1.1 miles from the turnoff for the Bandy Creek trailheads. Jacks Ridge Road is the dirt road to the right just after you cross the county line. The road is open to vehicles for 0.8 mile to a parking area at the beginning of the Black House Branch Trail; this road has not been upgraded and so is not suitable for passenger cars because of the deep sand and occasional mudholes. A vehicle can park beside West Bandy Creek Road if you want to begin there.

Description: From the junction with the Jacks Ridge Loop/Road, head left down a side road, which is the Black House Branch Trail. You'll see a bar gate restricting vehicle access; make your way around the gate and continue down the steep gravel road. At 0.1 mile, notice up to your right a small rock shelter as you begin to drop below the sandstone bluff of Laurel Fork Gorge.

The road passes a massive block of stone that has separated from the rim at 0.2 mile. At 0.3 mile the road curves right in its descent and finally curves left to a ford of the Laurel Fork of Station Camp Creek at 0.4 mile; hikers may find it a little more shallow upstream. Just before the ford, you'll see a camping spot on the left.

Across the creek, connect with the Laurel Fork Creek Trail for hikers, which to the left leads toward the West Entrance Trailhead. Turn right on the road, which is multiple-use for horses and hikers. At 0.5 mile is a junction with the Laurel Fork Creek Trail turning off to the right; this is a hiking trail and not open to horses. Stay with the road to the left to keep on the

Black House Branch Trail; the road is mostly hard-packed gravel, but you'll find occasional mudholes.

At 0.6 mile, the road fords Black House Branch on its way to join Laurel Fork; to the left notice the large rock overhanging the water. Ford the branch twice more at 0.7 mile and 0.8 mile. At 0.9 mile, pass through a more open area, and then the road curves to the right uphill. Switchback left and right as you make the ascent out of Laurel Fork Gorge.

At 1.4 miles the road skirts a clearing for a powerline and continues up past a gate to the top of the plateau at 1.5 miles. Through the woods, emerge in the open and pass under the powerline at 1.7 miles. Reentering the woods, you'll see an old roadway joining the main road on the right. At 2.0 miles you'll then reach a junction with a road that is the Fork Ridge Trail. To the left, it's 0.1 mile out to Fork Ridge Road and then right to the trails down to Charit Creek Lodge. To the right, the Fork Ridge Trail heads toward the confluence of Laurel Fork and Station Camp Creek.

10 | DUNCAN HOLLOW TRAIL ∩

Distance: 5.7 miles one-way
Difficulty: Moderate
Elevation loss: 720 ft
Cautions: Steep rocky descent, creek ford, motorized vehicles
Connections: John Litton Farm Loop 👫, Katie Trail ∩, By-Pass Trail ∩, Duncan Hollow Loop 🚲, Laurel Fork Creek Trail 👫, Fork Ridge Trail ∩, John Muir Trail 👫, Station Camp Creek Trail ∩

Attractions: This trail gives access to the Station Camp Creek area and can be combined with the Black House Branch Trail and the Station Camp Creek Trail or Fork Ridge Trail to make a loop for horse riders and mountain bikers.

Trailhead: Hikers and mountain bikers turn into the Bandy Creek Campground and park at the swimming pool. Horse riders head north on the North Bandy Creek Trail from the Bandy Creek Equestrian Trailhead. At 0.6 mile is a junction with the Katie Trail. Turn right to a junction with the Duncan Hollow Trail at 1.0 mile.

Description: From the swimming pool parking area by the John Litton Farm Loop trailhead on the right, hikers and bikers head down the gravel Duncan Hollow Road. The Duncan Hollow Trail follows this road, which is open to vehicles for the first 4.2 miles.

Cross the Scott State Forest boundary and reach a junction with the Katie Trail at 0.3 mile; this is where horse riders access the Duncan Hollow Trail.

At 0.9 mile, pass under a powerline and reach a fork. (The road to the right leads toward the John Litton Farm and is part of the farm loop.) Stay left.

At 1.2 miles, By-Pass Road on the left connects with the Jacks Ridge Loop. The Duncan Hollow Bike Loop, which has also been following the road, turns left here to make its loop route. Stay straight at this junction. Pass a couple of dirt roads to the right and at 2.7 miles enter an open area of old fields; notice the housesite to the left with blocks of stone from the chimney still piled in the center. Continuing on the road, reenter the woods, pass the traces of old roads to the left and right, and reach the end of vehicle access at 4.2 miles.

Stay straight on the old roadway as it begins its descent. Soon after, a small stream flows across the trail in wet weather. At 4.5 miles the trail drops below the rock bluff and then passes a rock shelter up to the right. The trail then makes a steep descent to a ford of Laurel Fork Creek at 5.4 miles. Here the Duncan Hollow Trail skirts the John Muir Trail (JMT) coming in on the right; there's a high bridge just to the right for hikers to cross the creek. On the other side is a junction with the Laurel Fork Creek Trail coinciding with the Fork Ridge Trail to the left. Use the North Bandy Creek/Katie/Jacks Ridge Loop, the Black House Branch Trail, the Fork Ridge Trail, and the Duncan Hollow Trail to make a loop of 14.6 miles from the Bandy Creek Equestrian Trailhead.

Turn right at this junction and join the JMT; the JMT and Duncan Hollow Trail coincide, but then turn left on the Duncan Hollow Trail while the JMT stays straight. At 5.6 miles the Duncan Hollow Trail fords Station Camp Creek and connects with the Station Camp Creek Trail at 5.7 miles. Horse and bike riders can use the North Bandy Creek/Katie/Jacks Ridge Loop, the Black House Branch Trail, the Charit Creek Lodge Trail, the Station Camp Creek Trail, and the Duncan Hollow Trail to make a loop of 14.9 miles from the Bandy Creek Equestrian Trailhead.

11 | DUNCAN HOLLOW LOOP 🚲

Distance: 5.0 miles
Difficulty: Moderate
Elevation change: 200 ft
Cautions: Mudholes, steep descents and ascents
Connections: John Litton Farm Loop 🚶, Duncan Hollow
 Trail ⋂, Katie Trail ⋂, By-Pass Road ⋂

Attractions: This short loop offers a good introduction to mountain biking the old roads and forest paths of the Big South Fork.

Trailhead: Across from the Bandy Creek Visitor Center, drive into the campground and bear left to park at the swimming pool. Hikers may use bike trails, but horses are not allowed here except on the Duncan Hollow and By-Pass Roads. Bike trails are blazed for one-way use.

Description: From the pool parking area, head down the gravel Duncan Hollow Road past the John Litton Farm Loop Trailhead on the right. At 0.3 mile the Katie Trail joins the road from the left. North from this junction the road is the Duncan Hollow Trail for horses and is also open to vehicle use.

At 0.9 mile, pass under powerlines and reach a right fork headed toward the John Litton Farm. The bike loop bears left off the road here but soon reconnects. At 1.2 miles the bike trail turns left on By-Pass Road. You'll pass an old road on the right that will be your return route. Stay with the main road left at the trace of an old road to the right at 1.8 miles.

At 1.9 miles the bike trail leaves the road straight ahead as By-Pass Road curves left. Veer left as another old road turns right. At 2.3 miles, turn right and descend to ford a small creek and turn right downstream. In a few yards, turn left to ascend from the creek. Reaching an old road, turn right. At 2.7 miles, the trail curves left and descends. Ascend to the top of a hill and turn right on another old road. The trail reconnects with By-Pass Road at 3.6 miles. Turn left to return to Duncan Hollow Road and ride back to the parking area at 5.0 miles.

12 COLLIER RIDGE LOOP 🚲

Distance: 7.3 miles
Difficulty: Moderate, strenuous section that may be avoided
Elevation change: 200 ft
Cautions: Stream crossings
Connections: Bandy Creek Campground Loop 🚶, North
    Bandy Creek Trail ⋂, Oscar Blevins Farm Loop 🚶, West
    Entrance Trail 🚶

Attractions: This more difficult mountain bike loop provides creek fords, steep descents and ascents, narrow passages, and traverses of bare sandstone.

Trailhead: Start at the Bandy Creek Trailhead.

Description: From the parking area, bike back to Bandy Creek Road and turn left. The Bandy Creek Campground Loop crosses the road where it changes to gravel, and at 0.1 mile, the North Bandy Creek Trail for horses crosses the road. Pass the Lora E. Blevins Farmstead and Katie

Blevins Cemetery at 0.6 mile, and then at 0.8 mile pass a Scott State Forest sign and turn left off the road onto a gravel path. At 0.9 mile cross the Oscar Blevins Farm Loop hiking trail.

The bike trail fords the north branch of Bandy Creek at 1.1 miles. At 1.2 miles the Oscar Blevins Farm Loop joins on the right; the hiking trail and bike trail follow an old roadbed. Soon after, stay left at a fork, which is the junction with the loop part of the bike trail; you'll return on the right fork.

At 1.5 miles, cross King Branch, then ride through the old Billie Blevins farmsite and at 1.7 miles continue straight as the Oscar Blevins Farm Loop turns left off the old roadway. The West Entrance Trail crosses the bike trail at 1.9 miles. Cross the south branch of Bandy Creek at 2.0 miles and then a smaller creek. Stay right at 2.2 miles. Ascend, sometimes on bare rock. At

Lora E. Blevins House

2.7 miles the bike trail turns right on a difficult section that is signed *advanced*. This route is a narrow, winding track, steep in places, and is not recommended for the inexperienced. As an alternative, continue straight to emerge onto TN 297 at 2.8 miles, turn right on the highway, and in 1.4 miles, turn right back into the woods to pick up the bike trail, thus avoiding the advanced section.

To ride the advanced section, turn right and descend on a narrow trail running among trees. At 2.9 miles the path drops over a low rock ledge; it's safest to walk here. Bottom out in a hollow and ascend. Along this section, the bike trail repeatedly moves up and down as it cuts across parallel ridges and hollows, sometimes making sharp right turns as it weaves across the landscape. Watch for stumps of shrubs and small trees that were cut to clear the path.

At 3.5 miles, cross an old roadbed. At 4.0 miles, jump a log deliberately left in the trail. Then at 4.7 miles, emerge into a grassy clearing along the highway; across the clearing, the trail reenters the woods. If you have ridden the highway instead of the advanced section, here is where you turn into the woods again and rejoin the trail.

At the clearing, head north on the bike trail. At 4.8 miles, turn right on an old road that is also the West Entrance Trail. The bike trail turns left off the road at 5.1 miles and the hiking trail stays with the road. The bike trail becomes mostly a single track winding through the woods.

Descend to close the loop at 6.6 miles. Bear left to recross the north branch of Bandy Creek and return to the West Bandy Creek Road at 7.0 miles. Turn right to return to the Bandy Creek Trailhead parking at 7.8 miles.

Map 2. Leatherwood Ford and East Rim

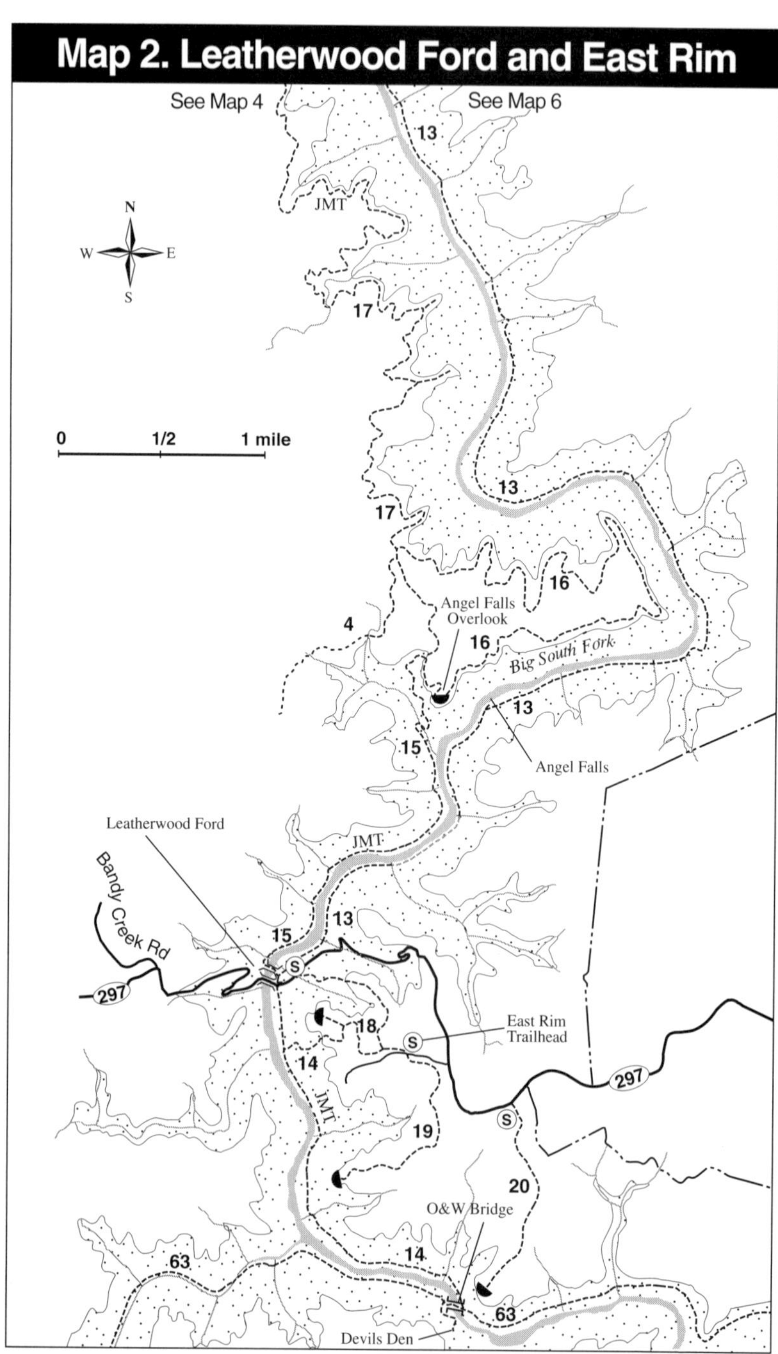

LEATHERWOOD FORD AND EAST RIM

Leatherwood Ford has been a main crossing of the Big South Fork River from the early years of settlement. Eventually a low-water bridge was built that still spans the river below the new highway bridge. After heavy rains this old bridge, now part of the hiking trail system, is often under water.

Here, boardwalks lead along the river and a universally accessible section of trail heads into the woods for a quarter mile. Leatherwood Ford is also a major takeout/put-in for paddlers running the river. Trails lead to Angel Falls (a large rapids in the river), Angel Falls Overlook (arguably the best view in the park), and the O&W Bridge (a railroad bridge left from a rail line that operated in the Big South Fork Gorge in the early twentieth century).

On TN 297, from the junction of Bandy Creek Road, head east to descend into the river gorge, cross the river over the bridge at Leatherwood Ford, and turn left into the river access on the east side of the river; you'll find restrooms and a large parking area. Coming from the east on TN 297, enter the park, pass the turn to the East Rim Overlook on the left, and descend into the river gorge to Leatherwood Ford at 2.2 miles from the east entrance. The John Muir Trail (JMT) comes from the south to cross the river on the old wooden Leatherwood Ford Bridge, which was the only way to cross the river before the new high bridge was built and the road paved.

13 ANGEL FALLS 🚶 / RIVER TRAIL EAST ∩

Distance: 8.1 miles one-way (*Angel Falls 2.0 miles one-way*)
Difficulty: Easy to Angel Falls, then moderate
Elevation change: 100 ft
Cautions: Can get muddy and overgrown beyond Angel Falls
Connections: John Muir Trail 🚶, Smith Ridge Trail ∩, Big Island Loop ∩

Attractions: Along this river trail featuring rock bluffs and a view of Angel Falls, wildflowers are abundant in the spring. Angel Falls is a huge rapids formed by boulders standing in the river. The rapids are all that's left of a

Angel Falls

low waterfall dynamited in the 1950s, probably by fishermen hoping to improve navigation on the river. Although the falls is no longer a waterfall, it's still an impressive sight, a churning sluice of water that rushes downstream.

Trailhead: To begin the Angel Falls Trail, walk to the far north end of the Leatherwood Ford parking area and follow the old road headed upstream, paralleling the river.

Description: Stroll through the shade of hemlocks, rhododendron, and mixed hardwood. Numbered posts corresponding to a brochure available at the Bandy Creek Visitor Center identify the trees; the posts begin along the sidewalk north of the gazebo. In spring columbine, trillium, geranium, and more line the trail. At 0.1 mile, cross a small stream on a footbridge. Then at 0.8 mile, the trail crosses Anderson Branch on another bridge. The reclaimed Anderson coal mine lies off to the right.

The trail passes a rock bluff on your right at 1.2 miles, where you'll have a good view of the river. At 1.3 miles, rockhop a small stream. Along the way, watch for a rock bluff on the right that contains a coal seam you can reach up and touch.

At 1.8 miles, a side path leading to the river and rejoining the main trail is the access for a portage around Angel Falls. At 2.0 miles is a trail junction. Take the left fork to a wooden deck overlooking Angel Falls. This side trail is the portage for boats to reenter the river downstream from the rapids. If you follow it down and explore along the river, use caution. If you slip on the rocks and fall in the water, the swift current will sling you against boulders and perhaps trap you underwater. A hiker drowned here in 1988.

From the junction going down to Angel Falls, bear right uphill to continue north on the River Trail East. Ascend to a gate at 2.1 miles; those on horses and mountain bikes coming from the other direction must leave horses and bikes here and walk down to Angel Falls.

The trail continues paralleling the river to the north, sometimes ascending over low ridges. At 3.2 miles the trail curves right to cross Bill Branch. The trail then ascends to the John Smith Place at 3.3 miles, which was Smith's homesite and once the location of a mining operation. (An old road that turns up to the right may eventually be part of a proposed Smith Ridge Trail. The trail will ford the river from the west and ascend out of the gorge to emerge into the back end of the Angel Falls Village development on the John J. Smith Road, which leads straight out to TN 297 northeast of the Black Oak Church. At this writing the route is unblazed and not maintained.)

The River Trail East descends from the John Smith Place and soon crosses a culvert that drains a hollow with huge boulders on the right. Beyond the John Smith Place, the trail can be muddy and, in summer, overgrown. Ascend through a gently sloping grassy area to the site of an old mine on the right at 3.4 miles. The trail ascends above the mine area. Cross a small stream turned rust-colored with oxides it has picked up while draining the mine area.

Descend to river level at 3.9 miles and walk over river rock in the floodplain. Rockhop Rough Shoals Branch where it flows into the river. At 4.1 miles notice a chute resting atop a small rock overhang on the right, left from mining operations up the slope. At 4.2 miles, step over a wet-weather stream that has a trickle of a waterfall dropping off a rock wall to your right; in summer you'll see white wood aster.

The trail descends a sandy slope to a footbridge crossing of a stream near the river at 4.3 miles. The trail soon curves right up a hollow to cross a small stream flowing out of boulders with a rock overhang. Watch for tall stands of yellow coneflowers and sunflowers in late summer.

At 4.8 miles, pass a small pond hidden in the trees on the right and then hop on large stepping stones to avoid a wet area. At another pond, frogs leap into the water in summer and red cardinal flowers stand at the water's edge. The trail soon crosses a small stream draining a nearby mine area.

The trail passes over a knoll. Watch for stands of cane and reed. At 5.8 miles the trail drops to cross a wet-weather stream and soon after descends with waterbars to cross Blevins Branch.

At 6.2 miles, the trail drops to cross Mill Creek. Take care because both banks of the stream can be muddy. The trail then curves back to the left to once more parallel the river. The trail curves right at 6.4 miles to go up another hollow to drop down stone steps to a creek crossing. Notice large beech trees in the area.

The trail crosses several small streams before passing into the parking area at Station Camp Crossing at 8.1 miles. Connect with the Station Camp Road; the Big Island Loop turns off the road to the right soon after the road crosses Slavens Branch. At low water only, you can ford the river to the other side to connect with the Station Camp Creek Trail and the JMT.

14 O&W BRIDGE / DEVILS DEN 🚶🚶

Distance: 3.0 miles one-way
Difficulty: Moderate
Elevation change: 100 ft
Cautions: Creek crossings, short steep ascent
Connections: Angel Falls 🚶🚶, John Muir Trail 🚶🚶, Leatherwood
Ford Loop 🚶🚶

Attractions: Enjoy river and bluff views along this trail to the O&W Railroad Bridge. Wildflowers are plentiful in the spring. Beyond the bridge, a section of the JMT leads past a waterfall to Devils Den.

The O&W Railroad Bridge was a link in the now-abandoned O&W Railroad that connected Oneida with Jamestown to the west, a rail line of 37 miles. The O&W Bridge was erected in 1915 and abandoned in 1954; the rails were pulled up and sold as scrap when the trains stopped operating. The bridge has a Whipple Truss design that was used between 1847 and 1900. This 200-foot bridge was once on another railroad but was brought here and adapted for use by the O&W. Very few Whipple Truss bridges survive today.

Trailhead: From the Leatherwood Ford River Access, the Angel Falls Trail heads to the north while the JMT crosses the old Leatherwood Ford Bridge to head north on the other side of the river. To head toward the O&W Bridge, walk south under the TN 297 bridge to a trail junction. (If you climbed the rock steps on your left to the highway above, you'd be on the Leatherwood Ford Loop.) Continue straight into the woods headed south; this is also the JMT, blazed with a blue silhouette of Muir.

Description: With the river on your right, cross a wooden bridge and meander through a fern and wildflower gathering and boulder displays. This part of the trail is graveled and smooth and has occasional benches to make it universally accessible. Watch for platforms and stairs to the right

O&W Bridge

that let you wander among boulders at the river's edge. At 0.3 mile, the universally accessible portion of the trail ends as the path becomes a walk on an old roadbed paralleling the river. Drop through a drainage that leads right to the river at a large pool across from the mouth of Bandy Creek on the river's west side.

Devils Den

This section of the JMT is also part of the Leatherwood Ford Loop. At 0.5 mile is a junction where the loop turns left up the steep slope toward the East Rim Trailhead. Continue straight ahead to stay on the JMT. Cross a small creek, dry at times, and then follow the trail down right as the old road continues left uphill. At 0.8 mile, begin a climb up the slope on rock steps and switchbacks.

At 1.0 mile, the trail rejoins an old road and descends to once more reach a level area paralleling the river. Where the river curves to the left, you can perhaps see through the trees across the river to the confluence of North White Oak Creek. Stay with the road now, crossing occasional wet-weather streams, sometimes on footbridges, until at 2.1 miles you'll have your first view of the O&W Bridge and pass huge boulders to the left of the trail. As you near the bridge, you'll encounter a house-sized boulder that fell from the rim and landed in the roadway. The trail turns down right to go around the boulder and arrives at the O&W Railbed and the bridge over the Big South Fork at 2.3 miles.

At the bridge, the road to the left is the old railbed that leads toward Oneida; you can drive down this rough, rocky road out of the community of Verdun, probably not suitable for passenger cars. A wooden stairway drops to the river's edge on the upstream side of the bridge, where you can sit on broad boulders beside the rushing river.

The JMT turns right to cross the O&W Bridge over the Big South Fork. Enjoy the view of yellow cliffs behind you where the bluff towers overhead. Below, rapids stretch upstream before the river fades around the bend. On the other side of the bridge, watch for where the JMT turns down to the left, following an old roadway.

The roadbed dips through a hollow and ascends, and then at 2.5 miles the trail turns off right on a footpath. Up the path is a boulder-choked stream where the trail switchbacks up to the right. The trail climbs through more switchbacks over a rise and descends to a rockhop crossing of the stream among large boulders; there's a waterfall up to the right. The trail ascends to a rock wall, with the 40-foot waterfall on your right at 2.7 miles.

Turn left at the rock wall to climb out of the small gorge, switchback right, and descend, curving right to rockhop the stream above the falls and then descend again to cross another branch of the stream. At the second crossing, the trail turns up right, winding up the slope to cross bare rock to a turn down right to Devils Den, an almost perfect half-dome rock shelter, at 3.0 miles.

An old roadbed continues past the shelter turnoff, which may be the future route of the trail. The JMT currently ends at Devils Den, but plans call for the trail to continue south toward Honey Creek, where it will link with another existing section and then eventually follow the Clear Fork River all the way to the southern boundary of the park at Peters Bridge, which would add about 23 miles to the trail.

15 | ANGEL FALLS OVERLOOK 🥾

Distance: 3.0 miles one-way
Difficulty: Moderate
Elevation gain: 400 ft
Cautions: Stream crossings, steep ascent, boulder passages, narrow ledge crossing, ladder, bluffs at the overlook
Connections: Angel Falls 🥾, Grand Gap Loop 🥾, John Muir Trail 🥾

Attractions: This route takes you along the river, past rushing streams, through boulder passages, and atop the plateau for one of the best views of the Big South Fork Gorge. The first part of the trail, along the river, is a wonderland of wildflowers in spring: crested dwarf iris, bluets, cinquefoil, penstemon, fire pink, geranium, purple phacelia, foamflower, mayapple, marsh blue violets, trillium, bloodroot, dwarf dandelion, eared coreopsis, and more. If you are just out for a stroll, this part of the trail is a good one in spring.

Trailhead: From the Leatherwood Ford River Access, the Angel Falls Trail heads to the north and the JMT heads south toward the O&W Bridge.

The Big South Fork Gorge from Angel Falls Overlook

To get to Angel Falls Overlook, hike the JMT north on the other side of the river. Walk across the old Leatherwood Ford Bridge and climb the stairs into the woods. Then turn right. If there has been a recent rain, the old bridge may be under water; in that case, walk across the highway bridge to get across the river and turn down steps on the right side of the bridge and bear left on a makeshift path to pick up the trail at the old bridge crossing.

Description: Now along the trail, with rock bluffs on your left laced with laurel blossoms in May and the river drifting below on your right, you will encounter several side streams with cascades that you cross on bridges or by rockhopping as you meander through a hemlock and mixed hardwood forest.

At 1.8 miles, turn up Fall Branch where it joins the Big South Fork. The trail has slumped at this confluence where uprooted trees have fallen and clogged the stream channel. At 2.0 miles the trail crosses a curved bridge over Fall Branch, which roars and rushes through boulders as it hurries to the river. On the other side, turn right and walk downstream with a rock bluff on your left and the stream on your right. The trail then switchbacks to the left to begin an ascent out of the gorge.

The trail is mostly a continuous climb with switchbacks, stone steps, and boulder passages. Where the trail runs into a large boulder, turn left (hikers turning the wrong way and coming back have worn a path to the right). After more switchbacks and an ascent through boulders, you'll reach the rimrock below Angel Falls Overlook. Bear left along the tall rock bluff. The trail then levels off for a time, with the valley of Fall Branch on your left. Pass under a large rock overhang and cross a wet-weather stream that forms a waterfall down the rock ledge on your right.

Bridge over Fall Branch

At 2.6 miles, the trail switchbacks right up through rocks onto a rock shelf; there's a cable to hang onto. Notice the iron deposits in the rock face along the ledge. The trail turns into a small gorge created by the stream you just crossed. A short ladder helps you up to another level; the trail then ascends through a hemlock and rhododendron cove sandwiched between gorge walls. Toward the upper end stand large beech trees.

When you arrive at the head of the small gorge at 2.8 miles, the trail connects with the Grand Gap Loop. Turn right to get to the Angel Falls Overlook for a grand view of the river in another 0.2 mile. With the river sweeping by vertical rock walls, this is perhaps the best view in the park and one of the best on the entire Cumberland Plateau. Angel Falls is hidden in trees below. You can continue along the Grand Gap Loop to the left past other views to get a glimpse of the rapids below.

Retracing your steps, you'll have a total round trip hike of 6.0 miles.

16 | GRAND GAP LOOP 𝕩

Distance: 6.8 miles *(Grand Gap Overlook 1.2 mile
  one-way)*
Difficulty: Easy
Elevation change: Mostly level
Cautions: High bluffs
Connections: John Muir Trail 𝕩, Fall Branch Trail 𝕩

Attractions: This loop offers spectacular views of the Big South Fork Gorge
and Angel Falls while circling on top of the plateau.

Trailhead: From the Leatherwood Ford River Access, hike the JMT north
on the other side of the river. Walk across the old Leatherwood Ford Bridge
to the west side of the river, climb the stairs, and turn right, downstream.
At 2.0 miles, cross a curved bridge over Fall Branch, the last reliable source
of water for the next section of trail.
Following the route to the Angel Falls
Overlook, ascend to the top of the plateau to the Grand Gap Loop at 2.8
miles. (See Trail 15.)

Description: Once you get to the
Grand Gap Loop, you can turn right or
left to hike the loop. To the left is the
continuation of the JMT. Turn right to
get to Angel Falls Overlook in 0.2 mile.
The trail circles left from the overlook,
paralleling the gorge rim past other
views, where you can see Angel Falls
far below.

The rest of the trail for most of the
loop periodically swings away from
the gorge then returns, remaining
fairly level but with a few ups and
downs. You'll be passing through the
typical pine and mixed hardwood uplands forest of the plateau top. In
spring, a few wildflowers appear in
this drier environment: yellow star
grass, violet wood sorrel, and infre-
quent yellow lady's slipper.

After the first overlooks, the trail
swings away from the gorge rim and
passes a small rock overhang in a bluff

*View of Angel Falls from the
Grand Gap Loop*

on the left. At 0.4 mile, pass a larger overhang that is actually an arch. Walk into the rock opening, and you'll see that the overhang has separated from the bluff by the widening of a joint, creating a natural arch about 8 feet high and 50 feet long.

Soon after the arch, the trail passes by another rock overhang and later curves left over a ridge. You may notice a dirt road to the left that runs down the middle of the Grand Gap Loop and is accessed off the old Duncan Hollow Road out of the Bandy Creek Campground. The other side of the loop is fairly close on the other side of the road.

At 1.0 mile, the trail makes a sharp switchback right and winds down to the gorge rim at 1.2 miles, where a short path takes you onto a rock overlook that provides wide-angle view of Angel Falls upstream. This Grand Gap Overlook is well worth the walk.

Turn away from the gorge again. At 1.4 miles the trail crosses a little footbridge over a seep that comes from under a rock overhang. Later, the trail enters a hemlock woods at 1.7 miles. At 1.9 miles, pass by a broken rock bluff on the left and blocks of stone on the right that have separated from the bluff.

The trail joins an old roadbed at 2.1 miles at Grand Gap. Turn right on the road, and then in a few yards turn left off the roadbed back onto a footpath. Pass another rock overhang at 2.2 miles and then top out on a bluff at 2.4 miles. The trail then switchbacks left and climbs over a small ridge. The Grand Gap Loop nearly comes together in the middle, which you will not even notice unless someone walks by on the other side.

At 3.7 miles the trail comes to a bluff overlooking a tributary gorge of the Big South Fork. Massive stone walls stand across the way. Farther on, the trail emerges at an overlook of the river gorge where another canyon to the left joins the main river channel. The trail gradually curves around to the left.

At 4.5 miles, this north side of the loop and the south side of the loop nearly come together. The trail ascends with switchbacks left and right over a ridge and then turns down right. Descending, switchback down and at 5.2 miles swing around an open area that was once the homesite of Alfred and Elva Smith. Alfred was a logger for the Stearns Coal and Lumber Company. When the lumbering operations were discontinued in the 1940s, the Smiths left their plateau retreat, leaving behind their son Archie, who was only 5 months old when he died of pneumonia in 1932.

At 5.5 miles is a junction with the JMT. Turn left on the JMT to complete the Grand Gap Loop. Cross the road that runs through the middle of the loop at 5.6 miles and reach a junction with the Fall Branch Trail to the right (which leads 1.9 miles to the John Litton Farm Loop). Stay straight.

The trail curves left to cross an old roadbed and reach the grave of Archie Smith at 6.1 miles, bounded by logs and marked by a headstone. Continue along the JMT, returning to the gorge of Fall Branch on the right. At 6.7 miles, a broad sandstone bluff offers a view down the gorge to the left as Fall Branch flows toward the Big South Fork. The trail then turns up the small gorge that contains the JMT down to Leatherwood Ford and closes the loop at 6.8 miles at the junction where the Grand Gap Loop begins. Turn right down the JMT to return to Leatherwood Ford in another 2.8 miles. The total round-trip hiking distance from Leatherwood Ford is 12.4 miles.

17 · JOHN MUIR TRAIL

Distance: 42.4 miles one-way
Difficulty: Moderate
Elevation change: 500 ft
Cautions: Steep ascents and descents, creek fords, bluff dropoffs
Connections: Grand Gap Loop, Fall Branch Trail, Duncan Hollow Trail, Laurel Fork Creek Trail, Station Camp Creek Trail, Terry Cemetery Loop, River Trail West, Maudes Crack Overlook, No Business Trail, Dry Branch Trail, Stoopin' Oak Road, Rock Creek Loop, Sheltowee Trace, Rock Creek Trail, Hidden Passage Trail

Attractions: Maybe the best 4- or 5-day backpack in the Southeast, the JMT leads by gorge overlooks, tumbling streams, pioneer homesites, rock walls, and standing buttes. This national historic trail commemorates the 1867 journey through this plateau country by the noted conservationist and founder of the Sierra Club. Although Muir became famous wandering the Sierras in California, the Cumberlands were the first mountains he explored. The trail is blazed by a blue silhouette of John Muir.

Trailhead: The easiest southern access for the JMT is at Leatherwood Ford River Access on TN 297.

John Muir blaze

The JMT actually extends south from Leatherwood Ford 2.3 miles to the O&W Bridge and will eventually extend farther south to Peters Bridge at the southern boundary of the park. These mileages begin at Leatherwood Ford.

Description: Walk across the old Leatherwood Ford Bridge to the west side of the river and turn right, downstream. At 2.0 miles, cross a bridge over Fall Branch, the last reliable source of water for the next section of trail. Following the route to the Angel Falls Overlook, ascend to the top of the plateau to the Grand Gap Loop at 2.8 miles.

Turn left at the junction to continue the JMT. Pass an overlook of the Fall Branch Gorge at 2.9 miles. The trail passes the grave of Archie Smith at 3.5 miles and reaches a junction with the Fall Branch Trail to the left at 4.0 miles. It's 0.1 mile down the trail to a tributary of Fall Branch that usually has water. Continuing straight on the JMT, cross a dirt road and reach a junction at 4.1 miles where the Grand Gap Loop comes in from the right and the JMT continues left, headed north. Of course, you can hike the Grand Gap Loop to this point.

The trail now wends through the woods, paralleling the rim, with an occasional gorge view. At 4.7 miles, cross an old road. At 4.8 miles, watch for a left turn in the trail; cross bare rock with reindeer moss and pines in pockets of thin soil.

Watch for a right turn uphill at 5.1 miles. The trail crosses a small creek at 5.8 miles, where you might find water; to the left is a pouroff where water coming out of the bluffs drops to the creekbed. At 6.2 miles, cross an old roadway and then watch for a turn left at 6.3 miles.

The trail at 6.6 miles crosses a drainage on a footbridge. Cross another footbridge, and then at 7.0 miles a short stairway takes you down a low bluff. Turn left and follow the JMT out along the bluff to a good view of the sandstone rim of the river gorge.

At 7.6 miles, the trail makes a right turn to a junction; the main trail turns left and a side path straight ahead leads to a gorge overlook on a point. At 8.2 miles is another junction where the main trail turns left and a side trail straight ahead leads out to another overlook; a side cove on the left joins the river gorge. The JMT heads up this tributary cove to descend through a couple of switchbacks and cross a footbridge over a side drainage and then reach a bridge over the main tributary creek at 10.3 miles. This is the only reliable source of water on the 13-mile stretch from Fall Branch to Laurel Fork. You'll find some areas for camping just upstream.

The trail now heads up the other side of the cove back toward the river. Bear left to parallel the river and eventually bear left up Duncan Hollow. Penetrate deep into the hollow and cross a ridge. At 12.9 miles, the trail crosses an old road. Cross a saddle and then ascend to join an old road at 13.2 miles. Follow the road to the right. At 13.6 miles, the trail turns to the left off the road and begins a descent toward Station Camp Creek.

The trail crosses a footbridge over a small drainage and descends into a beech cove. Cross another footbridge and circle the point of a ridge and switchback right down to face a massive block of stone; turn left down stone steps to get around the obstruction. The trail makes a series of switchbacks to complete the descent. At 14.8 miles the trail passes above the confluence of Laurel Fork and Station Camp Creek and follows Laurel Fork upstream. Drop into the overgrown floodplain where the Duncan Hollow Trail comes down to ford the creek; you'll find a high bridge to walk over Laurel Fork at 15.0 miles.

On the other side, the Laurel Fork Creek Trail leads to the left. Turn right to stay with the JMT. At another junction soon after, the Duncan Hollow Trail turns to the left. The JMT bears right along an old road, but soon turns left to cross Station Camp Creek on a bridge at 15.1 miles. After crossing the bridge, the JMT bears right through an overgrown area to rejoin the old road, which has forded the creek. Turn left. At 15.4 miles, the trail turns left off the road, which continues toward the Station Camp River Crossing. The JMT passes through an overgrown area where you may still see foundations and building debris. A subsistence farming community once thrived on Station Camp Creek. The community had a grocery store, post office, and school, and managed to survive into the early 1960s in the face of a dwindling population.

At 15.5 miles is a junction with the Station Camp Creek Trail. To stay on the JMT, keep straight up an old road, which is also the River Trail West. At 15.6 miles, the JMT bears left, while the horse trail continues along the road.

The trail climbs above the road to traverse a broad shelf; at 16.0 miles, cross a bridge over a drainage. Soon after, the JMT rejoins the road. At 16.4 miles, as the road nears Parch Corn Creek, the trail bears left through an overgrown area. Cross a bridge over a side drainage and reach a long bridge over Parch Corn Creek at 16.6 miles.

On the other side of the bridge, you'll encounter the old Parch Corn Road, one leg of the Terry Cemetery Loop. You can turn left for 0.2 mile to reach the site of a cabin built by John Litton in 1881. The cabin burned in 1998; only the chimney remains. The JMT turns right on Parch Corn Road from the bridge crossing and then leaves the road to the left. The road continues down to connect with the road/horse trail along the river after it has forded Parch Corn Creek. As the JMT continues north it weaves on and off the old river road, which is still the River Trail West. The trail is obscure through here, so you may want to just follow the road.

At 16.9 miles, the trail swings away from the road to cross a bridge over Harvey Branch. Cross two more bridges over smaller streams. Watch for rock foundations and piles of stone from cleared fields, remnants of settlements along the road that connected the main communities at Parch Corn and No Business Creeks. At 18.1 miles, the Watson Cemetery Road, the other side of the Terry Cemetery Loop, leads down from Terry Cemetery Road; the road crosses the JMT to connect with the River Trail West. At 18.3 miles, the JMT curves left up a side road to a ford of Big Branch.

The JMT continues to parallel the road until at 18.5 miles it turns uphill to the left; if you have been walking the road instead of the trail, watch for this junction up the slope to your left. The old road continues north another mile to the mouth of No Business Creek, where the River Trail West ends.

Turn left uphill to continue on the JMT. Swing right up Big Branch Hollow on an old roadway that is sometimes steep. At 19.2 miles, the trail bears right off the road. Continue up to cross another road. The trail switchbacks right and left, crisscrossing this old roadway. If leaves are off the trees, you'll see two huge stone pillars standing on the ridge up to your right.

The trail makes a switchback right, with a tall sandstone bluff standing ahead. At 19.4 miles, the trail tops the ridge. The pillars you saw from below stand to the right.

The JMT turns back left over the ridge and circles the rock bluff with some of the most intricate rockwork in the park, with lines and scrolls and multi-colored stone. The trail crosses a ridge below the point of the bluff and circles left to cross a saddle between the main bluff and a sandstone knob on the right.

Maudes Crack

At 19.7 miles, the JMT switchbacks right to begin a descent toward No Business Creek. Just at the turn, you'll see a passageway to the left where a path turns off to head up to Maudes Crack, a large break in the rock bluff where you can climb to the top of the plateau. On the JMT, descend into a valley of sandstone buttes, several to the left, while you pass below Burke Knob to the right.

After many switchbacks, bottom out at 20.5 miles and turn left to cross two footbridges over Betty Branch. Then turn right to reach a long bridge over No Business Creek. On the other side, good camping spots lie to the right, but camp in this floodplain only during dry times of the year.

The trail bears left to enter the former community of No Business and pass the foundations for the old boarding house; the pillars are solid sandstone slabs. The community adopted the creek's name, which is attributed to a woman whose husband brought them to settle the isolated region; she repeatedly told him they had no business being there. The community eventually had two stores, a school, and a post office and survived into the 1960s.

The trail passes through a grassy area and up to a junction with an old road at 20.7 miles. This road is a horse and hiking trail: the No Business Trail for horses and the Dry Branch Trail to the right and the JMT to the left for hikers.

Hiking left along the road, parallel No Business Creek upstream. Watch for foundations and the remains of fences. At 21.4 miles, an old road turns down to ford the creek; you'll see foundations across the way. At 21.5 miles, watch for the shell of an old truck where a side stream crosses under slabs of rock in the road; tumbled-down log barns rest in the overgrown field to the left. Soon after, pass the Stoopin' Oak Road headed up the slope to the

John Muir Overlook

right. At 21.6 miles, the JMT fords Tacket Creek, the last reliable source of water for the next leg. Then at 21.9 miles, the JMT turns right off the old road; the No Business Trail continues on to connect with the Longfield Branch Trail.

Turning right, begin a long climb to the top of the plateau. The trail switchbacks right and left and then hits an old roadway at 22.1 miles; turn right. Watch for a left turn off the road at 22.2 miles; the turn is easy to miss. Make several more switchbacks to climb a ladder up a low bluff and walk up stone steps to a left turn. After a couple more switchbacks, the trail runs into a slope of bare stone at 23.0 miles. Scramble up the stone and watch for the trail turning right. You'll finally reach the top at 23.1 miles. The trail then swings left to the bare rock of the John Muir Overlook at 23.2 miles, a panoramic view of the No Business Creek Gorge.

From the overlook, head right along the bluff. The trail drops to cross a narrow ridge separating No Business Creek Gorge from Tacket Creek Gorge. At 23.4 miles, turn left on an old road. Then at 23.8 miles, the trail turns left off the road just before you reach posts blocking vehicle access from the other direction, which is the short way in to the John Muir Overlook.

The next section of trail is uneventful. Cross old roads at first and later a number of footbridges over small streams. At 28.6 miles, bear right to reach a short ladder up a low bluff. At 30.7 miles, ascend to cross Divide Road. The trail then descends with switchbacks to cross Massey Branch on a bridge and connect with the Rock Creek Loop at 31.2 miles.

The JMT follows the Rock Creek Loop to the right. At 32.4 miles is a junction with the Sheltowee Trace, and then all three trails coincide as the path turns left and follows Rock Creek upstream. At 35.8 miles is a junction with the Rock Creek Loop turning up left and the JMT/Sheltowee Trace turning down right to ford Rock Creek. On the other side, turn left upstream to cross into Pickett State Forest, outside the recreation area. A concrete piling perched on a rock on the other side of the creek once supported a railroad bridge, probably part of the Stearns Coal and Lumber Company operations.

Connect with the Rock Creek Trail at 36.0 miles. At the junction, you have the option of continuing straight on the Rock Creek Trail, passing a junction with the Tunnel Trail and fording the creek three times to reach TN 154 at 37.9 miles. From there, if you want to walk farther, walk to the right on the highway to cross the bridge over Rock Creek and turn left back into the woods. In the next few miles, make 27 fords and two bridge crossings of Rock Creek. At 42.9 miles, you'll reach Boundary Road and the end of the JMT.

The other option at the junction with the Rock Creek Trail is to turn left. Ford to the other side of Rock Creek and make a steep ascent out of the gorge. At 37.5 miles, connect with the Hidden Passage Trail. Turn left. Pass by Thompson Overlook and continue on to emerge at the trailhead for the Hidden Passage Trail on TN 154 at 42.4 miles.

18 | LEATHERWOOD FORD LOOP 🚶🚶

Distance: 3.6 miles
Difficulty: Moderate
Elevation change: 550 ft
Cautions: Short section along highway
Connections: Sunset Overlook Trail 🚶🚶, John Muir Trail 🚶🚶

Attractions: The upper part of the loop offers scenic views and blooming laurel in mid-May; in early spring, you'll walk through gatherings of wildflowers on the lower elevations and along the river. The return trail follows a wagon road and passes an old farm pond.

Trailhead: Head up the east side of the river gorge from Leatherwood Ford on TN 297, and at 1.6 miles turn right on the paved road across from the park headquarters, where a sign directs you to the East Rim Overlook. If you're entering the park from the east on TN 297, turn left at 0.6 mile from the park's east entrance sign. At 0.3 mile along the road to the East Rim Overlook, park on the right at the East Rim Trailhead. You'll see the old Leatherwood Ford Road leading into the clearing. On the other side of the paved road, the Sunset Overlook Trail heads south.

Description: On the trailhead side of the road, walk to the left, paralleling the road, until you enter the woods and the trail becomes more obvious. In 0.2 mile you'll reach the loop part of the trail. Turn left for the best approach.

Pass through a low area that has water in wet seasons, join an old road for a short distance, and then drop among rocks to a side trail at 0.6 mile; the path leads to the right 0.1 mile to an overlook of the river with the bridge at Leatherwood Ford.

Back on the main trail, descend, following a small stream and passing below rock bluffs to eventually rockhop the stream. The trail works through several switchbacks before it reaches the river at 1.6 miles. This section of the trail wanders through wildflowers in spring: foamflower, penstemon, geranium, columbine, Solomon's seal, phlox, cinquefoil, crested dwarf iris, bloodroot, fire pink, mayapple, dwarf dandelion, and more.

At the river, the trail joins the JMT. To continue the loop, turn right on the JMT. The trail parallels the river and eventually becomes a gravel path leading to Leatherwood Ford at 2.1 miles.

Next to the TN 297 bridge, before going under, turn right and go up the rock steps beside the bridge. After topping out on the highway, walk up the road, which passes over a creek, to a right turn into the woods.

The trail climbs steeply from the highway through a number of switchbacks. You'll see an old road off to the right and then cross it at 2.6 miles. This is the old Leatherwood Ford wagon road that once led down the bluff

Leatherwood Ford Overlook

to the river ford and that you saw at the trailhead; the old road was used as the route for the water line running to the restrooms at the river, so you'll see some scars left from the digging and occasional metal plates that cover access to the water line.

At 2.7 miles the trail approaches the creek you crossed on the road as it cascades among boulders on its way down the slope, making a small waterfall in a cove of rhododendron and hemlock. The trail switches left and then passes through more switchbacks to cross the old road again at 2.9 miles. The trail then swings right to follow the road up the ridge.

Once you reach the top of the gorge, the trail turns right off the road to follow the border between field and forest until you cross a footbridge and pass over the earthen dam for an old farm pond on your left at 3.3 miles. A short hike through the woods returns you to the beginning of the loop at 3.4 miles; turn left to return to the trailhead at 3.6 miles.

19 | SUNSET OVERLOOK TRAIL 🚶‍♂️

Distance: 1.3 miles one-way
Difficulty: Easy
Elevation change: Level
Cautions: High cliffs
Connections: Leatherwood Ford Loop 🚶‍♂️

Attractions: This trail crosses small streams, passes old farm ponds, and leads to an overlook with a panoramic view of the river gorge and Leatherwood Ford.

Trailhead: Head up the east side of the river gorge from Leatherwood

Ford on TN 297, and at 1.6 miles turn right on the paved road across from the park headquarters, where a sign directs you to the East Rim Overlook. If you're entering the park from the east on TN 297, turn left at 0.6 mile from the park's east entrance sign. At 0.3 mile along the road to the East Rim Overlook, park on the right at the East Rim Trailhead for the Leatherwood Ford Loop. On the other side of the paved road, the Sunset Overlook Trail heads south.

Description: Cross the road from trailhead parking and take the trail into the woods. Swing left to emerge on a gravel road at 0.1 mile that leads off the paved road up to a small building at a shooting range for law enforcement officers. Cross the road and pass a farm pond on the left. This path was once a nature trail; you may still see some old posts with interpretive numbers.

Parallel a small creek on the left and then turn to cross the creek on a bridge at 0.3 mile. The trail skirts the back of a maintenance and office area that you'll see through the trees to the left. Then curve right to cross an earthen dam creating another pond at 0.4 mile; a footbridge takes you over the spillway. Then join an old roadway and turn to the right.

At 0.6 mile, the trail turns right off the road. But then at 0.7 mile, the trail rejoins the road; turn right. Pass the trace of old roads to the right and left as you stay with the main roadway. At 1.1 miles the roadway narrows to a path in a small open area with two large beech trees on the left.

Continue on the path out the point of the bluff and descend to the edge of the gorge with switchbacks left and right down to the bare rock of Sunset Overlook, with a great view of the river gorge. To the right, you'll see the TN 297 bridge at Leatherwood Ford and to the left the North White Oak Creek drainage.

20 | O&W OVERLOOK 🚶🚶

Distance: 1.1 miles one-way
Difficulty: Moderate
Elevation loss: 140 ft
Cautions: Begins on private land, so stay to the trail; not blazed, mudholes, high cliffs
Connections: None

Attractions: This old road takes you to a panoramic view of the river gorge and the O&W Bridge. Until developed, this route should be attempted only by experienced outdoorspeople.

Trailhead: Just inside the park's east entrance on TN 297, you'll see a dirt road on the south side of the highway. Park at the east entrance sign and walk up to this road on the left, or pull in the road and park to the side so you do not block access; the road can be muddy. There are no-trespassing signs because the road crosses private land at first, but the signs were erected to keep hunters and others from leaving the roadway. The owners of the land have given permission for people to hike up the road.

Description: Head up the old road into the woods. Unless there has been dry weather, you'll soon encounter deep mudholes. You'll have some ups and downs and a somewhat steep, rutted descent as you walk out the ridge.

Cross the unmarked boundary into the park and at 0.8 mile pass an old roadway to the left as the main road curves right. At 1.0 mile is the end of the road. Walk the footpath that leads straight into the woods down to the edge of the river gorge; bear right along the rim to then switchback left down to a bare rock overlook at 1.1 miles. You'll see the O&W Bridge down to your left, where it spans the river, and have a grand view of the river gorge to the right as the Big South Fork heads toward Leatherwood Ford. Be careful exploring along the edge of the bluff, and do not climb on rocks at the edge; it's a long way down.

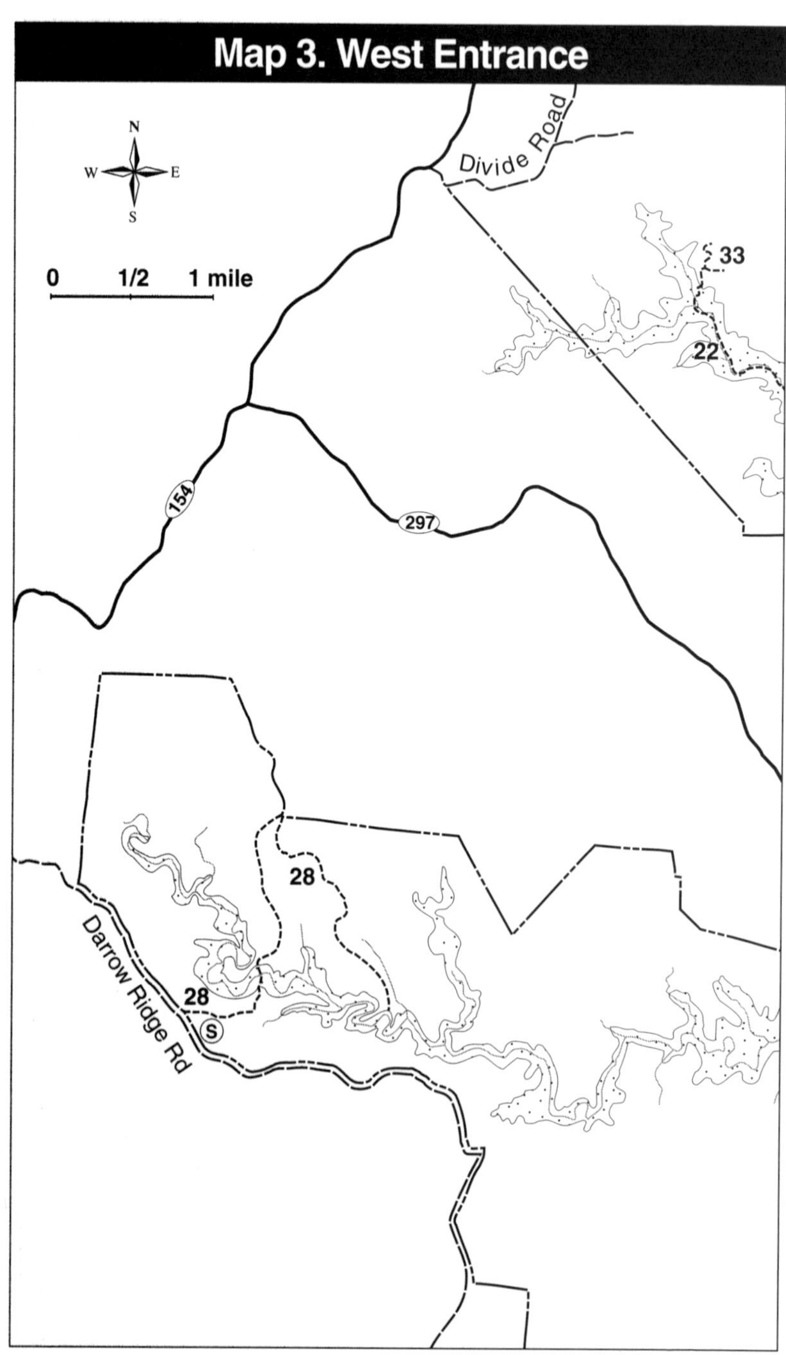

Map 3. West Entrance
N
W   E
S
0   1/2   1 mile
Divide Road
33
22
154
297
28
28
S
Darrow Ridge Rd

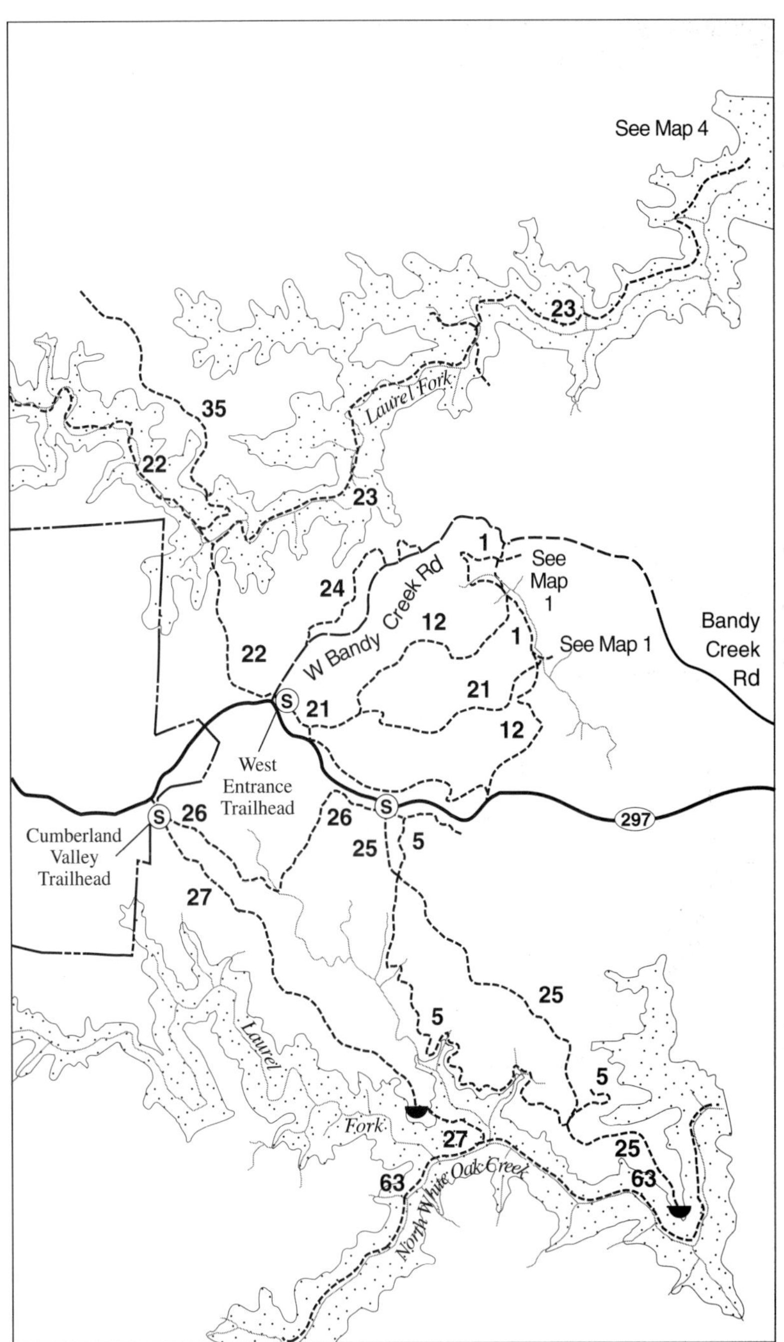

See Map 4
See Map 1
See Map 1
Bandy Creek Rd
Laurel Fork
W Bandy Creek Rd
297
West Entrance Trailhead
Cumberland Valley Trailhead
Laurel
Fork
North White Oak Creek
35
22
23
24
22
12
1
1
21
12
S 21
S 26
26
25
5
27
5
25
5
27
25
63
63
23

The West Entrance Trailhead is the first attraction for visitors approaching the recreation area from the west. Trails connect with the Bandy Creek area and head north to Middle Creek and south to North White Oak Overlook. Here you can also access a difficult mountain bike trail designed for advanced riders.

On the west side of the river, just inside the West Entrance to the BSFNRRA on TN 297, turn into the parking area for the West Entrance Trailhead on the north side of the road. If you're coming from the Bandy Creek Visitor Center, the trailhead is 3.9 miles west along TN 297 from the Bandy Creek Road turnoff. You can also reach the trailhead from the visitor center by continuing on the Bandy Creek Road, which becomes the gravel West Bandy Creek Road and swings around to rejoin TN 297; the trailhead parking is to your left.

21 | WEST ENTRANCE TRAIL 𝕸

Distance: 2.4 miles one-way
Difficulty: Easy
Elevation loss: 200 ft
Cautions: None
Connections: Salt Pine Trail 𝕸, Collier Ridge Loop 🚲,
Oscar Blevins Farm Loop 𝕸

Attractions: This easy walk connects the West Entrance Trailhead with the Oscar Blevins Farm Loop and the Bandy Creek area.

Trailhead: The West Entrance Trail begins to the right of the parking area for the West Entrance Trailhead.

Description: At first, walk through scrub pine and hardwood as the trail parallels the highway to the east. Then at 0.1 mile, curve away from the road; watch for climbing fern on the right of the trail and a large pine on the left. The trail soon curves back to skirt the highway once more before turning back into the woods.

At 0.4 mile the trail joins an old road that is part of the Collier Ridge Loop. Keep straight ahead around a sign that indicates no jeeps, horses, or motorized bikes on this section. The trail follows the old road until at 0.8 mile the bicycle trail forks to the left and the hiking trail continues on the old road to the right. Then at 0.9 mile, the trail turns right off the road and begins dropping.

The trail switchbacks left at 1.0 mile and becomes more closed in by mixed pine and hardwood. You'll see a number of small pine trees. Later you'll find yourself on an old roadbed again. At 1.6 miles the trail reaches the south branch of Bandy Creek that wanders through thick laurel. Four footbridges help you across a boggy area where a small stream crosses the trail. At 1.7 miles, enter Scott State Forest.

Watch for trailing arbutus in bloom in spring along the trail; you may have to lift up the leaves of the low-growing plant to see the pink-white flowers. At 2.0 miles pass through a white pine and hemlock grove. Then at 2.2 miles, the trail crosses another old road that is the other side of the Collier Ridge Loop; keep straight.

At 2.4 miles is a junction with the Oscar Blevins Farm Loop. To the left on the loop, you can walk 1.0 mile to the Oscar Blevins Farm, which is now a historic site, and then on to the Bandy Creek Trailhead in another 1.6 miles. Or you can reach the Bandy Creek Trailhead in 1.0 mile by turning right on the loop.

22 SALT PINE / LAUREL FORK CREEK TRAILS TO THE MIDDLE CREEK AREA 🚶🚶

Distance: 5.6 miles one-way
Difficulty: Strenuous
Elevation change: 420 ft
Cautions: Many creek crossings impassable in high water, steep stone steps
Connections: West Entrance Trail 🚶🚶, Laurel Fork Creek Trail to Station Camp Creek 🚶🚶, Slave Falls Loop 🚶🚶

Attractions: Along these trails into the Middle Creek area, you'll enjoy isolated backcountry while following the Laurel Fork of Station Camp Creek upstream within the Laurel Fork Gorge.

Trailhead: Start at the West Entrance Trailhead parking area where the West Entrance Trail leads to the right.

Directions: To reach the Middle Creek area, go left, walking west from the parking area and paralleling TN 297; this Salt Pine Trail is proposed to become a multiuse path that horses and mountain bikes may also use.

Cross the gravel West Bandy Creek Road and continue heading west into the woods. At 0.1 mile the trail crosses an old roadbed at an angle. Soon after this crossing is an old route back to your right; stay straight. At 0.2 mile, watch for where the trail curves left back toward the highway; hikers who have missed the trail have created a path straight ahead. Continuing, the trail runs behind a fenced area on your left that holds living quarters for seasonal rangers off TN 297. The trail joins an old roadway and begins a gradual descent.

The trail crosses an expanse of sandstone at 1.3 miles that signals your approach to the Laurel Fork Gorge. Bear right off the old roadbed and begin descending steeply along steps carved into the rock. The trail then rejoins the old road to continue the descent toward Laurel Fork. At 1.5 miles watch for a rock step on the right side of the trail that indicates a right turn away from the road. Pass through woods and descend through three switchbacks to once again meet the road. This swing to the right has cut off a steep section of the roadway.

Continue your walk down the road; drop into rhododendron and level out to a trail junction at 1.7 miles with the Laurel Fork Creek Trail. (To the right, the trail leads toward Station Camp Creek.) Turn to the left to head toward the Middle Creek area.

Almost immediately, ford Laurel Fork; the creek is wide and hardly ever is low enough to rockhop. This is the first of 18 times you'll ford Laurel Fork, so be prepared. At times of high water, the creek may be impassable; if you are not sure you can make it across (remember that you'll have to do it many times), come back another day.

Once on the other side of the creek, turn left and walk upstream. You'll be walking along an old roadbed; for most of this walk, the trail off and on follows the old road. The walk is through the floodplain of the creek, sandy in places and shrouded in pine, hemlock, and scattered hardwood. Cross several small tributaries. The occasional dense stands of hemlock along the way make good campsites except in flood seasons. The trail passes through stands of mountain laurel, for which the creek is named.

At 1.9 miles the trail curves left away from the old road into a hemlock grove and then curves right into a more open area. The trail reconnects with the road and heads up a slope to a junction with an old roadway up to the right that is the proposed extension of the Salt Pine Trail, impassable for now on this lower end. From here on, the Laurel Fork Creek Trail will continue to be for hikers only. Bear left here and walk down the road to the second creek ford at 2.0 miles.

Ford the creek four more times. At 2.6 miles, the trail veers left away from the road and crosses an oxbow of the creek that in low water is dry. Cross the other side of the oxbow before rejoining the old road. Ford again at 2.9 miles.

The trail crosses a small side stream and passes through a large patch of climbing fern. Be alert in this section; the trail veers away from the road several times, crossing another small side stream along the way. Ford again at 3.4 miles; notice the rock bluff to your left.

The trail rejoins the road only to veer away again to the left to move along a secondary roadbed. At 3.6 miles, watch for where the trail turns off to the right to rejoin the original road; the turn is easy to miss. Ford five more times. At 4.3 miles, cross a side stream in an overgrown area where the trail is not well marked. Follow what appears to be the most traveled path; you should soon see a blaze. The trail then passes through the boggy area of a side stream.

At 4.5 miles, drop into the creek, but do not ford to the other side. In a few feet, the trail comes out on the same side of the creek; you've just bypassed a slough on the east side. The trail then follows an island between two sloughs; notice the rock wall to the east with a wet-weather waterfall. The trail curves left, back toward the creek, and at 4.7 miles turns left at a camping spot to ford the creek. Ford twice more and then ford Laurel Fork for the last time at 5.1 miles.

Then at 5.2 miles, the trail fords Ben Creek, a tributary of Laurel Fork. At this crossing, the old road continues up the tributary, but do not follow it. Just on the other side of Ben Creek, the trail heads to the right up the slope. Pause for a moment to scan for a small natural arch at the top of the low ridge just ahead on the west side of Ben Creek. Also as you walk up the trail, look back to your left at the ridgeline to see the arch.

The trail climbs from the creek in a moderately steep ascent. After a couple of switchbacks, come to steps cut in the rock bluff at 5.3 miles. The steps can be slippery when wet. The trail then curves back left over the bluff. You'll see to your left the deep cove you were headed into before climbing up the bluff. At 5.4 miles, stay left where an old trail heads up the slope. Make a couple more switchbacks as you continue to climb out of the gorge of the Laurel Fork, and finally come to a trail junction at 5.6 miles with the Slave Falls Loop. Turn left on the loop to make your way to the Sawmill Trailhead in 1.1 miles and the Middle Creek Trailhead in 2.9 miles.

23 | LAUREL FORK CREEK TRAIL TO STATION CAMP CREEK 👫

Distance: 6.9 miles one-way
Difficulty: Moderate
Elevation loss: 350 ft
Cautions: Numerous creek fords impassable in high water
Connections: Salt Pine Trail ∩, Black House Branch Trail ∩, Fork Ridge Trail ∩, Duncan Hollow Trail ∩, John Muir Trail 👫

Attractions: The Laurel Fork of Station Camp Creek passes through Laurel Fork Gorge, crossing the stream several times to reach Station Camp Creek. As you follow Laurel Fork, you'll walk through a bottomland of rhododendron, hemlock stands, small pines, and a variety of hardwoods. The trail often is sandy and often follows an old roadway. The creek washes up against sandstone bluffs. Small side streams cross the path to join Laurel Fork. In fall, floating leaves of yellow and red create swirls of color in the slowly moving water.

Trailhead: From the West Entrance Trailhead parking area, go left, walking west and paralleling TN 297 along the Salt Pine Trail 1.7 miles to the junction with the Laurel Fork Trail. Turn to the right to head toward Station Camp.

Description: At 0.1 mile, you'll reach the edge of Laurel Fork, which

Falls on Laurel Fork

you must ford. In the next 2 miles, you will ford the creek 11 times. These fords can be dangerous in times of high water, so you should plan to do this hike during dry times of the year.

The trail follows an old roadway, fording the creek several times. Then at 1.2 miles the old roadbed curves left down to the creek, but the trail continues straight to the seventh crossing just downstream. After the eighth ford, the trail becomes faint in an overgrown area, but stay generally left along the creek bank and you'll soon find the way open again. In a hemlock stand, watch for a boulder on the right that has several trees growing on top; it's a good campsite. Just beyond the boulder, ford the creek for the ninth time at 2.0 miles.

At 2.8 miles, you'll reach a junction with the Black House Branch Trail for horses. You can loop back to the West Entrance Trailhead here by turning to the right where the horse trail fords Laurel Fork and heads up a road 0.4 mile to connect with the Jacks Ridge Loop. Turn right on the loop and walk 0.8 mile out to West Bandy Creek Road, where you can turn right again and walk up the gravel road 1.9 miles back to the trailhead on TN 297.

To continue on the Laurel Fork Creek Trail, stay straight on the Black House Branch Trail, which is the road that runs beside the creek. At 2.9 miles, the hiking trail turns off to the right while the horse trail/road continues to the left.

Turning right, the Laurel Fork Creek Trail passes through a grassy area and then a hemlock wood to parallel Laurel Fork downstream and then to ford the creek at 3.0 miles. The trail crosses the inside of a meander of the stream, with good campsites in a hemlock wood. Camp in the floodplain of the creek only in dry seasons. Ford the stream again at 3.1 miles.

The trail climbs to the left and stays on this northwest side of Laurel Fork, moving up and down, crossing side drainages, passing large hemlocks, white pines, and beeches. Pass around a large boulder to the left, and then watch for a switchback right and left soon after at 3.7 miles. Pass between two boulders and by a huge white pine on the left and then descend, turning right and left at 3.8 miles. The trail curves left up a cove to cross a rhododendron-filled side creek at 4.0 miles. Two more times, make right and left turns as the trail works its way upstream. At 4.6 miles, curve left around a moss-covered block of stone.

At 5.0 miles the trail joins a road to the left. Pass through an area of large pines. You'll lose the trace of the roadway for a time. Watch for an area where trees grow on top of rocks on both sides of the trail. You'll be back on the roadway again. Then listen for falling water in the creek below, where a nice little waterfall beckons. Watch for a block of stone on the right beside the trail at 5.2 miles; on the far side, a 50-yard path leads down to a precarious overlook where a jumble of house-size boulders constrict the stream to the 6-foot, two-step spout.

At 5.6 miles, the trail leaves the old roadbed to the left, but soon rejoins.

Then at 5.7 miles, watch for where the trail leaves the road to the left; at the turn you'll see a medium-sized birch standing on its roots; it once grew atop a fallen log that has decomposed.

The trail descends to cross a drainage on stepping stones and then passes along the edge of the creek and joins an old road at 6.0 miles. Bear left on the road.

Pass through a hemlock wood and then at 6.4 miles enter a more open area of grown-up fields that was part of the subsistence community around the confluence of Laurel Fork and Station Camp Creek.

The trail passes through a wooded area and then more old fields to cross a small side stream and reach a junction at 6.7 miles with the Fork Ridge Trail. The horse and hiking trails then coincide along the old road, paralleling the creek to a junction at 6.9 miles, with the Duncan Hollow Trail fording Laurel Fork from the right and the JMT crossing the creek from the right on a high bridge. Station Camp Creek is just beyond on the JMT.

24 | WEST BANDY CREEK TRAIL 🚲

Distance: 4.2-mile loop
Difficulty: Strenuous
Elevation change: 160 ft
Cautions: Not for beginning mountain bikers; steep and narrow sections, creek ford
Connections: None

Attractions: The bike trail off West Bandy Creek Road presents challenges for the experienced mountain biker.

Trailhead: Start at the West Entrance Trailhead parking area.

Description: Ride out onto TN 297; turn west and then turn right on the gravel West Bandy Creek Road. At 0.7 mile, watch for a bike trail sign on the left that marks the beginning of the mountain bike trail. At this writing, the trail has not yet been blazed, but you might still find blue flags occasionally marking the route from when the trail was originally constructed.

As you head left into the woods the trail narrows and curves left downhill. At 0.9 mile the trail switchbacks right at a low bluff. Soon after, connect with an old road; right will take you out to West Bandy Creek Road. Turn left on the road, and in a few yards turn right off the road. You'll soon encounter a steep downhill section and a steep uphill. At 1.2 miles, ride across bare rock with pines and reindeer moss and then encounter another steep down and up.

At 1.3 miles, join the faint trace of an old road to turn right and connect with another road. Turn right and then turn left off that road. Drop into another steep downhill at 1.4 miles, this time down bare rock. Curve right at the bottom and emerge onto an old road at 1.5 miles; again, turning right will take you out to West Bandy Creek Road. Turn left and then watch for a right turn off the road at 1.6 miles. Then begin a downhill section with a right turn into a steep descent into a cove and join another old road at 1.7 miles. Turn left here to ford a small creek and bear right uphill to a right turn. Follow the road you are now on into a steep ascent.

At 1.8 miles, at the top of the ascent, connect with another road. Turn right and emerge on West Bandy Creek Road. Turn left on the road and at 2.4 miles you'll see the bike trail turning left back into the woods along an old roadway.

The old road curves left; then bear left off the road to join another road to the right. At 2.5 miles, the trail turns right off the road and curves down the slope to cross a drainage at 2.6 miles. The trail ascends out of the cove, bearing right.

The trail joins an old roadway headed north; at 2.9 miles, stay straight on a side road as the road you're on curves right. Soon after, cross the top part of the Y of an old roadway, bearing right up the left branch of the Y to emerge on West Bandy Creek Road at 3.1 miles.

Turn right along the road to complete the loop back to the trailhead. Reach the beginning of the bike trail on the right at 4.1 miles and then emerge back on TN 297 and turn left back to the West Entrance Trailhead at 4.8 miles.

25 | GAR BLEVINS / NORTH WHITE OAK OVERLOOK TRAILS ∩

Distance: 3.9 miles one-way
Difficulty: Moderate
Elevation loss: 140 ft
Cautions: Loose gravel
Connections: Groom Branch Trail ∩, North White Oak Loop ∩

Attractions: This ride follows the old Gar Blevins Road and the Narrows Road for the shortest access to the North White Oak Overlook. You'll have a good view of the North White Oak Creek Gorge; you can even see a patch of the creek below as it flows east toward the river. The O&W Railroad once ran along the north side of the creek, but trees shroud the old railbed so you can't see it.

Trailhead: The old road begins on the south side of TN 297 1.0 mile east of the West Entrance Trailhead parking area. You can park at the trailhead

Mountain bikers on Gar Blevins Trail

and bike east on TN 297 to get to the Gar Blevins Trail. Or start at the beginning of the road; the first few yards of the road are paved, so you can pull in and park to the side so that you do not block access.

Description: Follow the old Gar Blevins Road into the woods; you'll reach a junction at 0.1 mile with the Groom Branch Trail. Continue straight on Gar Blevins Road. At 0.3 mile the road crosses the upper part of the North White Oak Loop and from here cuts through the middle of the loop.

This first section of the trail has been improved, so you'll encounter gravel where there used to be ruts and rock ledges. An open field lies on the left at 0.7 mile. Beyond the field the road is still a dirt track through the forest. Cross the Scott State Forest boundary at 1.2 miles.

At 1.5 miles, the road curves right and comes to a fork. (The road to the right travels down to cross the west side of the North White Oak Loop in 0.3 mile.) Bear left to stay on the Gar Blevins Trail. You'll reach another fork at 2.0 miles; the left fork is now so overgrown, you may not even notice the intersection. This left fork was the continuation of the Gar Blevins Road; the Gar Blevins Trail continues straight on the right fork, following what was once the Narrows Road that eventually extends out a narrow point of land. At 2.1 miles, cross the state forest boundary again; the sign marking the boundary faces the other direction.

The road crosses the lower part of the North White Oak Loop at 2.3 miles and continues straight, headed for the overlook. The part of the road out to the overlook has been proposed to be called the North White Oak Overlook Trail. The trail stays level at first and descends before beginning a long steep ascent over a knoll and up to the top of a second knoll at 2.8 miles. From here, there are a couple of steep descents. At the bottom, you may notice an overgrown trail to the left that was once an alternative route for horses that swung around to rejoin the main trail 0.1 mile back up the road.

The main trail then ascends to hitching rails for the overlook at 3.9 miles.

At the hitching rails, leave horses and bikes and walk 30 yards up to a long flight of stairs that takes you on a ridge of rock that leads out to the overlook. From here, return to your starting point, or take the North White Oak Loop east or west for longer return routes.

26 | GROOM BRANCH TRAIL ∩

Distance: 2.4 miles one-way
Difficulty: Easy
Elevation change: 120 ft
Cautions: None
Connections: Gernt Trail ∩, North White Oak Loop ∩, Gar Blevins Trail ∩

Attractions: This horse trail connects the Cumberland Valley Trailhead with the Gar Blevins Trail and the North White Oak Loop and is part of the Cumberland Valley Loop.

Trailhead: Drive west from the West Entrance Trailhead on TN 297, exiting the park and in 1.0 mile reaching the Hitching Post Grocery on the left. Beside the grocery, turn left on Gernt Road which has been upgraded for 0.2 mile to the Cumberland Valley Trailhead, where the Groom Branch Trail begins on the left.

Description: Headed east, the Groom Branch Trail descends from the trailhead, passing through coves; in wet weather, streams of water often pass under the road. At 0.7 mile, ascend to a junction with an old roadway to the left that emerges on TN 297 in half a mile, providing additional access west of the West Entrance Trailhead; there is no parking at that location.

Turn right to stay on the Groom Branch Trail, which descends steeply. After a level section, the trail turns left and descends to a crossing of Groom Branch at 1.2 miles. The stream is small and shallow, but the crossing can be muddy.

Ascend steeply from the creek and continue up to an intersection at 1.9 miles with another old road that leads straight ahead to the highway in 0.1 mile; the way is blocked by fallen trees. Turn right to continue along the trail, swinging through the head of a cove and ascending to an intersection with the Gar Blevins Trail at 2.4 miles. To the left it's 0.1 mile out to TN 297. To the right the Gar Blevins Trail crosses the North White Oak Loop in 0.2 mile. Stay straight ahead on the Groom Branch Trail about 70 yards to connect with the North White Oak Loop. There, you can turn right or left to circle the loop and return to this intersection.

27 | GERNT TRAIL ∩

Distance: 3.3 miles one-way *(East Laurel Overlook 2.8 miles one-way)*
Difficulty: Moderate
Elevation loss: 560 ft
Cautions: Deep sand, steep rocky descent
Connections: Groom Branch Trail ∩, O&W Railbed ∩

Attractions: This old road gives access to East Laurel Overlook and the O&W Railbed. Along the railbed was once a mining and lumber camp run by the Bruno Gernt family, who settled the community of Allardt to the south of the park in the 1880s. Here coal and lumber were loaded on the O&W trains that operated in the Big South Fork watershed in the first half of the 1900s. The trains picked up coal and lumber at several loading stations along the track and hauled them east to Oneida, where the material was transferred to the Southern Railway and shipped out of the region.

Trailhead: Drive west from the West Entrance Trailhead on TN 297, exiting the park and in 1.0 mile reaching the Hitching Post Grocery on the left. Beside the grocery, turn left on Gernt Road for 0.2 mile to the Cumberland Valley Trailhead. The Groom Branch Trail leads to the left from the trailhead, while the Gernt Trail continues straight.

Description: Ride from the trailhead straight ahead on the old Gernt Road. The tread is deep sand. Long stretches of sand may cause mountain bikes to lose traction. The old road mostly stays level across the surface of the plateau.

At 1.0 mile, as the road descends bare sandstone, an old homesite lies

Gorge of the Laurel Fork of North White Oak Creek from East Laurel Overlook

to the right, a clearing marked by yucca plants. The road crosses the trace of an old road at 1.3 miles.

At 1.7 miles, pass through a pine woods and at 2.7 miles reach a fork in the road. The left fork is the continuation of Gernt Road as it begins its descent toward North White Oak Creek; the way is blocked by a bar gate to prevent vehicle access.

Before turning left to make the descent, keep straight to get to the East Laurel Overlook; posts at the fork also prevent vehicle access straight ahead. In 0.1 mile from the fork is the end of the road at a hitching rail. A footpath to the right leads through the woods 200 yards and down to an impressive overlook of the gorge of Laurel Fork of North White Oak Creek; bare sandstone cliffs stand above a slash of water in the trees below.

Back at the junction, take the left fork to descend into the gorge. The route is steep, rough, and rocky. Watch for low ledges in the roadway. Drop below a rock bluff and continue descending into a right curve and bottom out at 3.2 miles. Then continue on a level section of road with the O&W Railroad bed to your left until you pass between posts blocking vehicle access and reach a junction with the old railroad bed at 3.3 miles.

From the Cumberland Valley Trailhead, you can cover a long loop, called the Cumberland Valley Loop, by heading east on the Groom Branch Trail, cutting across the top of the North White Oak Loop, descending to the O&W Railbed on the Coyle Branch Trail, turning west on the railbed, and ascending back to the trailhead on the Gernt Trail, a total of 13.5 miles.

28 LAUREL FORK OF NORTH WHITE OAK CREEK 👥

Distance: 3.7 miles one-way
Difficulty: Strenuous
Elevation change: 250 ft
Cautions: Creek ford, mudholes, unmarked route
Connections: None

Attractions: On this unofficial route, you'll get to see a large arch in formation and the gorge of the Laurel Fork of North White Oak Creek. This route should be attempted only by experienced outdoorspeople. At this writing part of the route is blocked by fallen trees; check with the Bandy Creek Visitor Center to see whether the way has been cleared. The way to the Laurel Fork is not marked because there is as yet no official trail into the area, so it is possible to get lost. Pay attention to where you are going so if you lose the way, you'll at least be able to get back out. Although there is no official trail, these backroads are used by those who know the region.

The Laurel Fork contains some of the cleanest water that flows into the Big South Fork. This acreage is sometimes called the Willamette Tract because Willamette Timber, based in Salem, Oregon, helped to secure the land by acquiring it from another company for the Nature Conservancy, which purchased the 1,200 acres to preserve it until the federal government appropriated the funds to acquire it for the BSFNRRA.

Trailhead: From the West Entrance Trailhead, head west on TN 297 to the junction of TN 154. Turn south toward Jamestown. In 3.6 miles, turn left on Darrow Ridge Road. In 0.8 mile the pavement ends. Continue down the gravel road, which begins to follow the boundary of the BSFNRRA on the left. At 1.5 miles from the end of the pavement, a dirt road to the left is the beginning of the hike. Before you get there, the gravel ends and the Darrow Ridge Road can be muddy; if so, park to the side and walk down the road to the left turn.

Laurel Fork Gorge

Directions: At first the old road is a rutted track with some large mudholes that span the width of the road; you'll be able to walk around in the woods. At 0.4 mile a sign indicates the end of vehicle access. Cross bare rock as the old road begins a descent toward Laurel Fork. A side road leads off to the left. Descend more steeply down a broad rock slope at 0.6 mile. Then watch for a path on the left that drops from the road to a large rock shelter. If you explore inside, you'll find the structure is a natural arch in formation; toward the back, an opening has eroded in the rock ceiling. In time, the hole will widen, separating the overhead rock from the back wall, leaving a graceful span of stone.

The road descends steeply to a ford of the Laurel Fork of North White Oak Creek at 0.8 mile. On the other side, ascend from the creek. The road once went to the left but is now overgrown. Stay straight up the slope; do not take the path to the right along the creek. Ascend a steep path and at 0.9 miles bear right on another old roadway that ascends over sandstone rock.

At 1.1 mile, top out to enter a clearing; to the right you'll see broken cement, probably the plugging of a gas or oil well. Continue up the old roadbed. At 2.0 miles, cross the boundary out of the BSFNRRA and turn right onto a side road, which curves back to the left; immediately turn right again on a less-used side road that heads back toward Laurel Fork. You'll soon reenter the park. This is the section that has been blocked by fallen trees.

At 2.8 miles, keep right as the road forks, and at 3.1 miles, keep left at another fork. At 3.7 miles is the edge of Laurel Fork Gorge, with nice views into the narrow chasm. The creek meanders through this region, having created promontories projecting from both sides of the gorge that are nearly interlaced like shuffled cards. Locals call this Sawtooth Canyon. You can explore left and right along the gorge rim; to avoid unnecessarily trampling lichen growing on the rock surfaces, stay with paths others have made. Then retrace your route back to your vehicle.

Map 4. Middle Creek

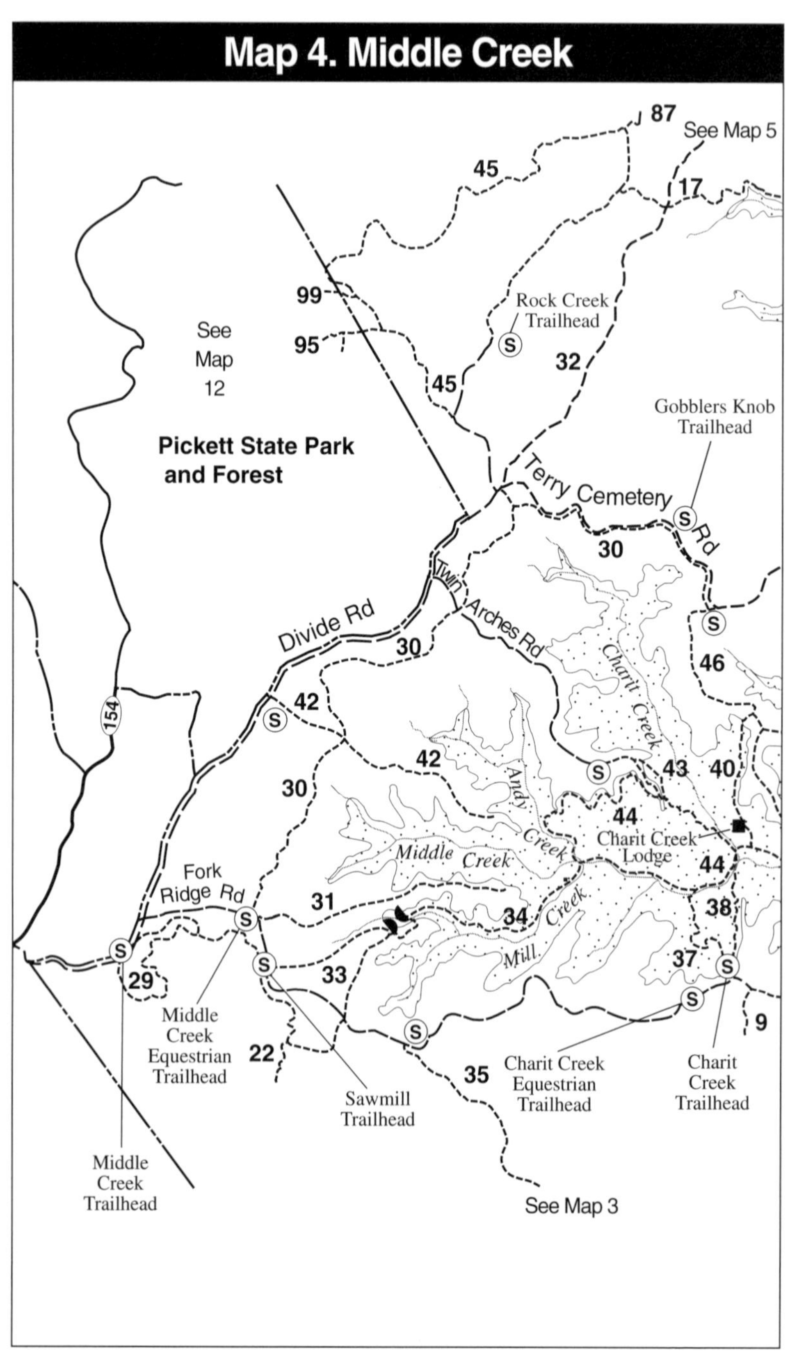

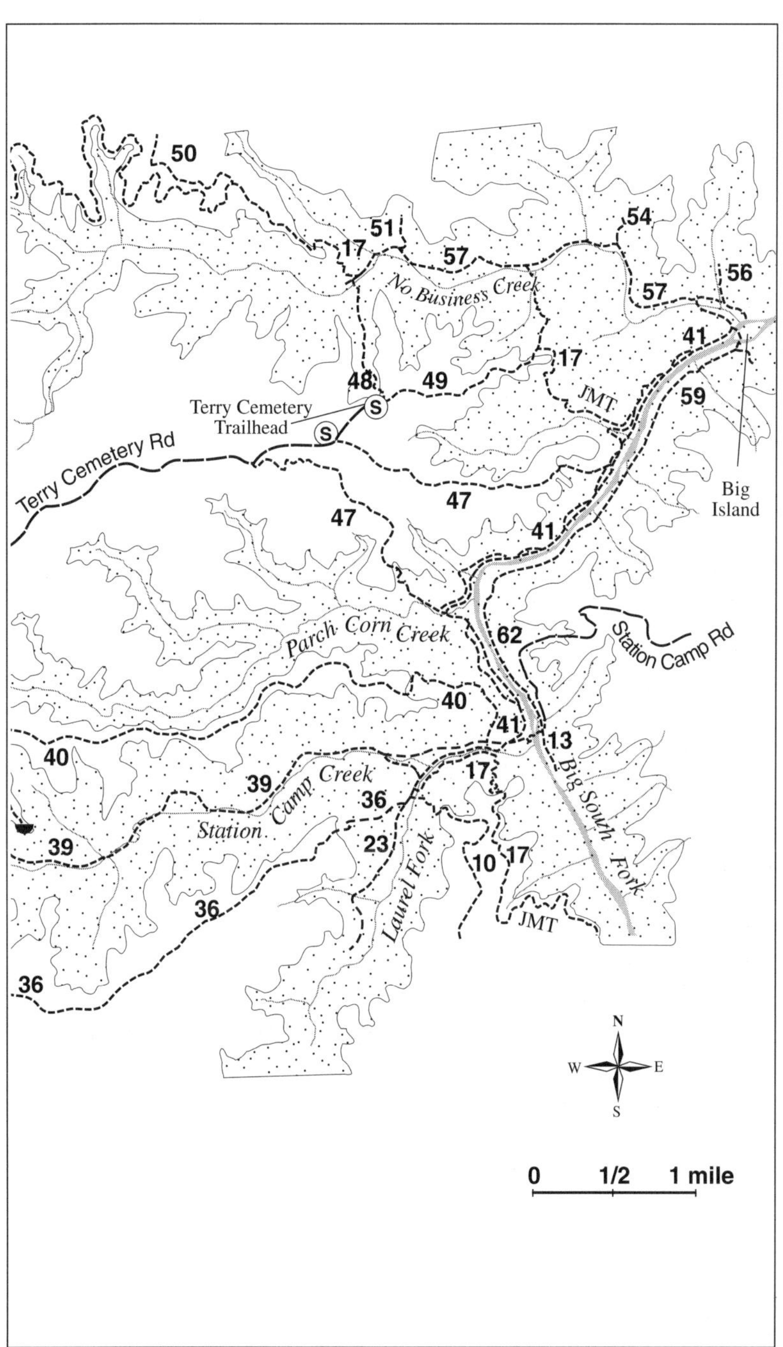

50
51
17
57
54
56
No Business Creek
57
41
17
48
49
JMT
59
S
Terry Cemetery Trailhead
S
Big Island
Terry Cemetery Rd
47
47
41
Parch Corn Creek
62
Station Camp Rd
40
41
13
40
39
Station Camp Creek
17
40
39
36
23
Laurel Fork
10
17
Big South Fork
36
JMT
36
N
W E
S
0   1/2   1 mile

MIDDLE CREEK

The Middle Creek Section of the recreation area contains some of the most isolated and interesting land in the park. You'll walk to the massive structure of Twin Arches, view slender Slave Falls, stand atop Maudes Crack, and wander along Rock Creek.

From Bandy Creek or the West Entrance Trailhead, drive west on TN 297 to its junction with TN 154; Jamestown lies to the left, and this is your approach to the BSFNRRA if you come to the park from the west. Head north on TN 154 from this junction. At 1.9 miles, before Pickett State Rustic Park, turn east on the gravel Divide Road. Pass rental cabins being constructed on private land on the right. The Middle Creek Trailhead and parking area lie on the right in 0.8 mile.

From the Middle Creek Trailhead, continue east on Divide Road for 0.2 mile to turn right on Fork Ridge Road. This gives you access to the Middle Creek Equestrian Trailhead at 0.7 mile from the beginning of Fork Ridge Road, the Sawmill Trailhead at 1.4 miles, the Salt Pine Road at 3.5 miles, the Charit Creek Equestrian Trailhead at 5.8 miles, and the Charit Creek Hikers Trailhead at 6.0 miles.

Other trails in the Middle Creek area are accessed by continuing up Divide Road past Fork Ridge Road. The road to Twin Arches turns off to the right at 4.2 miles from the beginning of Divide Road; it's 2.0 miles to the trailhead. The turn to the Rock Creek Trailhead is on the left at 4.7 miles; it's 1.3 miles to the trailhead at the Hattie Blevins Cemetery. Terry Cemetery Road turns to the right off Divide Road at 4.9 miles; along that road, the Gobblers Knob Trailhead lies on the left at 1.4 miles, and the Terry Cemetery Trailhead lies just past the cemetery at the end of the road at 5.7 miles.

29 | MIDDLE CREEK NATURE LOOP 👫

Distance: 3.5 miles
Difficulty: Moderate
Elevation change: 100 ft
Cautions: Occasional stream crossings, boulder passages, mudholes on last section
Connections: Middle Creek Connector Trail 👫

Attractions: This loop takes you by an impressive array of cliff walls and rock overhangs. At the end of May, you'll find blooming laurel. White-

Rock shelter on Middle Creek Nature Loop

tailed deer bound away at your approach. The Shawnees called the Cumberland Plateau Ouasioto, meaning "mountains where the deer are plentiful."

Trailhead: Start at the Middle Creek Trailhead.

Description: From the trailhead sign, walk into the forest along an old road about 50 yards to a sign indicating the Middle Creek Nature Trail both straight ahead and to the left. To hike the nature trail clockwise, turn left into the woods on a footpath.

Along this first section, the trail parallels Divide Road. The trail then curves away from the road to the right, and at 0.5 mile it skirts Fork Ridge Road, which turns off Divide Road. Descend gradually and then more steeply with a few switchbacks to a junction at 1.0 mile with the Middle Creek Connector Trail. (This trail leads left 0.8 mile to the Slave Falls Loop.

From that loop, you can also access the Twin Arches, Charit Creek, and Bandy Creek areas in long hikes.)

To continue the Middle Creek Nature Trail, bear right. Cross a stream on planks and curve right to a rock bluff on the right with the creek running along the base of the rock wall. The trail now swings out and in, each time nearing the rock wall, often where rock shelters have formed. Pass several of these rock overhangs forming hollows in the rock walls, some quite large. Most have a trickle of water running from underneath, part of the erosion that helped create the recesses. Cross these streams easily on stepping stones. Occasionally, the trail meanders under the overhangs along their sandy floors and through boulders piled in front of the openings. A recent rain will leave small waterfalls that drop off the lips of rock overhead. Watch for falling ice in winter.

Rock shelters are often habitat for sensitive plant species. Stay on the trail to avoid unnecessary trampling of vegetation.

At 1.8 miles the trail climbs through rocks and then descends to cross a small creek on a footbridge. Skirt the rock wall again with alum root, moss, and fern-covered ledges. At 2.3 miles, the trail crosses a boardwalk over a low area growing tall fern. Keep straight ahead when the trail crosses an old logging road at 2.4 miles. Reach another rock shelter at 2.7 miles and then ascend stone steps; notice up to the right a pedestal of rock supporting the ledge.

The trail curves right to ascend above the rock bluff and follow an old roadbed through the woods. When the trail links up with a dirt road at 3.1 miles, turn right. Skirt some mudholes along the road to complete the loop at 3.5 miles.

30 | GOBBLERS KNOB TRAIL ∩

Distance: 7.2 miles one-way
Difficulty: Easy
Elevation change: 120 ft
Cautions: Steep ascents and descents
Connections: Middle Creek Trail ∩, Long Trail ∩

Attractions: Connecting the Middle Creek Equestrian Trailhead with Terry Cemetery Road, this trail for horse-drawn wagons provides a route north not open to motor vehicles.

Trailhead: From the Middle Creek Trailhead, continue east on Divide Road. In 0.2 mile, turn right on Fork Ridge Road. Then at 0.9 mile turn left to the Middle Creek Equestrian Trailhead.

Description: The Gobblers Knob Trail straight ahead is the continuation of the road into the trailhead. The reason it looks like a road is that it serves as a route for horse-drawn wagons from here to Terry Cemetery Road; no bicycle use is proposed. This is also the beginning of the Long Trail that traverses the park all the way to Blue Heron in Kentucky.

As you descend from the trailhead on the gravel path, cross a clearing (probably an old homesite). Back into the woods, the trail swings left into a descent and then curves right to bottom out where a stream passes under the road in a culvert at 0.2 mile. An old bridge may still remain to the left that was abandoned when the new trail was constructed.

Ascend from the stream and wind through the woods to descend to a ford of Middle Creek at 1.4 miles. The trail then ascends to an intersection with the Middle Creek Road (the proposed Middle Creek Trail) at 1.8 miles. Stay straight across the road on the Gobblers Knob Trail.

The trail dips through a hollow and ascends past a low overhang on the left at 2.2 miles. Dip through another hollow and then cross under a powerline at 2.4 miles. At 2.7 miles is an old roadway to the left that leads up to Divide Road, but that route is not a trail.

The road swings through several coves and eventually crosses the Twin Arches Road at an angle to the right at 3.9 miles. Then curve left into a steep, winding descent. At 4.2 miles, the road curves right at rock outcrops on the left and dips through some low areas to ascend to a fork at 5.1 miles. Left at the fork leads steeply up to Divide Road at Three Forks at 5.5 miles (this is the route of the wagon road that continues up Divide Road into Kentucky). Right at this fork leads up to Terry Cemetery Road at 5.6 miles. There the Gobblers Knob Trail turns right to parallel the road. At 6.4 miles, a side path on the left turns to cross Terry Cemetery Road to a parking area that is the Gobblers Knob Trailhead. The Gobblers Knob Trail continues straight, paralleling Terry Cemetery Road, to a junction at 7.2 miles with the Hatfield Ridge Trail.

31 | BOOGER BLEVINS ROAD ∩

Distance: 1.9 miles one-way
Difficulty: Moderate
Elevation loss: 560 ft
Cautions: Unmarked route
Connections: None at this writing

Attractions: A Booger Blevins Trail will provide access from the Middle Creek Equestrian Trailhead to Charit Creek Lodge along this old roadway. This proposed trail should be attempted only by experienced outdoorspeople.

Trailhead: From the Middle Creek Trailhead, continue east on Divide Road. In 0.2 mile, turn right on Fork Ridge Road. Then at 0.9 mile turn left to the Middle Creek Equestrian Trailhead. From the trailhead, go back out on Fork Ridge Road and turn left 0.1 mile to the Booger Blevins Road on the left. Eventually there may be a connector through the woods from the trailhead to the old road so you can avoid riding or walking on Fork Ridge Road.

Description: Turn left on Booger Blevins Road and stay with the old road past traces of other roads to the left and right and through a couple of dips. The road is mostly level as it heads out along the top of a ridge; this section of the trail is open to motorized vehicles. At 1.3 miles the road makes an obvious curve right. You'll reach the end of the road at 1.9 miles.

If the trail has not yet been constructed, the way from here will be impassable because of down trees. The trail will drop off to the left, still following the old roadway, and continue out along a ridgeline. The route will eventually descend steeply to the bottom of a cove, where it will intersect at 2.7 miles with the Slave Falls to Jakes Place Connector. Just to the left that trail crosses two footbridges over Middle Creek to connect with the Twin Arches/Charit Creek Loop at Jakes Place. Horses and bikes are not allowed on these trails. Plans call for the Middle Creek Trail, which also will emerge at this junction, to continue straight ahead toward Charit Creek Lodge. The trail will ford Mill Creek and follow Station Camp Creek downstream to connect with the Charit Creek Lodge Trail in another 1.2 miles.

32 | LONG TRAIL Ω

Distance: 26.9 miles one-way
Difficulty: Moderate
Elevation loss: 900 ft
Cautions: Creek and river fords
Connections: Gobblers Knob Trail Ω, Middle Creek Road Ω, John Muir Trail 👥, John Muir Overlook 👥, Stoopin' Oak Road Ω, Mark Branch Trail 👥, Sheltowee Trace 👥, Laurel Hill Trail Ω, Cat Ridge Road Ω, Kentucky Trail 👥, Laurel Branch Trail Ω

Attractions: This combination of horse trails makes for a long ride through the northern region of the park and includes two alternative routes that make long loops back to the trailhead.

Trailhead: From the Middle Creek Trailhead, continue east on Divide Road. In 0.2 mile, turn right on Fork Ridge Road. Then at 0.9 mile turn left to the Middle Creek Equestrian Trailhead.

Description: From the Middle Creek Equestrian Trailhead, head north up the Gobblers Knob Trail. At 5.1 miles, the trail forks. (To the right you can reach Terry Cemetery Road and turn right to ride an alternative loop of the Long Trail: turning on the Hatfield Ridge Trail to the Hatfield Ridge Loop and descending to Charit Creek Lodge and then taking the Charit Creek Lodge Trail up to Fork Ridge Road, which you'd ride west to complete a 14.3-mile loop back to the Middle Creek Equestrian Trailhead.)

To continue the Long Trail north, stay to the left at the fork, following the route of the wagon trail. Emerge on Divide Road at 5.5 miles at Three Forks, where the Terry Cemetery Road begins. Now head north on Divide Road. At 7.4 miles the JMT crosses the road. At 8.6 miles, cross the state line into Kentucky; Divide Road becomes the Peters Mountain Road. Daniel Boone National Forest borders the road on the left and the BSFNRRA borders the road on the right.

At 9.4 miles, an unmarked road on the right leads toward the John Muir Overlook. At 10.2 miles, pass Forest Development Road (FDR) 6300 on the left. Then at 10.7 miles, pass the Stoopin' Oak Road on the right. At 11.2 miles, Peters Mountain Road passes FDR 6105 on the left (which gives access to the Mark Branch Trail). Then at 11.7 miles, you'll reach an intersection with the Peters Mountain Trailhead up to your right. The Sheltowee Trace, headed west, turns off the road to the left. Also to the left, FDR 139 joins the intersection. Continue straight, now on FDR 6101, which is the route of the Sheltowee Trace north. At 11.9 miles, turn right on Laurel Ridge Road.

Beginning at 12.1 miles, you'll see clearings in the hollow to the left where the Forest Service has cut the trees on national forest land.

The Laurel Hill Trail turns right at 13.4 miles on the old Laurel Hill Road. (This is also an alternative loop of the Long Trail. Go down the Laurel Hill Trail to connect with the Miller Branch Trail that drops to Big Island at the mouth of No Business Creek; ford the creek and continue south on the River Trail West, nearly impassable in wet weather in winter and spring because of mud, to connect with the Station Camp Creek Trail leading west to Charit Creek Lodge, where you'll pick up the Charit Creek Lodge Trail to reach Fork Ridge Road and ride west to complete a 30.8-mile loop at the Middle Creek Equestrian Trailhead.)

To continue on the Long Trail north, stay straight on Laurel Ridge Road from the junction with the Laurel Hill Trail. At 14.6 miles, pass the Cat Ridge Road to the right that leads toward the Big South Fork and intersects with the Kentucky Trail in 1.7 miles; a proposed Cat Ridge Trail will follow this road. Pass the Blevins–Kidd Cemetery on the left at 14.7 miles and continue straight on Laurel Ridge Road.

The road drops to cross a fork of Puncheoncamp Branch at 16.0 miles and then ascends. At 20.6 miles, the Sheltowee Trace turns off to the left, although at this writing the trail is closed because of storm damage. Continue straight on Laurel Ridge Road.

Begin descending and pass a side road on the left blocked by metal posts at 20.9 miles. At 21.3 miles, pass the Kidd Cemetery on the right and encounter a massive rock outcropping called Stepping Rock on your left. The road continues along the side of the rock. At 22.2 miles, climb steeply onto Stepping Rock; before the Forest Service improved the road, several ledges created steps up the rock. On top, the road curves right. Pass roads right and left and pass the old Bald Knob School at 23.7 miles.

Continuing on Laurel Ridge Road, now also called the Devils Creek/Beech Grove Road, enter an S-curve and pass Bald Knob Road at 24.1 miles.

Stay straight up Laurel Ridge Road. Pass houses right and left and then turn right at 25.0 miles on Waters Cemetery Road, just before the Beech Grove Baptist Church. Down Waters Cemetery Road, just before the Barr Cemetery on the right, turn left at 25.3 miles on a road that leads to Dick Gap Overlook. At 25.8 miles, the horse trail turns right off the road, which continues on to parking in another 0.5 mile, where a 0.3-mile walk to the left takes you to Dick Gap Overlook of Blue Heron. The path to the overlook leads down to your left and is not open to horses or bikes; the view is worth the short walk. An old roadway leading from the overlook parking reconnects with the horse trail, which has paralleled the road to that junction at 26.3 miles.

Down the horse trail, pass another old roadway to the right and curve left in a steep descent to intersect with the Kentucky Trail at 26.5 miles; this is also the Catawba Overlook Loop. The hiking and horse trails coincide for a short distance before the hiking trail continues straight while the horse trail stays on the old road as it curves right in a steep and rocky descent.

Pass below rock bluffs and an overhang to cross at 26.7 miles the lower part of the Catawba Overlook Loop, not open at this writing because of slides along the trail to the right. Continue descending steeply to reach a ford of the Big South Fork at 26.9 miles; attempt the ford only at low water. Emerge from the river at the river access ramp at the Blue Heron Mining Community, where you can end your ride or connect with the Laurel Branch Trail that leads upstream to connect with the Lee Hollow Loop.

33 | SLAVE FALLS LOOP 👥

Distance: 3.8 miles (*Slave Falls 1.3 miles one-way*)
Difficulty: Easy; side trip to Slave Falls moderate
Elevation change: 300 ft
Cautions: Footbridges
Connections: Slave Falls to Jakes Place Connector 👥, Laurel Fork Creek Trail 👥, Middle Creek Connector Trail 👥

Attractions: Slave Falls is a slender waterfall where a primary tributary of Mill Creek splashes into a rock gorge with a large rock shelter behind. The hard sandstone that caps the Cumberland Plateau creates such dramatic

Indian Rock House

geologic formations. Where water finds a break in the sandstone, it erodes the softer layers below, creating a waterfall. Erosion continues to remove the rock underlying the sandstone lip of the waterfall, hollowing out natural amphitheaters behind. The name of the falls comes from stories that runaway slaves hid in such rock shelters. Later on the trail, Indian Rock House opens in a tall rock bluff.

Trailhead: From the Middle Creek Trailhead, continue east on Divide Road. In 0.2 mile, turn right on Fork Ridge Road. From the beginning of Fork Ridge Road off Divide Road, pass the Middle Creek Equestrian Trailhead at 0.7 mile and reach the Sawmill Trailhead on the left at 1.4 miles. From the Sawmill Trailhead, walk left, paralleling the road 0.1 mile to engage the Slave Falls Loop at a junction. Turn right to walk the loop clockwise.

Description: The trail passes through a mixed pine–hemlock–hardwood forest. You'll see many down trees and broken branches caused by a snowstorm in 1998. At 0.3 mile, the trail dips through a hollow and follows it down on your right. Then at 0.6 mile, cross a plank footbridge over a small creek, one of the many headwater streams of Mill Creek. The trail passes through another depression at 0.7 mile. At 1.0 mile, you'll get your first glimpse of the gorge that contains Slave Falls. The trail soon after joins an old roadway and bears left.

The trail then curves right through another hollow and up to a junction at 1.1 miles; turn right to continue on the Slave Falls Loop. Straight ahead is the Slave Falls to Jakes Place Connector. Before turning on the loop, continue straight ahead 100 yards to a side path on the left that leads to Slave Falls in 0.2 mile. Descend among thick understory, down rock steps and stone ledges, and then along a rock wall through blocks of stone and under a low overhang to an overlook of 60-foot Slave Falls.

Back at the junction on the Slave Falls Loop, at a total walk of 1.5 miles after visiting the falls, turn uphill to complete the loop. Ascend on an old road to pass between two posts limiting vehicle access and then follow the road, lined with bluets in spring. At 2.1 miles the road reaches a junction with another old roadway, where you turn left to emerge on Fork Ridge Road. Cross the road to reenter the woods.

The trail curves left and soon joins an old roadway coming in from the left. Walk up this roadway, staying straight past another old road on the right. At 2.3 miles at a fork in the road, the trail follows the road to the right but soon turns right onto a footpath. The trail now winds through the woods, crossing a bridge over a drainage below a low rock shelter on the right at 2.4 miles. Also cross three footbridges over drainages that are usually dry. At 2.6 miles the trail joins an old road and turns right to ascend over a ridge and curves left down to a junction with the Laurel Fork Creek Trail at 2.7 miles. Stay right to complete the Slave Falls Loop.

The trail soon curves left but then bears right to descend into a hollow. In a second hollow, join an old road to the left that leads up to the Indian Rock House at 3.0 miles. Set in a massive rock wall up to the right, this is one of the largest rock shelters in the park.

After passing the rock shelter, the trail dips through a shallow drainage and ascends to a left turn off the old road; the roadway continues out to the

Fire Tower Road above the Sawmill Trailhead. The trail now wanders through the woods. At 3.3 miles, drop into a hollow and bear right on a boardwalk crossing a wet area in front of a low overhang. Up from the hollow, the trail passes through a couple of more open areas growing small trees that are rejuvenating fields or old blow-down areas. At 3.7 miles is a junction with the Middle Creek Connector Trail to the left (which connects with the Middle Creek Nature Loop in 0.8 mile). Stay to the right at this junction; cross Fork Ridge Road and close the loop. Turn right to return to the Sawmill Trailhead at 3.8 miles.

34 | SLAVE FALLS TO JAKES PLACE 👫

Distance: 2.5 miles one-way
Difficulty: Easy
Elevation loss: 350 ft
Cautions: Boulder passages
Connections: Slave Falls Loop 👫, Twin Arches/Charit Creek
Loop 👫

Attractions: This connector from the Slave Falls Loop to the Twin Arches/ Charit Creek Loop at Jakes Place passes Needle Arch and a similar arch in formation. The slender Needle Arch was formed by the widening of a joint, or break in the rock. Erosion separated the top of the arch from the ridge behind; simultaneously, runoff and seepage removed the softer rock and earth beneath the arch, leaving a 50-foot span. This delicate arch consists of the Pennsylvanian sandstone, which makes this formation possible. Only when the rock is especially erosion-resistant can such a thin ribbon of rock remain suspended.

Trailhead: From the Middle Creek Trailhead, continue east on Divide Road. In 0.2 mile, turn right on Fork Ridge Road. From the beginning of Fork Ridge Road off Divide Road, pass the Middle Creek Equestrian Trailhead at 0.7 mile and reach the Sawmill Trailhead on the left at 1.4 miles. From the Sawmill Trailhead, walk left, paralleling the road 0.1 mile to engage the Slave Falls Loop at a junction. Turn right. Walk the Slave Falls Loop 1.1 miles to its junction with the Slave Falls to Jakes Place Connector and continue straight ahead toward Jakes Place.

Description: In 100 yards down the connector trail, a side path leads 0.2 mile down to Slave Falls. The connector continues straight ahead. At 0.1 mile, the trail turns right, with an abandoned section of trail straight ahead; the path once passed above Needle Arch. Now the trail descends to the right and turns left to swing in front of the natural arch at 0.2 mile.

From Needle Arch, the trail ascends right and swings left along the slope of the valley of Mill Creek on the right. Follow a rock ledge on your left. At an overhang, you'll see an arch in formation overhead, a small hole that eventually may widen to separate a span of stone from the rock wall in a process similar to the formation of Needle Arch.

At 0.3 mile, the trail ascends to a junction with the original route of the trail; you'll see the abandoned path to the left. Turn right.

The trail turns left over a ridge and descends across a slope, crossing footbridges over two drainages. At 0.7 mile, cross another drainage where uprooted trees and broken branches from a 1998 snowstorm are piled. The trail descends to ford the Mill Creek tributary that forms Slave Falls, then ascends to a junction at 0.8 mile. A side trail left leads 0.2 mile to another view of Slave Falls; along the way, ascend curving right and then

Needle Arch

switchback left to descend, stepping down a rock ledge on a plank footbridge and then a boardwalk over a wet area to the falls overlook.

From the side path to Slave Falls, continue on the main trail, which parallels this tributary that soon joins Mill Creek. The trail then follows Mill Creek downstream. Along the slope, cross numerous drainages on stepping stones. Watch for plenty of wildflowers in spring: crested dwarf iris, foamflower, wild geranium, phlox. Cross a drainage at 1.5 miles; the side stream to the left forms a small waterfall where it spills over a rock wall.

At 2.1 miles, the trail switchbacks right and left down to creek level, where it's often wet. Cross boardwalks over some of the muddiest areas. As the trail nears a footbridge crossing Middle Creek, you'll see the trace of an old roadway up the ridge to the left; this is the route of the proposed Booger Blevins Trail, which on this lower end is impassable. Straight ahead, cross two footbridges over Middle Creek to a junction with the Twin Arches/Charit Creek Loop at 2.5 miles. Jakes Place lies to the left. To the right, the loop crosses Andy Creek on a footbridge; the three creeks (Mill, Middle, and Andy) converge here to form Station Camp Creek. Charit Creek Lodge, at the confluence of Charit Creek with Station Camp Creek, lies 1.5 miles to the right along the loop.

35 | SALT PINE ROAD ⋂

Distance: 2.5 miles one-way
Difficulty: Strenuous
Elevation loss: 360 ft
Cautions: Unmarked route, overgrown, fallen trees, mudholes
Connections: Laurel Fork Creek Trail 🥾

Attractions: This old road is proposed as a horse trail that will provide easy access from the Middle Creek area to the West Entrance Trailhead. This route should be attempted only by experienced outdoorspeople.

Trailhead: From the beginning of Fork Ridge Road off Divide Road, pass the Sawmill Trailhead at 1.4 miles and continue up Fork Ridge Road. The road forks; the dirt right fork leads 0.3 mile to the site of an old fire tower where only the tower's foundations remain; stay with the gravel left fork. At 3.5 miles, you'll reach Salt Pine Road, with room for a vehicle to park beside the road.

Description: Following the road into the woods, bear right around a berm and pass a road on the right that parallels Fork Ridge Road. Continue up Salt Pine Road. You may encounter trees down across the road if it has not been cleared recently.

At 0.3 mile, pass the trace of a roadway to the left, and then the road splits for a short distance to avoid ruts. Pass the trace of another old road to the left at 0.9 mile and penetrate woods where small pines overhang the trail at 1.2 miles. The road ascends steeply to top a knoll at 1.5 miles, where you'll cross another old roadway.

Soon begin a steep descent into the gorge of the Laurel Fork of Station Camp Creek. Curve right and descend across bare rock and then bear left at 2.2 miles. The road continues to descend and curve right into berms that once blocked vehicle access at 2.4 miles. On the other side, continue on a level section along the side of the slope before curving left into more descent.

The old road from here has become overgrown and impassable. When the trail is constructed, it will bottom out and connect with the Laurel Fork Creek Trail at 2.7 miles. To the right is hiking only. The proposed horse trail route will turn left up the Laurel Fork Creek Trail to ford Laurel Fork and reach a junction at 3.0 miles with the other part of the Salt Pine Trail that leads up to the West Entrance Trailhead at 4.7 miles.

36 | FORK RIDGE TRAIL ∩

Distance: 4.0 miles one-way
Difficulty: Moderate; strenuous on lower section
Elevation loss: 660 ft
Cautions: May be closed at the beginning of a steep, rocky
   descent on lower section
Connections: Charit Creek Lodge Trail ∩, Black House
   Branch Trail ∩, Laurel Fork Creek Trail 🚶, John Muir Trail 🚶,
   Duncan Hollow Trail ∩

Attractions: This trail follows the old Fork Ridge Road east to give access to the Station Camp Creek area. This old forest road travels along Fork Ridge before making a steep descent to Laurel Fork Creek.

Trailhead: From the beginning of Fork Ridge Road off Divide Road, pass Salt Pine Road at 3.5 miles and reach the Charit Creek Equestrian Trailhead on the left at 5.8 miles. Begin the ride or hike here.

Description: Ride or walk up Fork Ridge Road 0.1 mile to where the road curves sharply left; the Charit Creek Lodge Trail continues along the road to the left and the Fork Ridge Trail heads straight into the woods on the continuation of the old hard-packed roadbed that was the eastward extension of Fork Ridge Road. Four-wheel drive vehicles are also allowed to continue along the road.

Continuing east, pass through a junction of old roadways; stay with the main gravel road. At 0.2 mile is a junction with the Black House

Branch Trail (which heads toward Bandy Creek on the right). Continue straight on the Fork Ridge Road.

The road continues east through a pine and hardwood forest along the spine of Fork Ridge, the ridge separating Laurel Fork Creek to the right and Station Camp Creek to the left. You'll see an occasional old roadway off to the left.

At 2.0 miles, you'll see an old roadway off to the left as the main road curves left. At 2.3 miles the road heads into an S-curve to get over onto this roadway that has paralleled the main road.

The road curves left to descend below a bluff and reach the end of vehicle access at 2.8 miles. The trail continues along the base of the bluff, following the roadbed that now has soft tread.

Pass over a ridge at 3.0 miles with a roadway off to the right and begin a long, steep, rocky descent with rock ledges into Laurel Fork Gorge. The trail is closed here at this writing because of the steep descent and down timber that blocks the way. The Fork Ridge Trail will eventually be reconstructed to avoid this

Chimney at housesite

steep descent, so the current route probably will not be cleared of debris.

Experienced hikers may continue on, but the way is difficult. In the descent, curve left to continue down a small cove. Pass a jumble of boulders in the cove's drainage. The trail curves right and left to finally bottom out in a grassy area at 3.7 miles. The remains of an old chimney stand on the left as a reminder of the subsistence communities that lived along Laurel Fork and Station Camp Creeks.

At 3.8 miles is a junction with the Laurel Fork Creek Trail. Stay left on the old roadway that parallels Laurel Fork downstream; here the Fork Ridge and the Laurel Fork Creek Trails coincide. At 4.0 miles is a junction with the Duncan Hollow Trail, which fords Laurel Fork to the right, and with the JMT, which crosses Laurel Fork to this side of the creek over a high bridge.

The Fork Ridge Trail can be combined with the North Bandy Creek/

Katie/Jacks Ridge Loop, the Black House Branch Trail, and the Duncan Hollow Trail to make a loop ride out of Bandy Creek of 14.9 miles.

37 | CHARIT CREEK LODGE TRAIL ∩

Distance: 1.5 miles one-way
Difficulty: Moderate
Elevation loss: 540 ft
Cautions: Steep descent, creek ford
Connections: Fork Ridge Trail ∩, Charit Creek Trail 🚶, Twin Arches/Charit Creek Loop 🚶, Station Camp Creek Trail ∩, Hatfield Ridge Loop ∩

Attractions: This horse trail follows Charit Creek Road down to Charit Creek Lodge, which has overnight lodging, meals, and a stable (reservations recommended).

Charit Creek Lodge

Trailhead: From the beginning of Fork Ridge Road off Divide Road, pass Salt Pine Road at 3.5 miles and reach the Charit Creek Equestrian Trailhead on the left at 5.8 miles. Mount up and continue east on Fork Ridge Road 0.1 mile to where the Fork Ridge Trail continues straight on the old roadbed while the existing road turns sharply left, now as the Charit Creek Road.

Description: Continuing down the gravel Charit Creek Road, pass parking for the Charit Creek Trail for hikers on the right at 0.1 mile. Then make your way around a bar blocking vehicle access to begin the steep descent toward Charit Creek Lodge.

At 0.2 mile the road curves left in its descent and soon after curves right. Continuing the descent, pass an old roadway on the left at 0.8 mile that will be the end of the Middle Creek Trail when it is constructed. The road bottoms out and fords Station Camp Creek at 1.0 mile. At 1.1 miles, the Twin Arches/Charit Creek Loop joins the road from the left. Soon, the Charit Creek Trail for hikers crosses a bridge over Station Camp Creek to join the road. At 1.5 miles is a footbridge over Charit Creek; horses and mountain bikes must ford the creek to enter the lodge area.

On the other side, you'll see a trailhead to the left for the Station Camp Creek Trail/Hatfield Ridge Loop. If you're staying at the lodge, do not ride horses through the lodge complex; turn right down a trail that follows Charit Creek to its confluence with Station Camp Creek and then turn down Station Camp Creek to follow the path to the stables at the far side of the complex.

38 | CHARIT CREEK TRAIL 朮

Distance: 0.8 mile one-way
Difficulty: Moderate
Elevation loss: 500 ft
Cautions: Stairs, steep descent
Connections: Charit Creek Lodge Trail ∩, Twin Arches/
   Charit Creek Loop 朮, Station Camp Creek Trail ∩,
   Hatfield Ridge Loop ∩

Attractions: This trail leads to an old homesite that is now Charit Creek Lodge, which offers meals and lodging. Charit Creek was named for a girl, Charity, who drowned in the creek; the stream was originally called Charity's Creek.

Charit Creek Lodge consists of several structures, including a large central building with two cabins to the right and a solar bathhouse to the rear. An old barn stands to the left, and a corncrib, now used as a residence, sits in front. The lodge operates as a concession. You can get meals with your lodging; reservations are needed. (See the address and telephone number in the Appendix.) Horse riders can board their horses in the stables.

The Charit Creek/Station Camp area was once the home of Jonathan Blevins, one of the early settlers. He came with his family to the region in the late 1700s and later moved to this area in the 1850s. The main lodge building incorporates an old cabin, built around 1816, that Blevins could have used as the home for his family. Some locals speculate that he may have lived a mile and a half farther down Station Camp Creek at the housesite near where he is buried in the Hatfield Cemetery. He died in 1863 from bee stings.

Later, others lived at Charit Creek: Jonathan Burke and William Riley Hatfield, both of whom lie in a small cemetery just east of the lodge complex in the open area above the stables, and Oscar Blevins with his father, John, who were descendants of Jonathan Blevins and who built the present barn, a corncrib, and a blacksmith shop behind the lodge. The last family to live here, the Phillipses, sold the homesite around 1963 to Joe Simpson, who operated it as the Parch Corn Hunting Lodge until 1982; Simpson brought in logs from other cabins in the area to expand the main building and erect the two outlying cabins. When the complex was purchased for the park, it operated as a hostel and was renamed Charit Creek, after the creek that flows beside the main structure. Later, the buildings were converted to a lodge.

Trailhead: From the beginning of Fork Ridge Road off Divide Road, pass the Charit Creek Equestrian Trailhead at 5.8 miles and continue up Fork Ridge Road. At 5.9 miles the road curves left. At 6.0 miles, you'll find trailhead parking on the right. The road, blocked by a gate farther down, leads all the way to the lodge and is used as the horse trail. The hiking trail begins at the far end of the parking area.

Description: Descend through a couple of switchbacks and cross a footbridge over a small drainage to reach a stairway at 0.1 mile that drops into the head of a hollow; a wet-weather waterfall trickles off the bluff to the left. Turn right at the bottom of the stairs, following the rock bluff. The trail then turns away from the bluff and descends in a forest dotted with large beeches.

At 0.2 mile, the trail switchbacks left just before a huge decaying log in the forest. After a switchback right, watch for a boulder up to the right in the grip of a tree growing on top. As you continue to descend into the cove, the trail makes several switchbacks. Where the trail turns left to pass through large boulders at 0.6 mile, watch for stone crop, trillium, and rue anemone growing on the rock. Along the way you'll also see hepatica, chickweed, phlox, violets, cinquefoil, and more in spring. Once through the boulders, turn right.

Continue the descent to Station Camp Creek where a high swinging bridge takes you across the creek. The trail merges with the Twin Arches/ Charit Creek Loop on the old road to the lodge. Turn right to pass downstream and reach a bridge over Charit Creek to the lodge at 0.8 mile. Just downstream, Charit Creek joins Station Camp Creek, which runs in front of the lodge.

Behind the lodge, near the bridge over Charit Creek, is a junction for horse trails. The Station Camp Creek Trail/Hatfield Ridge Loop leads to the right.

39 | STATION CAMP CREEK TRAIL Ω

Distance: 4.1 miles one-way
Difficulty: Moderate
Elevation loss: 130 ft
Cautions: Several creek fords
Connections: Charit Creek Lodge Trail Ω, Charit Creek Trail ⚤,
    Twin Arches/Charit Creek Loop ⚤, Hatfield Ridge Loop Ω,
    Duncan Hollow Trail Ω, John Muir Trail ⚤, River Trail
    West Ω, Big Island Loop Ω

Attractions: This trail follows an old road that meanders along Station Camp Creek Valley to the Big South Fork. The road once connected the various settlements along Station Camp Creek, which supported a community of subsistence farms in the 1800s and early 1900s. All that remain are the old cabins at Charit Creek Lodge, roadways, and a few cemeteries.

Trailhead: Hikers follow the Charit Creek Trail and horse riders and mountain bikers follow the Charit Creek Lodge Trail down to Charit Creek Lodge. At the back northwest corner of the lodge complex, you'll find the trailhead. (To the left, across the footbridge over Charit Creek, you can also access the Twin Arches/Charit Creek Loop.)

Description: Head right up the road behind the lodge complex. An abandoned roadway that heads straight up the slope used to be the return route for the Hatfield Ridge Loop; because of erosion problems, the trail was rerouted. Pass a block wellhouse on the left to bear right and reach a newer junction with the Hatfield Ridge Loop at 0.1 mile; the Station Camp Creek Trail is the lower part of the Hatfield Ridge Loop. Continue straight on the old road, which is hard-packed gravel but eventually gives way to a dirt track with occasional mudholes in wet weather.

Descend to the edge of Station Camp Creek and then ford a tributary stream at 0.9 mile. You'll see an old roadway up to the left on the other side. The road becomes sandy; pass a huge boulder on the right, with another roadway up to the left, and soon after reach a ford of Station Camp Creek at 1.2 miles. This is the first of several fords that make this trail impassable in high water.

Ford the creek again at 1.3 miles at another huge rock. You'll find a good campsite to the right on the other side. Soon after, ford again. At 1.4 miles, the trail enters the creek but then comes out on the same side. Ford at 1.5 miles. Soon after, the trail enters a clearing that was once a farmsite; a roadway leads off to the left. Stay straight through a pine woods and the side road rejoins the main road when you emerge from the woods. The road then curves to the edge of the creek and reaches a path up to the left at 1.7 miles that leads 50 yards to the Hatfield Cemetery, where you'll find the grave of Jonathan Blevins, one of the earliest settlers of the region. He may have lived at Charit Creek but probably lived here, near where he is buried.

At 1.8 miles, ford Station Camp Creek again (you'll also see a makeshift path to the left that avoids this and the next ford at 1.9 miles). After these two fords, the road passes over a ridge. Creeks run under the road at 2.5 and 2.7 miles. Up the slope in this vicinity lies the Owens Cemetery near an old housesite marked by yucca plants; the way is not easily found.

At 3.2 miles, the Duncan Hollow Trail joins on the right (this trail leads

Grave of Jonathan Blevins

down to a ford of Station Camp Creek and to a junction with the JMT). Continue straight. At 3.8 miles the Hatfield Ridge Loop turns up a road to the left. Stay straight, and at 3.9 miles the JMT crosses the road; the route to the left is also the River Trail West. Stay straight and make a muddy descent to pass an overgrown trail to the left; bear right to a junction at 4.0 miles with an unofficial side path to the right (which connects with the Duncan Hollow Trail). Turn left to reach the mouth of Station Camp Creek and then bear left along the creek down to the ford at 4.1 miles. Attempt the Station Camp Crossing only at low water. You must skirt a section of big rocks instead of making the ford straight across; if you cannot see the river bottom, you probably should not try it. On the other side of the river, you can connect with the Big Island Loop.

40 | HATFIELD RIDGE LOOP ∩

Distance: 9.9 miles *(Charit Creek Overlook 2.1 miles one-way clockwise)*
Difficulty: Moderate
Elevation change: 500 ft
Cautions: Creek fords, steep ascent and descent
Connections: Twin Arches/Charit Creek Loop 🏃, Station Camp Creek Trail ∩, Duncan Hollow Trail ∩, Hatfield Ridge Trail ∩

Attractions: This loop, which includes the Station Camp Creek Trail, offers a route out of Charit Creek Lodge to an overlook of Station Camp Creek Valley.

Trailhead: Hikers follow the Charit Creek Trail and horse riders and mountain bikers follow the Charit Creek Lodge Trail down to Charit Creek Lodge. At the back northwest corner of the lodge complex, you'll find the trailhead. (To the left, across the footbridge over Charit Creek, you can also access the Twin Arches/Charit Creek Loop.)

Description: To ride or hike counterclockwise, follow the old road east that is the Station Camp Creek Trail. Pass the return of the Hatfield Ridge Loop at 0.1 mile on the left and continue on the Station Camp Creek Trail with several fords to pass the Duncan Hollow Trail to the right and reach a junction with the far end of the Hatfield Ridge Loop at 3.8 miles.

Turn left up the steep road to continue on the Hatfield Ridge Loop. The road levels off as it circles the end of Hatfield Ridge; you'll encounter an occasional mudhole. At 4.4 miles the trail turns left up a cove on the north side of Hatfield Ridge; you'll soon begin ascending the flank of the ridge. At 4.5 miles, the road switchbacks left in the ascent and, soon after, switchbacks right. As you near the top of the ridge, you'll see rock bluffs up to the left. Switchback left again and curve right at the point of the ridge to reach the top at 4.7 miles.

The trail now heads west along the ridgeline with some up and down, but it's mostly a level gravel roadway. In summer, watch for patches of blueberries on the floor of the mixed pine, hardwood, and laurel forest. At 7.2 miles, skirt the head of a hollow to the right. Then at 7.4 miles, pass a no-vehicle sign to stop motorized traffic coming from the other direction.

At 8.5 miles, a side trail left leads 0.7 mile out to the Charit Creek/ Station Camp Overlook. Turning down this side road, you must skirt some mudholes to make your way out this point of the ridge. Near the end, pass hitching rails where horses should be left. The overlook gives you a good view of Station Camp Creek Valley and Charit Creek Lodge. Back on the main trail, continue heading west from this side trail.

You'll reach a Y-junction at 8.8 miles. To the right is the 0.9-mile Hatfield Ridge Trail (which follows an old roadway to the Terry Cemetery Road and a junction with the Gobblers Knob Trail). Stay straight and then turn left to begin the descent to Charit Creek Lodge; pass through posts blocking vehicle access. The descent becomes more steep, and a shallow creek crosses the roadway at 9.4 miles, with a dripping waterfall to the left. Pass a low overhang along a rock wall on the left as you descend into a forest of large beech trees. The tributary of Charit Creek you're following drops rapidly, with spillways in the creekbed.

At 9.5 miles is a junction with the abandoned route straight; turn left along the newer route. The trail is level at first, but then descends in a beech forest to a junction with the Station Camp Creek Trail at 9.8 miles. Turn right to get back to the Charit Creek Lodge at 9.9 miles.

41 RIVER TRAIL WEST ∩

Distance: 4.4 miles one-way
Difficulty: Easy to strenuous
Elevation change: Mostly level
Cautions: Creek fords, muddy in spring
Connections: Station Camp Creek Trail ∩, John Muir Trail 𝄞,
  Big Island Loop ∩, Terry Cemetery Loop ∩, No Business
  Trail ∩

Attractions: This horse trail follows the old road along the west side of the river that once connected the Station Camp and No Business Communities.

Trailhead: Hikers follow the Charit Creek Trail and horse riders and mountain bikers follow the Charit Creek Lodge Trail to Charit Creek Lodge. At the trailhead at the back northwest corner of the lodge complex, pick up the Station Camp Creek Trail and follow it 3.9 miles to a junction with the River Trail West on the left. You can also access the trail from the east side of the river off the Big Island Loop by using the Station Camp Crossing river ford; ford the river only at low water. After making the crossing, ride 0.2 mile up the Station Camp Creek Trail to the junction with this trail north.

Description: The junction with the River Trail West is also the junction with the JMT for hikers coming from the south. The horse and hiking trails coincide with the old road headed north along the river. At 0.1 mile, the hiking trail turns off to the left but interweaves with the old road all the way to No Business Creek, so you may see hikers as the hiking and horse trails converge.

The trail stays with the old road the entire way. At 1.1 miles, ford Parch Corn Creek; soon after is a junction with the old Parch Corn Road (which is one leg of the Terry Cemetery Loop). At 0.3 mile left up this road, you can reach the site of a cabin built in 1881 by John Litton, part of the subsistence community that existed along Parch Corn Creek.

From Parch Corn Creek, continue up the old road, which is sometimes called the Big Branch Trail. Ford Harvey Branch at 1.4 miles. Cross other drainages along this road; they may be flowing in wet weather. At 2.0 miles, watch for foundation stones up to the left, remains of settlements along this road that connected the Parch Corn and No Business Creek Communities. The Watson Cemetery Road comes in from the left at 2.6 miles (which is the other side of the Terry Cemetery Loop). Stay straight; at 2.8 miles, ford Big Branch.

At 3.0 miles, the JMT, on the hillside up to your left, reaches a junction where it turns left up the slope. The River Trail West continues north on the old road; an old hiking trail also follows this route. At 3.3 miles, ford a small stream flowing toward the river.

The trail passes large blocks of stone that have fallen from the rim of the river gorge. As you near No Business Creek the tread becomes softer. When you reach the ford at Big Island at 4.0 miles the tread is mostly sand and mud, well compacted in the dry seasons of summer and fall but nearly impassable with spring flooding, which dumps silt at this location. This section of trail may be rerouted or closed during the spring.

At the mouth of No Business Creek, you can ford across to Big Island in the middle of the river and then across to the east side to connect with the Big Island Loop. Ford only at low water. The bank on the east side is muddy also. You can also ford to Big Island and then cross back, passing upstream around the mouth of No Business Creek to pick up the No Business Trail.

From the river ford, the River Trail West turns left up an old road, paralleling No Business Creek upstream. Near the river this road is muddy, and so at first the horse trail goes up the bank straight ahead before making the turn left in order to skirt some of this mud. You'll see good campsites to the right, but camp in the floodplain only in the dry seasons. Rejoin the road as it continues up from the river.

The road passes over a low ridge and then makes a descent, passing an old roadway up to the left. At 4.3 miles, ford No Business Creek. You must ford diagonally upstream several yards in order to pick up the trail on the other side and then connect with the No Business Trail at 4.4 miles.

42 | MIDDLE CREEK ROAD ∩

Distance: 1.8 miles one-way
Difficulty: Moderate
Elevation change: 160 ft
Cautions: Unmarked route
Connections: Gobblers Knob Trail ∩

Attractions: This forest road eventually will provide access from the Gobblers Knob Trail to Charit Creek Lodge; for now, you can preview this proposed trail. This route should be attempted only by experienced outdoorspeople.

Trailhead: From the Middle Creek Trailhead, continue north on Divide Road past Fork Ridge Road at 1.0 mile from TN 154. Divide Road from here north is mostly a single track, so watch for oncoming traffic. Pass the gravel Watson Branch Road on the left at 2.0 miles (which connects with Pickett State Rustic Park on the western boundary of the recreation area); stay straight. At 2.7 miles, Middle Creek Road begins on the right. There's room for one or two vehicles to park without blocking the road.

Description: The Middle Creek Trail will follow the old Middle Creek Road east toward Charit Creek Lodge. At 0.6 mile along the road, intersect the Gobblers Knob Trail that leads to the left toward Terry Cemetery Road at Three Forks in 3.8 miles and to the right toward the Middle Creek Equestrian Trailhead in 1.8 miles. The Middle Creek Road has been upgraded only to this intersection; beyond, the route will remain an old roadway through the woods until the trail is established. But you can follow this roadway east along the ridge that stands between Middle Creek to the south and Andy Creek to the north.

At 1.4 miles a couple of old roadways lead to the left. You'll reach a fork at 1.6 miles; the left fork leads 0.2 mile out to a powerline, where it deadends. The main road takes the right fork. Descend to eventually cross exposed sandstone to two posts blocking further vehicle access at 1.8 miles.

The trail drops off to a lower level to continue following the old roadway. At this writing, the path from here is too overgrown and there are too many down trees to continue. But when the trail is constructed, you can continue along the ridgeline and descend, eventually fording Middle Creek and at about 3 miles connect with the Slave Falls to Jakes Place Connector at approximately the same location as the proposed Booger Blevins Trail junction. The Middle Creek Trail will then continue straight, fording Mill Creek and following an old roadbed along Station Camp Creek to intersect at about 4 miles with the Charit Creek Lodge Trail, which follows the road down to Charit Creek Lodge.

43 | TWIN ARCHES TRAIL 🚶🚶

Distance: 1.4-mile loop
Difficulty: Easy
Elevation change: 150 ft
Cautions: Steep stairways
Connections: Twin Arches/Charit Creek Loop 🚶🚶

Attractions: The Twin Arches are two of the largest arches in the eastern United States and the most spectacular geologic formation in the Big South Fork area. Nowhere else do you find two large arches so close together and nearly aligned end to end. The North Arch has a span of 93 feet and a clearance of 51 feet. The South Arch is the largest on the Cumberland Plateau, with a span of 135 feet and a clearance of 70 feet.

Both arches were formed by headward erosion, a process in which a gully slowly erodes up a slope, perhaps one on both sides of a ridge, until the Pennsylvanian sandstone at the ridgeline is reached. The sandstone resists falling apart, so the rain and seeping water erode under and through less resistant underlying sandstone, eventually opening a hole in the ridge.

Notice that these arches occur in a very narrow spur of the plateau surface. This edge of the plateau is receding slowly. There probably was an arch beyond the South Arch; if you explore to the south, you'll see a gap in the ridge with a mound in between that is probably the remains of the collapsed arch. As the slow process of erosion continues, the South and North Arches will eventually collapse, causing the edge of the plateau to recede even farther. Other arches likely will form farther back as time goes on, probably where seeps now emerge from the rock wall.

Trailhead: From the beginning of Divide Road off TN 154, pass Fork Ridge Road to the right at 1.0 mile and the Middle Creek Road at 2.7 miles and reach a right turn on the Twin Arches Road at 4.2 miles. Down the Twin Arches Road, the Gobblers Knob Trail crosses the road at 0.3 mile, and you'll reach the trailhead at 2.0 miles.

Description: From the trailhead, enter a mixed pine and hardwood forest with laurel lining the path and descend to a junction with the loop part of the trail at 0.3 mile. Turn left to walk the loop clockwise.

Soon, descend two sets of wooden stairs. At the bottom, turn left and then right to stay on the trail. At 0.4 mile the trail crosses footbridges over two small flows of water seeping out of the rock wall to your right. At 0.6 mile, cross another footbridge over a seep and then reach the arch formation, approaching first the North Arch. The Twin Arches/Charit Creek Loop passes under North Arch.

Continue to your left, past the stairway to the top of the ridge, to a trail

South Arch

junction on the left where the Twin Arches/Charit Creek Loop leads toward Charit Creek Lodge. Just beyond this junction stands South Arch.

The Twin Arches complex also includes two tunnels. At the south end of South Arch, you'll find the West Tunnel, on the west side. The tunnel is 88 feet long and was caused by widening of a joint. A much smaller passage, East Tunnel, can be found on the east side between the two arches, under the stairway that leads to the top. Water moving through rock created the East Tunnel.

Ascending the stairway to the top of the ridge, you'll see bare rock and patches of reindeer moss. You can then turn left along the ridgeline onto the top of South Arch. With some difficulty, you can then climb to a peak atop the arch, from which you have wide views of the landscape. Take care; people have fallen from these arches.

From the top of the stairway, turn right to complete the loop, first walking across the top of North Arch. Ascend a steep flight of stairs that leads up a knoll. Passing across the knoll, you'll see a side path to the right to a viewpoint. The trail then descends some stairs. Pass another path to the right to a viewpoint and then close the loop portion of the trail at 1.1 miles. Retrace your steps back to the trailhead at 1.4 miles.

44 | TWIN ARCHES / CHARIT CREEK LOOP 🚶

Distance: 4.6 miles
Difficulty: Moderate
Elevation change: 400 ft
Cautions: Steps, boulder passages, stream crossings
Connections: Twin Arches Trail 🚶, Slave Falls to Jakes Place Connector 🚶, Charit Creek Lodge Trail Ω, Charit Creek Trail 🚶, Station Camp Creek Trail Ω, Hatfield Ridge Loop Ω

Attractions: The trail loops by Twin Arches, rock shelters, Jakes Place, and Charit Creek Lodge. The Jakes Place homesite dates to about the same time as the old log home that became Charit Creek Lodge. Several families lived at Jakes Place; Jacob Blevins, Jr., and his wife, Viannah, were the last. A grandson of Jonathan Blevins, Jacob was known as Jakey. He died in 1935, followed a decade later by Vi; they both lie in the Katie Blevins Cemetery near the Lora Blevins Farmstead at Bandy Creek.

Joe Simpson bought the old Blevins home at Jakes Place and had it dismantled and moved to Charit Creek, which at the time was a hunting lodge. The far bunkhouse cabin at the lodge is made from the logs of the house. Jakes Place was marked by a solitary stone chimney that has since toppled.

Former chimney at Jakes Place

Trailhead: From the beginning of Divide Road off TN 154, reach a right turn on the Twin Arches Road at 4.2 miles. Down the Twin Arches Road, reach the trailhead for the Twin Arches Trail at 2.0 miles. Hike the Twin Arches Trail 0.7 mile to the arches and pick up the Twin Arches/Charit Creek Loop under the North Arch and turn right.

Description: The trail skirts the rock bluff, passing by several rock shelters where in wet weather water trickles over the edge of the rock. Flowers are abundant in spring; you'll find laurel, iris, and columbine. At 1.0 mile, watch for an overhang where erosion has bored a hole through the rock, creating a tunnel to the ridgetop, a possible arch in formation.

The trail loops south, leaving the ridge. Begin dropping into the valley created by the confluence of the three creeks that form Station Camp Creek. At the lower elevations watch for fire pink, fleabane daisy, dwarf dandelion, cinquefoil.

Finally, descend into a cedar bottom to cross Andy Creek on a boardwalk and stepping stones. Just before the crossing, you'll see a stack of rocks from an old homesite or a cleared field. At 2.0 miles, the trail enters the meadow and farmsite of Jakes Place with the collapsed chimney to the left.

The trail continues through the meadow and soon reaches a junction with the Slave Falls to Jakes Place Connector to the right; Slave Falls is at a distance of 1.5 miles. Continuing on, recross Andy Creek on a plank bridge, just above the confluence where Middle Creek, Mill Creek, and Andy Creek form Station Camp Creek. Follow the trail as it parallels Station Camp Creek downstream. Watch for cool wading pools in the creek. At 3.1 miles, the trail joins a gravel road, which is the Charit Creek Lodge Trail. Bear left to walk the road to the lodge at 3.5 miles; the Charit Creek Trail, the hiking trail down to the lodge, joins the trail after crossing a bridge over Station Camp Creek. At the lodge, you can cross a bridge over Charit Creek to get to the lodge. Across the bridge, you can also connect with the Station Camp Creek Trail and the Hatfield Ridge Loop to the left.

From the bridge crossing to Charit Creek Lodge, the trail continues straight, first paralleling Charit Creek through a mixed hardwood forest.

This is a good section for wildflowers in spring; you'll see bluets, cinquefoil, crested dwarf iris, violets of several kinds, chickweed, rue anemone, and more. The trail then climbs steeply with many log steps and switchbacks until you arrive back at Twin Arches at 4.6 miles. Then return along the Twin Arches Trail to the parking area for a total distance of 6.0 miles.

45 | ROCK CREEK LOOP 👫

Distance: 7.5 miles
Difficulty: Moderate
Elevation change: 500 ft
Cautions: Mudholes, steep sections
Connections: John Muir Trail 👫, Sheltowee Trace 👫, Coffee Trail 👫, Rock Creek Trail 👫

Attractions: This trail follows part of an old railroad grade along Massey Branch as it drops to join Rock Creek at a junction where the JMT and the Sheltowee Trace converge. The three trails together travel along Rock Creek to the west.

Trailhead: From the beginning of Divide Road off TN 154, pass Fork Ridge Road to the right at 1.0 mile and the Twin Arches Road at 4.2 miles. At 4.7 miles, turn left toward the Hattie Blevins Cemetery; 1.3 miles down this road you'll reach the cemetery and the trailhead.

Description: Walk down the old road past the cemetery, which contains graves of the Blevins, Slaven, Burke, and Crabtree families. You'll have to skirt mudholes along the way if there has been recent rain. At 0.4 mile the road forks; stay right, watching for the red arrow blaze.

The road levels out along a ridgeline where at 0.8 mile the trail turns right off the old road. This turn is very easy to miss, so watch for a path to the right.

Following this trail to the right, begin a descent toward Massey Branch. After dropping into laurel and rhododendron, cross a side creek at 1.5 miles. The trail then follows Massey Branch downstream.

At 1.6 miles is a junction with the JMT to the right, which crosses Massey Branch on a bridge.

Continue straight with the Rock Creek Loop using the JMT. You'll see the blue silhouette of Muir as the trail blaze. The trail enters a gorge at 1.7 miles on an old railroad bed left from coal and lumbering times when the Stearns Coal and Lumber Company operated in the region. Cross old railroad ties and scattered coal. At 1.8 miles, Massey Branch spills over a ledge to form a small waterfall on your right.

At 2.7 miles, the trail bears right off the old railbed and switchbacks down to a junction with the Sheltowee Trace National Recreation Trail. From the right the Sheltowee Trace has traveled south through Kentucky, passing through the Yahoo Falls and Yamacraw Bridge sections of the park to reenter the park, cross Massey Branch, and make this connection with the JMT. Massey Branch joins Rock Creek off to your right, out of sight. All three trails coincide to the left. Along with the John Muir blaze, you'll occasionally see a white turtle blaze for the Sheltowee Trace.

The trail heads upstream, occasionally using the old railbed along Rock Creek. Cross footbridges and stepping stones over side creeks and traverse rock steps up slopes; a few times the trail turns up the slope and then drops back to creek level. Deep green pools in Rock Creek with sand and rock bottoms make great swimming holes in summer. The trail passes by several camping sites. At 5.6 miles is a junction with the Coffee Trail. (This side trail fords Rock Creek to the right and leads half a mile into Pickett State Forest to the Coffee Overlook at the end of Coffee Road.) This is also the Pickett State Forest boundary; you'll see orange blazes on trees ahead.

At 5.9 miles, you'll encounter old rails and a train car wheel and, just beyond, a junction with the Rock Creek Loop turning left. The JMT and the Sheltowee Trace drop down to ford Rock Creek and continue downstream on the other side of the creek.

To complete the Rock Creek Loop, turn left and make a long, steep climb up the slope. Along the way, at 6.2 miles, the trail passes under a rock shelter. Continuing the climb, you'll reach the top of the bluff, where the trail turns left. At 6.5 miles, the trail reaches an old roadway and turns left. At 6.7 miles, intersect with another old road; stay right. At 6.8 miles, the trail turns right onto another old road; watch for the blazes. Emerge onto the cemetery road at 7.0 miles. It's now a half mile left down the road to get back to the cemetery and the trailhead.

46 | HATFIELD RIDGE TRAIL ∩

Distance: 0.9 mile one-way
Difficulty: Easy
Elevation change: 50 ft
Cautions: None
Connections: Gobblers Knob Trail ∩, Hatfield Ridge Loop ∩

Attractions: This short trail connects Terry Cemetery Road and the Gobblers Knob Trail with the Hatfield Ridge Loop for access to Charit Creek Lodge.

Trailhead: From the beginning of Divide Road off TN 154, pass Fork Ridge Road to the right at 1.0 mile and the road to the Hattie Blevins

Cemetery at 4.7 miles. Continue up Divide Road to pass on the right the wagon road down to the Gobblers Knob Trail and turn right on Terry Cemetery Road at 4.9 miles at Three Forks. In 0.8 mile along Terry Cemetery Road, the Gobblers Knob Trail emerges on the right to parallel the road. At 1.4 miles, parking for the Gobblers Knob Trailhead lies on the left; from there, you would cross the road to connect with the Gobblers Knob Trail still paralleling the road on the right. You may begin your ride or hike here. But you can also continue up Terry Cemetery Road until at 2.1 miles the road curves to the left and there is a smaller parking lot on the right for the Hatfield Ridge Trail.

Description: From the upper access point, head straight into the woods on an old forest road that is the Hatfield Ridge Trail. Just down the trail is a junction with the end of the Gobblers Knob Trail (which leads 0.8 mile back to the Gobblers Knob Trailhead); continue straight.

The road dips through a low area along Hatfield Ridge and then ascends, curving left. At 0.5 mile, an old roadway leads up to the right; stay straight. The road descends past a low rock wall with a wet-weather waterfall at 0.8 mile. The trail reaches a junction with the Hatfield Ridge Loop at 0.9 mile. To the right, this loop descends into the Station Camp Creek valley to Charit Creek Lodge in 1.1 miles.

47   TERRY CEMETERY LOOP ∩

Distance: 6.1 miles
Difficulty: Moderate
Elevation change: 660 ft
Cautions: Steep ascents and descents, rocky footing, no blazes
Connections: John Muir Trail 🚶, River Trail West ∩

Attractions: This popular horse loop dips into the gorge of the Big South Fork on Watson Cemetery Road and returns up the old Parch Corn Road, passing by the site of the John Litton Cabin on Parch Corn Creek.

Trailhead: From the beginning of Divide Road off TN 154, drive for 4.9 miles, then turn right on Terry Cemetery Road at Three Forks. At 0.8 mile along Terry Cemetery Road, the Gobblers Knob Trail emerges on the right to parallel the road. At 1.4 miles, parking for the Gobblers Knob Trailhead lies on the left; from there you cross the road to connect with the Gobblers Knob Trail still paralleling the road on the right. A ride on the Terry Cemetery Loop probably should begin here, where there is adequate parking and room for loading and unloading horses. You might also park at the Terry Cemetery Trailhead at the end of the road.

Continuing up Terry Cemetery Road, at 2.1 miles in a curve to the left, there is parking on the right for the Hatfield Ridge Trail (which leads 0.9 mile to the Hatfield Ridge Loop).

From the Hatfield Ridge Trail, continue up Terry Cemetery Road. Parch Corn Creek Road starts on the right at 4.6 miles. You will return, completing the loop, on this road. At this writing, the road had not been cleared of debris from the 1998 snowstorm, but it should be soon; check with the visitor centers for the latest information.

Continue up Terry Cemetery Road, ascending steeply. At 5.2 miles, the Terry Cemetery Loop begins to the right on the old Watson Cemetery Road. A single vehicle can park beside the road.

Description: Proceed up the Watson Cemetery Road to begin the Terry Cemetery Loop. At 0.9 mile the road makes a short descent and continues out the ridge. The road narrows to a trail but still follows the old roadbed.

Watch for where the trail bears left off the ridge at 1.2 miles while a less-used path continues straight. Descending, curve to the right below rock outcrops. At 1.5 miles, the trail bears left to swing around the Watson–Pennington Cemetery and then rejoins the roadway. After the cemetery, the road fades into the forest (unless it has been upgraded), but just continue on the path through the woods.

Curve left off the ridge and descend into a cove to cross a small stream at 1.7 miles. Curve right and descend the cove. The trail makes a steep

John Litton Cabin before it burned

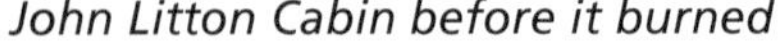

descent and then bottoms out at 2.1 miles to cross the JMT and connect with the old road along the Big South Fork that is the River Trail West.

Turn right on this old road. Before reaching Parch Corn Creek, you'll cross six creeks and drainages along the way, plus a few mudholes. The JMT occasionally comes out onto the road.

Just before the ford of Parch Corn Creek, turn right up Parch Corn Creek Road. Merge with the JMT for a short distance to where the hiking trail turns off left on a bridge over Parch Corn Creek at 3.6 miles. Continue straight up the old road to where it skirts the creek so closely that the roadway often is filled with water. If you're walking, either wade or rockhop along the edge to reach the site of the John Litton Cabin at 3.8 miles. The cabin burned in 1998; only the chimney remains. A path down to the left leads to a spring.

Continue up the Parch Corn Creek Road from the cabin. The ascent is steep and rocky. At 3.9 miles, cross a small tributary of Parch Corn Creek and then swing right to continue up the road. Cross the creek two more times in the ascent and finally reach the top of the plateau at 4.1 miles. Bear right to pass through posts blocking vehicle access and continue up the road.

You'll see low rock shelters at 4.8 and 4.9 miles. The trail curves left at 5.3 miles and then emerges on Terry Cemetery Road at 5.5 miles. Turn left to get back to the Gobblers Knob Trailhead in 3.2 miles. Or if you parked at the beginning of the Watson Cemetery Road, turn right to close the loop in a total of 6.1 miles.

48 | LONGFIELD BRANCH TRAIL ⋂

Distance: 0.7 mile one-way
Difficulty: Moderate
Elevation loss: 500 ft
Cautions: Steep descent, creek ford
Connections: Maudes Crack Overlook 🚶, No Business Trail ⋂

Attractions: This short trail descends into the No Business Creek Gorge to connect with the west end of the No Business Creek Trail, providing the shortest route into the site of the old No Business Community.

Trailhead: From the beginning of Divide Road off TN 154, continue up Divide Road and turn right on Terry Cemetery Road at 4.9 miles at Three Forks. Continue up Terry Cemetery Road past the Parch Corn Creek and Watson Cemetery Roads. At 5.5 miles along the Terry Cemetery Road (4.1 miles from the Gobblers Knob Trailhead), pass Terry Cemetery on the right, where the Roysden, Slaven, Watson, Miller, and other families are buried. Beyond the cemetery, you'll encounter a fork that is a loop; go either right or left to the end of the road and parking for the Terry Cemetery Trailhead at 5.7 miles.

Description: From the trailhead parking, continue down the old roadway, which is not improved beyond the trailhead. At 0.1 mile, turn left to go around a bar gate blocking vehicle access down the Longfield Branch Trail, which follows the old Longfield Branch Road. (Straight on the Terry Cemetery Road leads in 1.0 mile to Maudes Crack Overlook.) On the Longfield Branch Trail, descend the gravel roadway along the drainage of Longfield Branch, a tributary of No Business Creek. At 0.2 mile, pass a small overhang on the right with a small pool in front. To the left, Longfield Branch runs down a ravine.

Continue descending, and at 0.6 mile the road makes a sharp turn left. Continue down through two more curves in the road and reach the edge of No Business Creek at 0.7 mile. Ford the creek at an angle to the left to connect with an old road that runs along the north side of the creek and is the No Business Trail.

49 | MAUDES CRACK OVERLOOK 🚶🚶

Distance: 1.1 miles
Difficulty: Easy, strenuous down through Maudes Crack
Elevation loss: 100 ft
Cautions: Steep descent through crack to join the JMT
Connections: Longfield Branch Trail ∩, John Muir Trail 🚶🚶

Attractions: The top of the Maudes Crack bluff offers expansive views into the No Business Creek gorge. The crack is a passageway into the gorge providing a connection with the JMT. The passageway is named for Minnie Roysden, called Maude, who once lived in the area; she's credited with discovering the shortcut she used when bringing lunch to her husband and other workers who were cutting timber in the gorge. The men couldn't understand how she made the walk from the house to where they were working so quickly until she told them about the crack in the rock bluff.

Trailhead: From the beginning of Divide Road off TN 154, continue up Divide Road and turn right on Terry Cemetery Road at 4.9 miles at Three Forks. At 5.5 miles along Terry Cemetery Road, pass Terry Cemetery on the right. Beyond the cemetery, you'll encounter a fork that is a loop; go either right or left to the end of the road and parking for the Terry Cemetery Trailhead at 5.7 miles.

Description: Continuing up Terry Cemetery Road from the trailhead, pass the gated Longfield Branch Trail on the left and go just beyond the original beginning of the Longfield Branch Road; the trail and old roadway come together just down the slope. Stay straight on Terry Cemetery Road, which is not improved beyond the trailhead, so you must walk around occasional mudholes in the roadway.

The road rises until at 0.6 mile a downhill section begins, curving right and then left where the land drops away to the right into the valley of Big Branch, a tributary of the Big South Fork. You'll reach a side road to the right at 0.9 mile that has posts blocking further vehicle access; this old road also provides access to the JMT but at this writing it is impassable because of down trees. Terry Cemetery Road continues straight out a narrowing ridge, where at 1.0 mile it drops off to the left. The roadway dips through a saddle and extends out another point of the ridge and ends at a knoll.

From the end of the road, take the footpath to the left that passes over the side of the knoll and descends to Maudes Crack on your right at 1.1 miles. You'll see a break in the rock that extends down into the bluff. Straight ahead, the path reaches the plateau rim, with views into the No Business Creek gorge, Burke Knob to the right, and another sandstone butte to the left.

Maudes Crack

It is possible to climb down into Maudes Crack and scoot down the steep, rocky, sometimes muddy chute to emerge below the gorge rim; do not attempt this route unless you have some experience doing this kind of scramble. At the bottom, you'll see that the rift of Maudes Crack was formed when a piece of the bluff separated from the cliff.

When you emerge from the passageway, you can bear right along the rock bluff, turn right to pass between two large rocks forming a portal, and connect with the JMT. This junction is at the top of the JMT's descent into the gorge of No Business Creek. If you are not continuing on the JMT, retrace your steps to the Terry Cemetery Trailhead.

Map 5. Peters Mountain

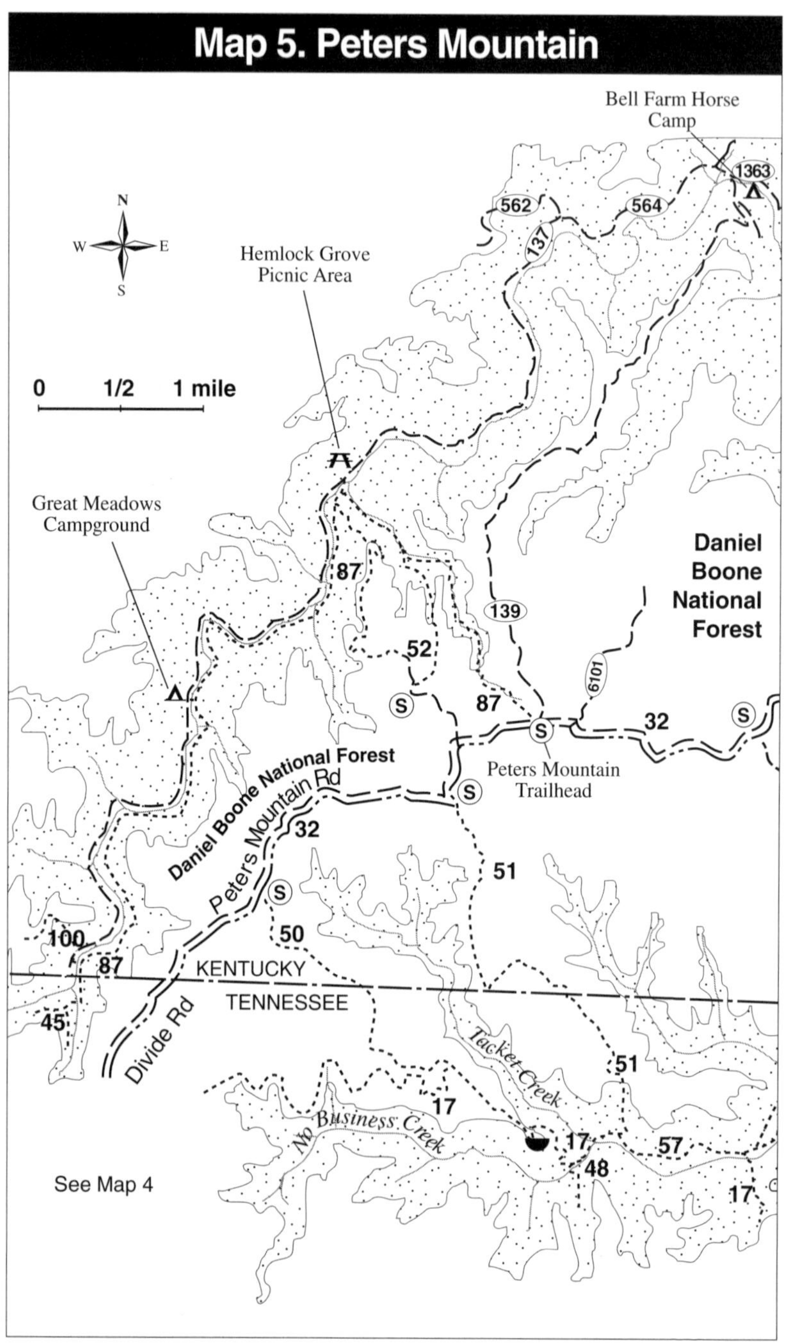

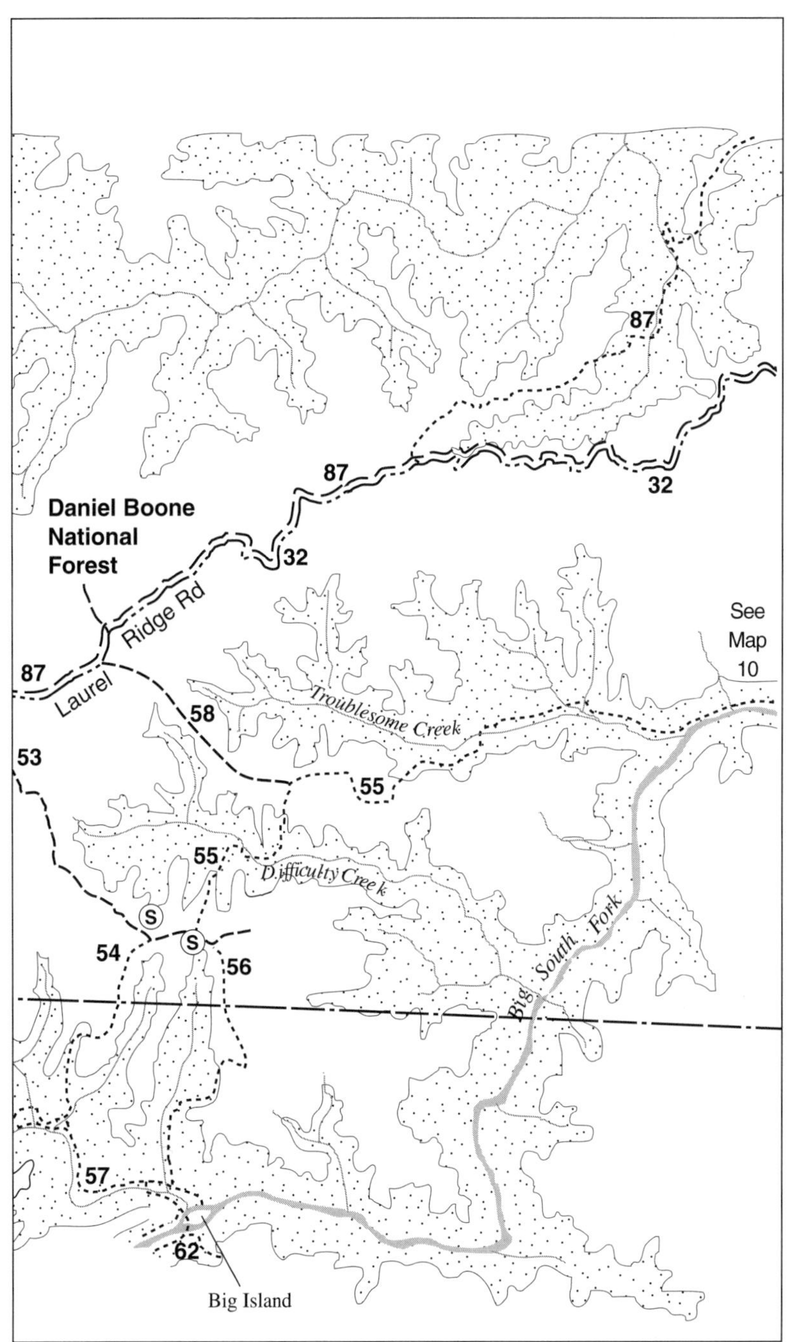

87
32
87
32
Daniel Boone National Forest
Ridge Rd
Laurel
87
See Map 10
58
53
Troublesome Creek
55
55
Difficulty Creek
S
Big South Fork
54
S
56
57
62
Big Island

The Peters Mountain section of the recreation area contains the most remote section of the park. The gravel Divide Road continues north from the Middle Creek area, crossing the state line into Kentucky, where it becomes Peters Mountain Road. Once in Kentucky, the road is flanked on the left by Daniel Boone National Forest and on the right by the BSFNRRA. Civilization is a long way off in any direction. Trails lead into both the national forest and the recreation area, featuring overlooks, arches, and cascading streams as well as providing additional access to the No Business Creek Gorge.

From the beginning of Divide Road off TN 154, the Terry Cemetery Road turns to the right at 4.9 miles. Continue north on Divide Road. Cross the state line at 7.9 miles, where Divide Road becomes Peters Mountain Road, and continue north. The Peters Mountain Trailhead lies on a knoll on the right at an intersection of forest roads at 11.2 miles. An alternate route to the Peters Mountain Trailhead is down FDR 139 from the western end of KY 1363.

50 | JOHN MUIR OVERLOOK 🚶🚶

Distance: 2.6 miles one-way
Difficulty: Moderate
Elevation loss: 200 ft
Cautions: Unofficial route, mudholes, steep dropoffs
Connections: John Muir Trail 🚶🚶

Attractions: At the John Muir Overlook, you'll have a sweeping view of the No Business Creek Gorge. In the early mornings, fog and mist drift through the valley. This route should be attempted only by experienced outdoorspeople.

Trailhead: Take Divide Road north from Terry Cemetery Road. The JMT crosses the road at 6.7 miles from TN 154. Cross the state line into Kentucky at 7.9 miles, where the road, now Peters Mountain Road, serves as the boundary between the Daniel Boone National Forest and the BSFNRRA. Watch for an unmarked road on the right at 8.7 miles, which is Chestnut Ridge Road. Pull in and park; the road will be muddy after a rain so you may need to park somewhere else; find a wide place in the road or go all the way to the Peters Mountain Trailhead to the north, and ride a bike or horse back to this location. This side road is passable only to four-

Morning mist gathering below John Muir Overlook

wheel-drive vehicles because of mudholes, and some of those get mired down. Hikers can go around any problem areas.

Description: Head down the road, which runs along the spine of Chestnut Ridge. Pass a field on the left and at 0.1 mile enter the woods. Stay along the main well-traveled dirt road as you pass traces of old roads right and left. At 1.0 mile, cross the state line into Tennessee.

The road bears right at 1.2 miles as another roadway heads left. At 1.3 miles, the road makes an obvious curve left where an old roadway continues straight. Pass another roadway to the right and reach a fork at 1.7 miles. Stay left.

After a time the road curves right and descends gently to a junction with the JMT at 2.0 miles. Posts block further vehicle access; horses and mountain bikes must be left here. Walk straight on the old roadbed, which is also the JMT. At 2.4 miles, the trail turns down right off the road. The trail drops with a couple of wooden steps onto a narrow saddle in the ridge separating Tacket Creek Gorge to the left and No Business Creek Gorge to the right. Then ascend rock and wooden steps and bear right along the bluff to where the JMT makes a sharp switchback left at 2.6 miles. Straight ahead is the bare rock bluff of the John Muir Overlook at the edge of the No Business Creek Gorge.

51 | STOOPIN' OAK ROAD ∩

Distance: 3.8 miles one-way
Difficulty: Moderate
Elevation loss: 600 ft
Cautions: Unmarked route, mudholes, steep and rocky descent
Connections: John Muir Trail ⚇, No Business Trail ∩

Attractions: This forest road descends into the No Business Creek area and, until developed as an official trail, should be attempted only by experienced outdoorspeople.

Trailhead: From the John Muir Overlook turnoff, continue up Peters Mountain Road. Pass FDR 6300 on the left and at 10.0 miles from TN 154 reach Stoopin' Oak Road on the right. Turn in and park to the right so you do not block the road; if it's muddy, there's a turnout on the right just down from the Stoopin' Oak turnoff. If you need more room to unload horses, drive on up Peters Mountain Road another mile to the Peters Mountain Trailhead and then ride back along the road to this turnoff.

Description: Head up Stoopin' Oak Road. You'll soon begin dropping below rock outcrops on the left. Pullouts on the left can serve as camping sites if you've brought water. At 0.3 mile, as the trail tops a ridge, pass another roadway to the left.

At 1.0 mile, the road makes a turn to the right where an old side road leads left. After a level section and some downhill, there's a steep ascent at 2.0 miles. Once you level off, the trail passes rock outcrops along the spine of the ridge. At 2.2 miles, a path on the left leads up into the rocks. The trail soon loops left over the point of the ridge. Tacket Creek flows in the valley to your right. The trail now heads down the other side of the ridge.

The road curves right into a descent at 2.5 miles, where a side path leads left up to a rock wall and a spring with water flowing from a pipe. The trail crosses the state line into Tennessee. You'll then reach an intersection of roads; continue straight. The roadway curves right on top of a knob. Drop to a small clearing where the road curves left at 2.8 miles to continue descending.

At 3.0 miles the road curves left to cross a small stream. The road continues straight and a side road leads left uphill, but turn right here to cross a larger creek and pass through posts preventing further vehicle access. Then begin the descent into the No Business Creek Gorge. At 3.2 miles, pass through a tall rock passageway to a steep descent as you drop below the rock bluff of the rim. The road eventually bottoms out at 3.8 miles to connect with the old road along No Business Creek. This is both the No Business Trail for horses and the JMT for hikers. Right along this trail will take you to the Longfield Branch Trail; left gets you to the Big South Fork at Big Island.

52 | MARK BRANCH / GOBBLERS ARCH TRAILS 🚶🚶

Distance: 4.0-mile loop
Difficulty: Moderate
Elevation change: 600 ft
Cautions: Creek crossings, steep ascent
Connections: Sheltowee Trace 🚶🚶

Attractions: The Mark Branch Trail and the Gobblers Arch Trail combine to form this scenic loop on national forest land. The route drops into a narrow gorge and swings through a natural arch.

Trailhead: Continuing north on Peters Mountain Road from Stoopin' Oak Road, watch for FDR 6105 on your left in 10.5 miles from TN 154. You'll see a low sign for the Mark Branch Loop. You can park here beside the road to begin this hike in the Daniel Boone National Forest. Or you might drive down FDR 6105 if it has been cleared of fallen trees; in wet weather,

Gobblers Arch

you may encounter mudholes. At 0.6 mile along the road, the trail turns off to the right; there's room to park a vehicle beside the road at the trailhead.

Description: From the trailhead 0.6 mile down FDR 6105, the Mark Branch Trail begins on an old roadway to the right blazed with white diamonds. You'll soon turn left off the roadway, descending to cross a shallow creek at the head of a hollow at 0.2 mile. The trail turns left to ascend to a rock bluff. Follow the bluff and then drop through another hollow and ascend to a right turn on an old roadbed at 0.4 mile.

At 0.5 mile, turn left off the roadbed to descend along the bluff of a narrow gorge and then descend into the rock gorge to cross a stream on a footbridge at 0.6 mile; in wet weather you'll see a small cascade up to your left. As you switchback up the other side, notice the large hemlock sitting on a boulder.

Descend back into the gorge. At 0.8 mile, the trail turns right off the shelf you're walking, drops through the hollow, and continues descending into the gorge. Switchback left in the descent and for a time follow an old railbed. At 0.9 mile, cross a creekbed and continue descending to a junction at 1.0 mile with the Sheltowee Trace at Mark Branch. Turn left to continue the loop.

Along the Sheltowee Trace, cross Mark Branch on stepping stones four times, then walk in the creekbed to a bend, where you'll climb above the creek. The trail crosses a couple of drainages and then emerges into an open area at a junction at 1.4 miles. The Sheltowee Trace turns left, but you can also follow a leg of the trace straight ahead to a ford of Rock Creek in 0.1 mile to get to the Hemlock Grove Picnic Area. You can access the Sheltowee Trace and walk the loop from this location on FDR 137.

At the trail junction, continue on the Sheltowee Trace to the left to a junction with the Gobblers Arch Trail on the left at 1.5 miles. The Sheltowee Trace continues straight to the Great Meadows Campground in another 2.0 miles.

On the Gobblers Arch Trail, make a steep ascent of the ridge, finally reaching the point of a rock bluff at 1.7 miles. This point on the rim marks the confluence of the Mark Branch and Rock Creek Gorges. The trail swings left and stays along the base of the rock bluff on the Mark Branch side. Watch for patches of columbine in spring.

Pass a deep alcove in the rock wall, which has a wet-weather waterfall. At 2.0 miles, the trail heads up a hollow; switchback right and ascend above the bluff. The trail now follows along the top, back to the bluff point, and then turns left to follow the bluff rim along the Rock Creek Gorge. At 2.6 miles is a short side path to a vista of the gorge, with the creek buried in trees below.

The trail follows along a low rock bluff and bears left to pass through Gobblers Arch, actually a low tunnel through the ridge, at 3.3 miles. On the other side, bear left to switchback up and walk out to FDR 6105, not open to vehicles at this point. Turn right and follow the road out to a turnaround where there is vehicle access at 3.5 miles. Then continue up the road to the beginning of the Mark Branch Trail at 4.0 miles. If you walked in, you'll have another 0.6 mile back to the Peters Mountain Road.

53 | LAUREL HILL TRAIL ∩

Distance: 2.4 miles one-way
Difficulty: Easy
Elevation loss: 140 ft
Cautions: None
Connections: Long Trail ∩, Sheltowee Trace 🏃, Burkes Branch Trail 🏃, Kentucky Trail 🏃, Miller Branch Trail ∩

Attractions: This trail, following an old roadway that has been upgraded, provides access to several backcountry trails that dip into No Business Creek Gorge and pass through the northern section of the park.

Trailhead: Continue northeast on Peters Mountain Road from the turn-off for the Mark Branch Trail to an intersection with FDR 139 to the left and FDR 6101 straight ahead, at 11.2 miles from TN 154. To the left, the Sheltowee Trace heads into the woods; on the right lies the Peters Mountain Trailhead. The Peters Mountain Trailhead can be a staging area for horseback rides and group gatherings, so a horseback ride will begin here. Smaller parties can continue to the beginning of the Laurel Hill Trail, where there is room for one or two smaller vehicles to park.

From this junction at Peters Mountain Trailhead, head straight up FDR 6101 (following the same route as the Sheltowee Trace and the Long Trail headed north). At 0.2 mile, turn right onto Laurel Ridge Road and continue on this gravel road. The Daniel Boone National Forest borders the road on the left; trees have been cut in the hollows on that side of the road. There's a junction at 1.7 miles with the Laurel Hill Trail to the right. The Sheltowee Trace and the Long Trail continue straight on Laurel Ridge Road. Park so you do not block access up either road.

Description: The Laurel Hill Trail heads up the old Laurel Hill Road. You may drive down the Laurel Hill Trail, but there are places where it is not suitable for passenger cars. An old roadway heads off to the left soon after you begin the trail. The road descends steeply. At 0.1 mile the old roadway on the left rejoins Laurel Hill Road. Continue descending, making a last steep descent at 0.4 mile.

The trail passes a clearing on the left at 0.8 mile. Past the clearing, another old roadway turns sharply back to the left. Begin an ascent out a narrowing ridge. The roadway soon levels off again, with the valley of No Business Creek to the right.

Pass a clearing on the left at 1.4 miles. The old roadway forks at 1.6 miles. The right fork is overgrown; stay left. Just beyond, the two forks come back together. At 1.8 miles, another fork on the right is overgrown; stay left. At 1.9 miles, the Burkes Branch Trail begins on the right. Just down that trail, the last overgrown fork joins the Burkes Branch Trail.

Continue straight on the Laurel Hill Trail. At 2.3 miles, the Kentucky Trail begins on the left, following an old roadway through two posts that block vehicle access. Stay straight to a junction at 2.4 miles with the Miller Branch Trail to the right, which is the continuation of the gravel roadway. The old Laurel Hill Road continues to the left, but is rapidly getting overgrown and is now impassable, although it may be developed as a trail in the future.

54 | BURKES BRANCH / DRY BRANCH TRAILS 🚶🚶

Distance: 2.2 miles one-way
Difficulty: Moderate
Elevation loss: 680 ft
Cautions: Steep descent
Connections: Laurel Hill Trail ∩, No Business Trail ∩, John Muir Trail 🚶🚶

Attractions: These hiking trails descend past rimrock into the No Business Creek Gorge to connect with the JMT.

Trailhead: From the Peters Mountain Trailhead, ride horses or bikes or hike north up FDR 6101 following the route of the Sheltowee Trace. Turn right on Laurel Ridge Road at 0.2 mile and continue to a junction at 1.7 miles, where the Laurel Hill Trail turns off Laurel Ridge Road to the right on the old Laurel Hill Road; you can also park one or two vehicles here to begin your hike. Turn up the Laurel Hill Trail, which is a gravel roadway, to a junction with the Burkes Branch Trail to the right in another 1.9 miles; four-wheel drive vehicles can make it to this trailhead.

Description: Turning right on the Burkes Branch Trail, walk past an old roadway to the right. At 0.5 mile, cross the state line into Tennessee and pass through posts blocking vehicle access. Soon after, listen for a wet-weather waterfall spilling over a rock wall at the gorge rim to your right. Descend bare sandstone to dip through a saddle. Over the next ridge, begin a serious descent into the gorge of No Business Creek. Somewhere in here, a proposed side trail will lead to the Burkes Branch Overlook.

At 0.9 mile, a side road comes in from the left. Soon after, watch for a cascade in the stream to your right. At 1.0 mile, pass massive rock that makes up the gorge rim. The old road descends steeply; at 1.2 miles, cross a small stream that is a tributary of Burkes Branch. Continue descending to a junction at 1.4 miles, where the Dry Branch Trail turns off on a footpath to the right. Straight ahead a few yards, the Burkes Branch Trail fords Burkes Branch and passes through posts to connect with the No Business Trail that follows the old road along No Business Creek.

Turning right on the Dry Branch Trail, pass through woods with Burkes Branch and the No Business Trail down to the left. At 1.6 miles the hiking trail swings next to the horse trail to turn up an old roadway while the horse trail continues on to ford Dry Branch. At 1.7 miles, the trail turns left off the roadway to a bridge crossing of Dry Branch. The trail also continues straight up the roadway, but it soon swings left to the bridge crossing, so just turn left at the first junction.

On the other side, pass through bottomlands and ascend to an old roadway at 1.8 miles and bear left. Cross two footbridges over small streams and reach a junction with the No Business Trail at 2.0 miles. Now the Dry Branch Trail and the No Business Trail coincide along the old roadway paralleling No Business Creek.

Pass an old roadway up to the right. At 2.1 miles, watch for a row of rocks on the right that may have been foundations for a house. A stream runs under the road. Watch for the foundation pillars of the old boarding house down to your left, with the massive bluffs of Burke Knob on the other side of the gorge. Where another stream passes under the road, you'll see stacked rocks to the right that seem to have formed a dam on the stream, but there are now so many spaces between the rocks that they do not hold back any water.

At 2.2 miles is a junction with the JMT coming in from the left, where the Dry Branch Trail ends. The JMT and the No Business Trail continue straight up the old road.

55 | KENTUCKY TRAIL 👥

Distance: 22.2 miles one-way
Difficulty: Moderate
Elevation loss: 880 ft
Cautions: Creek fords, mudholes, several ascents and
      descents
Connections: Laurel Hill Trail ∩, Cat Ridge Road ∩, Oil Well
      Branch Road ∩, Long Trail ∩, Sheltowee Trace 👥

Attractions: This long hike is a good backpacking route in the Kentucky section of the park. The first half of the trail consists of several designated sections: Difficulty Creek, Cat Ridge, Troublesome Creek, and Oil Well Branch.

In the early years when public attention turned to the Big South Fork River Gorge, wilderness designation was proposed for the Troublesome Creek region of the recreation area, about 26,000 acres. This suggestion was never pursued because of the more important steps of establishing the recreation area and purchasing the land. But the Difficulty Creek–Troublesome Creek area now traversed by the Kentucky Trail remains as primitive and isolated as before the park was established. The trail crosses numerous streams while traveling through a dense, verdant forest before emerging at the Blue Heron Mining Community.

The trail passes the first commercial oil well in the United States. The well was drilled in 1818 by Marcus Huling and Andrew Zimmerman, who were searching for salt on land owned by Martin Beaty. They drilled using a spring-pole rig supported on a post similar to the one standing in front of the well today. Instead of salt, Huling and Zimmerman found oil, which was virtually useless at the time, but Huling sold some of it as an ingredient in liniments. The original wooden casing has been replaced with metal pipe.

Beaty Oil Well

Trailhead: Begin this hike at the Peters Mountain Trailhead or continue north up FDR 6101 following the route of the Sheltowee Trace. Turn right on Laurel Ridge Road at 0.2 mile and continue to a junction at 1.7 miles, where the Laurel Hill Trail turns off Laurel Ridge Road to the right; you can also park one or two vehicles here. Turn up the Laurel Hill Trail, which is a gravel roadway, and pass a junction with the Burkes Branch Trail to the right at 3.6 miles; continue to a junction with the Kentucky Trail to the left at 4.0 miles. There is room for a vehicle or two to park at the beginning of the trail, but the Laurel Hill Road is not suitable for passenger cars in some places; four-wheel drive vehicles can make it easily.

Description: Turning left on the Kentucky Trail, pass through posts and walk along an old roadway to begin the Difficulty Creek section. The road narrows to a path and begins a descent toward Difficulty Creek. At 0.7 mile is a short set of stairs that the trail now bypasses. Out the ridge, the trail turns down to the right to continue the descent with a switchback and a curve to the right to drop below a rock bluff. Along the rock wall, at 0.9 mile, the trail turns left; straight ahead a path leads to a ravine headed by a waterfall.

The main trail heads down the ravine to cross a footbridge over a side stream and switchback down to a bridge crossing of the ravine stream at 1.3 miles. This is a tributary of Difficulty Creek, which you'll soon parallel downstream. The trail crosses a footbridge over a side stream and then reaches a large bridge over Difficulty Creek at 1.8 miles.

On the other side, turn right and continue downstream. Cross a bridge over a side drainage at 1.9 miles and curve right to descend stone steps to a bridge crossing of another tributary stream at 2.0 miles. Up steps on the other side, turn left on an old roadway. Soon the trail turns right up an old roadbed in a steep climb, bypassing a short footbridge no longer used. Watch for the trail to turn left off the roadway at 2.1 miles. The trail curves around the head of a hollow and continues up the trace of an old road. At 2.3 miles, bear right off the roadway, which leads to the Cat Ridge Road but has become overgrown and has down trees. On the path to the right, ascend to a junction with Cat Ridge Road at 2.4 miles. This dirt road leads down from Laurel Ridge Road and is proposed for a Cat Ridge Trail. Turn right on Cat Ridge Road.

The roadway heads out along a ridge and descends to where the Kentucky Trail turns on a path to the left at 3.0 miles to begin the Troublesome Creek section; the roadway continues straight but is mostly overgrown. At 3.4 miles, pass under an overhang and follow the trail up to the right.

A rock leaning against a larger rock signals a switchback left; within a few yards, switchback right. At 3.8 miles, the trail crosses the trace of a road dropping steeply down the slope. Descend to emerge on an old road at 3.9 miles; turn left. Watch for the trail to turn right off the road in 40 yards.

The path descends to a bridge crossing of a stream at 4.0 miles. Then switchback down to a long bridge crossing of Troublesome Creek at 4.3 miles. On the other side, bear left up stone steps and switch right as you ascend from the creek. The path joins an old roadbed. At 4.8 miles, bear left to ford Lone Cliff Branch just above its confluence with Troublesome Creek. On the other side, go left through an overgrown floodplain and turn right. Soon, you'll reach an old roadway up to the left that is the Lone Cliff Branch Road leading up to the Sheltowee Trace on Laurel Ridge Road. Bear right off the road into the floodplain of the creek to begin the Oil Well Branch section; you won't see much of a trail, but keep going and you'll find a roadway. Bear left to cross a small stream and turn right to a ford of Watson Branch at 5.0 miles. On the other side, pick up the old roadway and continue down Troublesome Creek.

At a fork at 5.5 miles, bear left. Continue bearing left as you leave Troublesome Creek and follow the old road north along the Big South Fork. At 5.7 miles, notice a huge block of stone in the river to your right, split in two.

At 6.0 miles, rockhop a streambed where a bridge has broken and scattered, unless it has been repaired. After a little rise, the trail curves left at 6.7 miles; off-trail, about 50 paces to the right, a pipe emerging from the ground is the old Beaty well, the first commercial oil well in the United States.

A little farther up the trail, you'll see another pipe sticking out of the ground on the left, probably another well. At 6.8 miles, ford Oil Well Branch. Pass an overgrown roadway up to the left; just after, a path leads up to the roadway. This is Oil Well Branch Road, which eventually will be the part of a proposed Oil Well Branch Loop that will travel west to turn up Lone Cliff Branch Road. Straight ahead, cross two branches of a small drainage and at 7.4 miles climb left around a boulder resting in the old roadway. Back on the roadbed, the trail crosses a rocky drainage.

At 7.7 miles, the trail turns up a road to the left. The road along the river continues straight but has become overgrown. As you ascend left steeply up the old road, cross two footbridges over a drainage, pass a low overhang on the left, and continue uphill to pass through posts and emerge on the gravel Bald Knob Road at 8.2 miles. Turn left. At 8.6 miles, pass the beginning of Oil Well Branch Road on the left; just up that road, you'll find the Hill Cemetery on your right. Continue up Bald Knob Road to reach the Ledbetter Place Trailhead at 8.8 miles.

Just up the road from the trailhead, at 8.9 miles, the Kentucky Trail turns right on a side road. At 9.0 miles, pass the King Cemetery on the right. At 9.3 miles the road fades into the landscape and the trail becomes a path. Pass through a hemlock grove and walk around the head of a hollow and descend to a road at 9.7 miles. Turn left to a bridge crossing of the south fork of Laurel Crossing Branch. On the other side, watch for the trail to turn off the road to the right. At 10.0 miles, cross the north fork of Laurel Crossing Branch on a bridge. Keep your eye on the blazes through the next complicated section that takes you through boulders and switchbacks.

At 11.1 miles is a junction with an old road. (To the left the overgrown road leads up to the back of the Waters Cemetery at the end of the Waters Cemetery Road.) Turn right.

The trail soon veers right off the road. Curve left and reach an old homesite at 11.3 miles. The trail passes through the clearing and then bears left on an old roadway. The road ascends and the trail veers off to the right at 11.5 miles. Dip through an old roadway and emerge at a field. Walk straight across to find where the trail reenters the woods. Emerge at another portion of the field; stay along the edge. At 11.7 miles, the trail turns right into the woods. Curve left to begin a descent at 11.9 miles. With switchbacks, you'll reach a junction with a side trail to Big Springs Falls at 12.4 miles. From here the Kentucky Trail continues north to pass Dick Gap

Falls and Catawba Overlook and reach the tram bridge over to the Blue Heron Mining Community at 15.8 miles (see Trail 75). The Kentucky Trail then continues north following the old tramroad on this west side of the Big South Fork (see Trail 74).

At 18.1 miles you'll see concrete piers that anchored a mining structure. Continue straight up the road, following a creek upstream. Work your way up the cove, crossing the stream and a couple of bridges to reach the drier plateau top.

At 19.8 miles, the trail crosses a bridge over a creek and then crosses the trace of an old road. Pass under a powerline and emerge on Wilson Ridge Road at 20.6 miles. Turn right on Wilson Ridge Road, not up the side road. At 20.8 miles, a side road leads to the right up to the Wilson Cemetery. At 20.9 miles the road passes a house on the left and the gravel part ends just beyond. The trail continues down the roadway, now a dirt track. At 21.0 miles, pass under a powerline. Stay left where the road forks at 21.3 miles. The trail turns left off the road at 21.5 miles.

Now on a path, round the point of Wilson Ridge and begin a serious descent, crossing the boundary of the national recreation area into Daniel Boone National Forest. With turns, switchbacks, and stone steps, descend the ridge to bottom out at a ford of Grassy Fork. Up from the creek, turn left and walk up to the end of the trail and a junction with the Sheltowee Trace at 22.2 miles. To the right, you can walk the trace to a ford of Rock Creek, where you reenter the recreation area and continue on to emerge at the Yamacraw Bridge crossing of the Big South Fork on KY 92 in 0.9 mile.

56 MILLER BRANCH TRAIL ∩

Distance: 2.1 miles one-way
Difficulty: Moderate
Elevation loss: 640 ft
Cautions: Steep descent
Connections: Laurel Hill Trail ∩, No Business Trail ∩

Attractions: This trail drops below the gorge rim to access No Business Creek on its eastern end at the confluence of No Business Creek with the Big South Fork.

Trailhead: From the Peters Mountain Trailhead, travel up Laurel Ridge Road and turn right on the Laurel Hill Trail to the junction with the Burkes Branch Trail at 3.6 miles from Laurel Ridge Road. Continue straight to where the Kentucky Trail turns left off the Laurel Hill Trail at 4.0 miles. Again continue straight to another junction at 4.1 miles with a dirt road to the left that is the old route of the Laurel Hill Road. The continuation of the gravel road to the right is the Miller Branch Trail. At this writing, the junction has not been signed.

Description: Down the Miller Branch Trail, join an old roadbed coming in from the right. At 0.6 mile, the gravel ends at the end of vehicle access. The roadway continues as a sandy track that begins a descent into the No Business Creek Gorge. A bar across the road blocks vehicle access.

The trail heads out a narrow ridge and descends across bare sandstone. As the roadway curves right at 0.8 mile, it leads into a steeper descent. At 0.9 mile, descend a steep bank, curving left. The trail soon curves right up a drainage to cross a small stream to the left at 1.1 miles.

The roadway continues to descend, curving left down the cove of Miller Branch and recrossing the drainage from above at 1.5 miles. Pass through a muddy section and eventually bottom out at a junction with the No Business Trail at 2.1 miles. To the left, you can access the Big Island Crossing of the Big South Fork in 0.3 mile. To the right, you can access the River Trail West in 0.3 mile, which you can turn down to ford No Business Creek and also reach the Big Island Crossing.

57 | NO BUSINESS TRAIL ∩

Distance: 3.1 miles one-way
Difficulty: Easy
Elevation gain: 80 ft
Cautions: Creek fords, mudholes
Connections: Big Island Loop ∩, Miller Branch Trail ∩, Big Branch Trail ∩, Burkes Branch Trail ⅗, Dry Branch Trail ⅗, John Muir Trail ⅗, Stoopin' Oak Road ∩, Longfield Branch Trail ∩

Attractions: This mostly level trail traverses the old community of No Business and connects several trails in the backcountry of No Business Creek Gorge. You'll see signs of civilization: old fence rows, rock foundations, remains of log barns, and even a rusting vehicle.

Trailhead: Because this is a connector trail, you must ride or hike other trails to get to it. To access the east end of the trail at the Big Island Crossing of the Big South Fork, ford the river from the Big Island Loop or take the River Trail West north from Station Camp Creek or the Laurel Hill Trail and Miller Branch Trail off Laurel Ridge Road.

Description: The No Business Trail begins on the north side of the mouth of No Business Creek, where the creek joins the Big South Fork River. You will be able to see Big Island in the middle of the river; at low water you can ford from the Big Island Loop on the east side of the river to

Truck remains at No Business

the island and then across to connect with the No Business Trail. From the No Business Trail, you can ford to the island and cross back to the same side of the river, going around the confluence of No Business Creek, to access the River Trail West. In spring, the banks of the river can be very muddy.

Headed west from the river on the No Business Trail, follow an old roadway that stays on the north side of No Business Creek. From the river shore, first pass over a low ridge and then traverse bottomlands along the creek, which can be muddy. At 0.3 mile is a junction with the Miller Branch Trail up to the right. Soon after, ford Miller Branch.

At 0.4 mile, the trail drops off to the left as a roadway continues straight. Soon after, watch for a rock wall up to the right that surrounds a collapsed barn and the foundations of a house with the base of a chimney still standing. The No Business Community of subsistence farms thrived along the creek in the late 1800s and early 1900s.

Cross a couple of small streams; there's a junction at 0.6 mile with a road down to the left. This is the River Trail West (which fords No Business

Creek and then follows an old road down the creek to the river at the Big Island Crossing).

Continue up the No Business Trail. As you ascend over a low ridge, you'll see the rock bluffs of Burke Knob across the gorge. Descending from the ridge, cross a couple of small streambeds and reach a junction at 0.9 mile with the foundations of a house on your left. The road straight ahead that is blocked by posts is the Burkes Branch Trail. The No Business Trail turns left here. Ford Burkes Branch and continue up the road, paralleling No Business Creek.

At 1.1 miles, the trail turns left at a road straight ahead that is part of the Dry Branch Trail. After making the left turn, ford Dry Branch at 1.2 miles and continue up the road along No Business. Crossing a couple of small streams that run across the trail in wet weather, you'll reach a junction at 1.6 miles where the Dry Branch Trail comes in from the right and joins the No Business Trail.

At 1.8 miles is a junction with the JMT coming in from the left. The Dry Branch Trail ends here and the No Business and John Muir Trails continue up the old road. This was a populated section of the No Business Community; watch for picket fences, stone foundations, and rows of rock. At 2.6 miles, look for the shell of an old truck where a side stream crosses under slabs of rock in the road and tumbled-down log barns rest in the overgrown field to the left. Soon after, pass the Stoopin' Oak Road that leads up to the right. At 2.7 miles, ford Tacket Creek. At 3.0 miles, the JMT turns off to the right and the No Business Trail continues straight.

Then at 3.1 miles, the trail ends at a junction with the Longfield Branch Trail that fords No Business Creek to the left. Straight ahead, the old roadbed continues but has become overgrown. That route may be developed as a trail in the future. You can turn up the Longfield Branch Trail to the Terry Cemetery Trailhead on Terry Cemetery Road in 0.6 mile.

58 | CAT RIDGE ROAD ∩

Distance: 2.3 miles one-way
Difficulty: Moderate
Elevation change: 110 ft
Cautions: Mudholes
Connections: Long Trail ∩, Sheltowee Trace ⋇, Kentucky Trail ⋇

Attractions: This old road has been proposed for a Cat Ridge Trail that will connect the Long Trail and Sheltowee Trace, which coincide along Laurel Ridge Road, with the Kentucky Trail to the east.

Trailhead: From the Peters Mountain Trailhead, head up FDR 6101 and turn right on Laurel Ridge Road. The Laurel Hill Trail turns off to the right at 1.7 miles, where one or two vehicles can park. Although Laurel Ridge Road has been upgraded during the last few years, from here on the road can get muddy in places and so may not be suitable for passenger cars. At 2.7 miles, the Cat Ridge Road turns off to the right. The road is not signed at this writing, so you must watch for the turn.

Description: The old Cat Ridge Road heads east from Laurel Ridge Road. Occasional large mudholes span nearly the entire width of the road in wet seasons. Pass a clearing to the right.

At 0.3 mile, the road descends across bare sandstone with plateau tablerock to the right and left. Level again, the roadway passes a clearing on the left and another on the right at 0.6 mile.

The road ascends steeply, crossing bare sandstone and passing a rock bluff on the left. The trail tops out where the road crosses more sandstone and descends, heading out a narrowing ridge.

Ascend to a fork with an old roadbed to the right. Stay left on the more well-worn roadway to reach a junction with the Kentucky Trail at 1.7 miles. To the right, this hiking trail heads toward Difficulty Creek. To the left, the Kentucky Trail joins the Cat Ridge Road to head toward Troublesome Creek.

Horses and mountain bikes may not turn right on the hiking trail but may continue down Cat Ridge Road. The road continues along a ridge and descends to a junction where the Kentucky Trail turns on a path to the left at 2.3 miles. The old roadbed continues straight, providing a route for anglers to continue east toward the river; the roadway may be overgrown. Horses and mountain bikes must return from this junction, where the hiking trail turns off to the left.

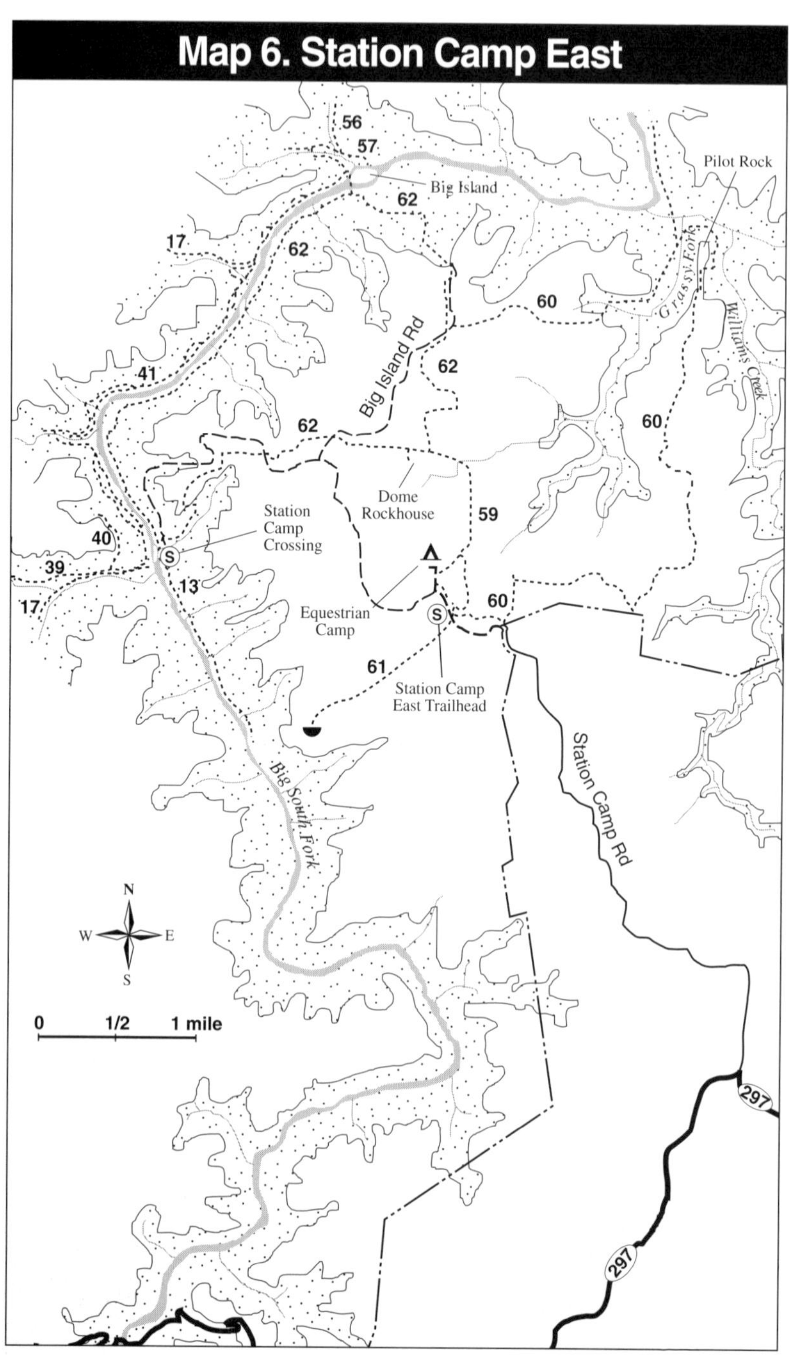

56
57
Big Island
62
Pilot Rock
17
62
60
Grassy Fork
Williams Creek
41
62
Big Island Rd
60
62
Station
Camp
Crossing
Dome
Rockhouse
59
40
39
13
60
17
Equestrian
Camp
61
Station Camp
East Trailhead
Big South Fork
Station Camp Rd
N
W   E
S
0   1/2   1 mile
297
297

The Station Camp East region of the recreation area contains an equestrian camp and several trails leading to overlooks, a domed rock shelter, and a massive block of stone sitting on the rim of the river gorge.

Outside the park on the east, where TN 297 makes a right-angle turn at the Terry and Terry Store, take the Station Camp Road west toward the river. The paved road becomes gravel at 3.7 miles. Cross the boundary into the park at 4.0 miles. At 4.5 miles, the Station Camp East Trailhead is on the right.

One of the Chimney Rocks

Just beyond is a right turn into the Station Camp East Equestrian Camp; hikers are welcome here too if they do not mind camping near horses, which are stalled around the perimeter of the camp. The Station Camp East Road continues toward the Big South Fork Gorge, passing the old Big Island Road to the right, which leads across the plateau toward Big Island. After beginning the descent into the river gorge, the Station Camp East Road passes Chimney Rocks, two pillars of stone on the left at 6.8 miles; from a parking area on the right, you can walk up to the 20-foot rocks.

Descending steeply into the gorge, the road bottoms out near the river at 8.5 miles. You'll pass a trail down to the Station Camp Crossing of the Big South Fork on the right, where you can ford the river at low water to access trails on the west side near the confluence of Station Camp Creek. Beyond the crossing the road ends at a parking area for trail access.

59 | DOME ROCKHOUSE ⋂

Distance: 2.2 miles one-way
Difficulty: Moderate
Elevation change: 200 ft
Cautions: Creek ford
Connections: Pilot/Wines Loop ⋂, Big Island Loop ⋂

Attractions: This hike or ride gives access to the Big Island Loop and the Dome Rockhouse. The entrance to this rock shelter opens to a recessed room where, once your eyes adjust to the dark, you'll see the large hemispherical ceiling from which the shelter gets its name.

Trailhead: Start at the Station Camp East Trailhead, where trails begin at the far right side of the parking area. This trail may also be accessed from the equestrian camp just down the road on the right; there a trail begins to the right just before the gate into the campground; there's also a short trail to the right connecting the camp with the trailhead.

Description: As you head into the woods, the Pilot/Wines Loop turns to the right. The trail straight ahead is also part of the Pilot/Wines Loop; stay straight. The trail winds down the ridge, but soon rises out of a bottomland to pass over a ridge. Descend into another hollow with sandy tread and pass up an eroded path to a junction at 0.7 mile. To the left lies the 0.6-mile trail from the equestrian camp.

Turn right. At 1.0 mile, cross a bridge over a drainage. The trail descends to a ford of Indian Rock Branch at 1.3 miles. Then cross a bridge over a side drainage. The trail climbs, switchbacks left, and reaches a junction at 1.6 miles with the Big Island Loop. Turn left to reach a junction at 2.1 miles with a 0.1-mile side trail to the left that leads to the Dome Rockhouse. After reaching a hitching area near the end of this side path, continue on foot to reach the rock shelter.

60 | PILOT / WINES LOOP ∩

Distance: 14.8-mile loop (Pilot Rock 7.2 miles one-way)
Difficulty: Moderate
Elevation change: 660 ft
Cautions: Creek fords
Connections: Station Camp East Overlook Trail ∩, Big Island Loop ∩

Attractions: This horse trail leads out to Pilot Rock, standing on the rim of the Big South Fork Gorge, and provides access to the Williams Creek area in a remote section of the park.

Trailhead: Start at the Station Camp East Trailhead; the trail begins at the far right side of the parking area.

Description: A few yards down the trail is a junction for the Pilot/Wines Loop. Where the trail continues straight ahead will be your return on the loop. Turn down right to follow the Pilot/Wines Loop counterclockwise. Head east, paralleling Station Camp Road. At 0.1 mile, the trail forks with the Station Camp East Overlook Trail up to the right. Stay with the left fork. The trail curves in and out around the heads of coves and at 1.0 mile ascends to a junction with the old Pilot Rock Ridge Road. To the right, you can reach Station Camp Road in 100 yards.

Turn left on Pilot Rock Ridge Road. The road curves right where a side road leads off left. Stay with the main road as side tracks lead off right and left. There's a fork at 1.4 miles; the right fork leads to a gate and private property, so stay left. At 1.8 miles, the trail turns right while a private side road continues straight. Descend, curving left, to a ford of a branch of Grassy Fork at 1.9 miles. The road ascends to an intersection of roads at 2.4 miles; stay straight, then make a sharp left and wind down into a cove.

At 4.4 miles, the trail intersects with an old roadway. At this junction, turn left and follow the old road out along Pilot Rock Ridge.

The trail ascends to the top of a knoll at 5.6 miles and curves right. Turn down left to cross a saddle in the ridge. With leaves off the trees, you can see the rock bluffs of Williams Creek Gorge to the right. The trail crosses another saddle and ascends to the top of a knoll at 6.5 miles; bear right again. Then make a steep descent and then a second descent that switchbacks left and right into a cove with rock bluffs. Ascend back to the ridgeline and continue out the narrow ridge to where the trail turns off right at 7.2 miles. At this turn, you can walk straight ahead on a path that takes you 100 yards to Pilot Rock, a massive 100-foot block of stone standing on the point of the ridge.

Making the right turn off the ridge, descend steeply to curve left and circle below Pilot Rock. At 8.1 miles, the trail forks; the left deadends in a few yards. Stay straight to continue a steep descent to the edge of Grassy Fork at 8.2 miles and a junction. (To the right, an old connector leads to a ford of Williams Creek and an old road north along the river that will be part of the Cub Branch Trail.)

At the junction beside Grassy Fork, turn left to continue on the Pilot/Wines Loop. At 8.4 miles, ford Grassy Fork and make a steep ascent with a switchback right. Level off and reach a junction with an old roadway at 8.8 miles. Turn left to cross a small drainage and begin another steep ascent, reaching the top of the plateau at 9.6 miles. Continue a gradual ascent to finally level off and pass a no-vehicle sign and emerge on the Big Island Road at 10.9 miles. The name *Wines* comes from the old Wines Road that wound along this ridge.

Turn left on the road; at 11.2 miles is a junction with the Big Island Loop. Turn left on the Big Island Loop to head back toward Station Camp East. The trail soon crosses the end of an old roadway. At 13.2 miles is a junction with the Big Island Loop to the right (the Dome Rockhouse is 0.6 mile down that trail). Turn left to complete the Pilot/Wines Loop, fording Indian Rock Branch and reaching a junction at 14.1 miles with the trail straight ahead that ascends to the equestrian camp in 0.6 mile. Turn left to return to the Station Camp East Trailhead at 14.8 miles.

61 | STATION CAMP EAST OVERLOOK TRAIL ∩

Distance: 0.8 mile one-way
Difficulty: Easy
Elevation change: 60 ft
Cautions: Some up and down
Connections: Pilot/Wines Loop ∩

Attractions: This short trail leads to an overlook that offers a broad view of the Big South Fork Gorge across from Duncan Hollow. The JMT travels the gorge rim on the other side.

Trailhead: From the Station Camp East Trailhead, head straight into the woods, then turn right on the Pilot/Wines Loop for 0.1 mile to a fork where the Station Camp East Overlook Trail turns up to the right.

Description: Ascending from the junction, cross Station Camp Road at 0.1 mile and continue west toward the river. The trail stays fairly level across the surface of the plateau following an old road, now a gravel horse trail.

At 0.6 mile the trail makes a sudden dip into a hollow and ascends back to the level. The trail dips through another hollow and then descends to a fork at 0.8 mile that is a turnaround at the end of the road. Go either right or left to the end at hitching rails. Then walk the footpath dropping down the slope of the rim to the overlook of the Big South Fork Gorge at 0.9 mile. You'll also see the tributary gorge of Mill Creek to the left.

There are no connections to this trail, so you must go back the way you came.

62 | BIG ISLAND LOOP ∩

Distance: 16.0 miles
Difficulty: Moderate
Elevation change: 620 ft
Cautions: Steep sections, small stream crossings, mudholes
Connections: River Trail East ∩, John Muir Trail ⋀⋀, Station Camp Creek Trail ∩, Pilot/Wines Loop ∩, No Business Trail ∩, River Trail West ∩

Attractions: This loop passes the Dome Rockhouse and traverses the plateau top before descending to the Big Island Crossing, where you can ford the river to Big Island and continue across to No Business Creek. On the return leg of the loop, the trail passes the Burke Cabin, which is used as a backcountry camp (first come, first served).

Trailhead: From the Station Camp East Trailhead, continue down the Station Camp Road, passing the equestrian camp on the right. If you have a horse trailer, you may begin this ride at the Station Camp East Trailhead or the equestrian camp rather than drive down the somewhat rough road into a long narrow parking area; from the trailhead you can ride the Pilot/Wines Loop, which connects with the Big Island Loop. Hikers and mountain bikers can continue down the Station Camp Road. At 2.3 miles from the Station Camp East Trailhead, the Big Island Loop crosses the road. But the best place to start the loop is down at the river, so continue down the gravel road, passing the Chimney Rocks. At 4.0 miles is Station Camp Crossing and the parking area at the end of the road. (At the south end of the parking area, the River Trail East heads toward Angel Falls. You can also ford the river here at low water to reach the JMT and Station Camp Creek Trail on the other side.)

Description: To walk or ride the Big Island Loop, head back up the road a few yards past the Station Camp Crossing down to the left. Just beyond,

Big Island Crossing

the Big Island Loop comes in on the left, which will be the return route. To cover the loop counterclockwise, continue up the road for 0.1 mile from the parking area to where the trail takes a sharp right turn off the road.

The trail follows an old roadbed until at 0.3 mile the trail turns up to the left, following another old road. You'll see rock outcrops on the left, and below on the right Slavens Branch flows down to the river, passing under the road just before the parking area.

At 0.7 mile, ascend to a junction with another old roadbed and turn left. The trail soon curves right, with the river now on your left. Continue to curve right up a hollow. The trail then curves left through the head of the hollow and into a long ascent. Top the ridge and descend through another hollow. As the trail ascends again, stay with the main roadbed as side roads lead off. At 2.2 miles, you'll reach the back of Slaven Cemetery, which is near Chimney Rocks.

The trail swings around the cemetery and then curves right to begin ascending again. The trail heads up a drainage steeply to the Station Camp Road at 2.7 miles. Cross the road to the right and reenter the woods. Descend into a cove. The trail crosses a bridge over a wet area and at 3.1 miles skirts an overhang where a trickle of water forms a small waterfall. Then ascend with a couple of switchbacks to cross an old road and then the gravel Big Island Road off Station Camp Road at 3.8 miles. The trail then descends, following a small streambed on the left.

At 4.4 miles is a junction with a 0.1-mile side trail to the right that leads to the Dome Rockhouse. After visiting the domed rock shelter, continue north. At 5.0 miles the trail ascends to a junction with the Pilot/Wines Loop; this is where those riding from the equestrian camp or the Station Camp East Trailhead will access the loop. Continue north (left) at this junction on the Big Island Loop.

The trail follows an old roadbed across the plateau surface headed back toward the Big South Fork. At 6.7 miles, the trail ascends to cross the end of an old road. At 7.0 miles, ascend to recross the gravel Big Island Road. This is where the Pilot/Wines Loop, coming down the road from the right, turns south on the Big Island Loop.

At 9.2 miles the trail comes out to the road again; turn left around a gate to descend steeply toward the river. Cross a small creek and reach a junction at 10.1 miles in the floodplain of the river. To get to the Big Island Crossing, you would follow the small stream down to the right to the river. Do not attempt a ford of the river except at low water; if you cannot see the bottom, you probably should not try it. On the other side, you can connect with the River Trail West and the No Business Trail. Both sides of the river can be very muddy.

The Big Island Loop continues south along the Big South Fork, following an old roadbed upstream; you'll probably encounter debris left from floodwaters. Along the way, cross several small streams on stepping stones. At 10.5 miles, notice up to the left the remains of an old cabin that burned.

At 11.3 miles, a trail turns up to spacious Burke Cabin, which has been maintained as a backcountry camp. The cabin sits on a knoll below a rock bluff where Cold Springs Branch spills down the hillside in a small waterfall. In spring the slopes above the creek are covered with wildflowers.

From the cabin, descend back to the main trail and continue on the old roadbed, crossing Cold Springs Branch. If there has been rain recently, the old roadbed will be pocked with mudholes, unless it has been upgraded. Some pools have been left by receding floodwaters. Here along the river, you'll see many wildflowers in spring, including occasional large patches of bluebells.

At 12.3 miles, an old car lies beside the trail, turned upside down. At 13.0 miles, moss-covered stone and then occasional rock walls mark an area that was once a farming community. Staying along the river, return to Station Camp Crossing at 16.0 miles.

Map 7. O&W Area

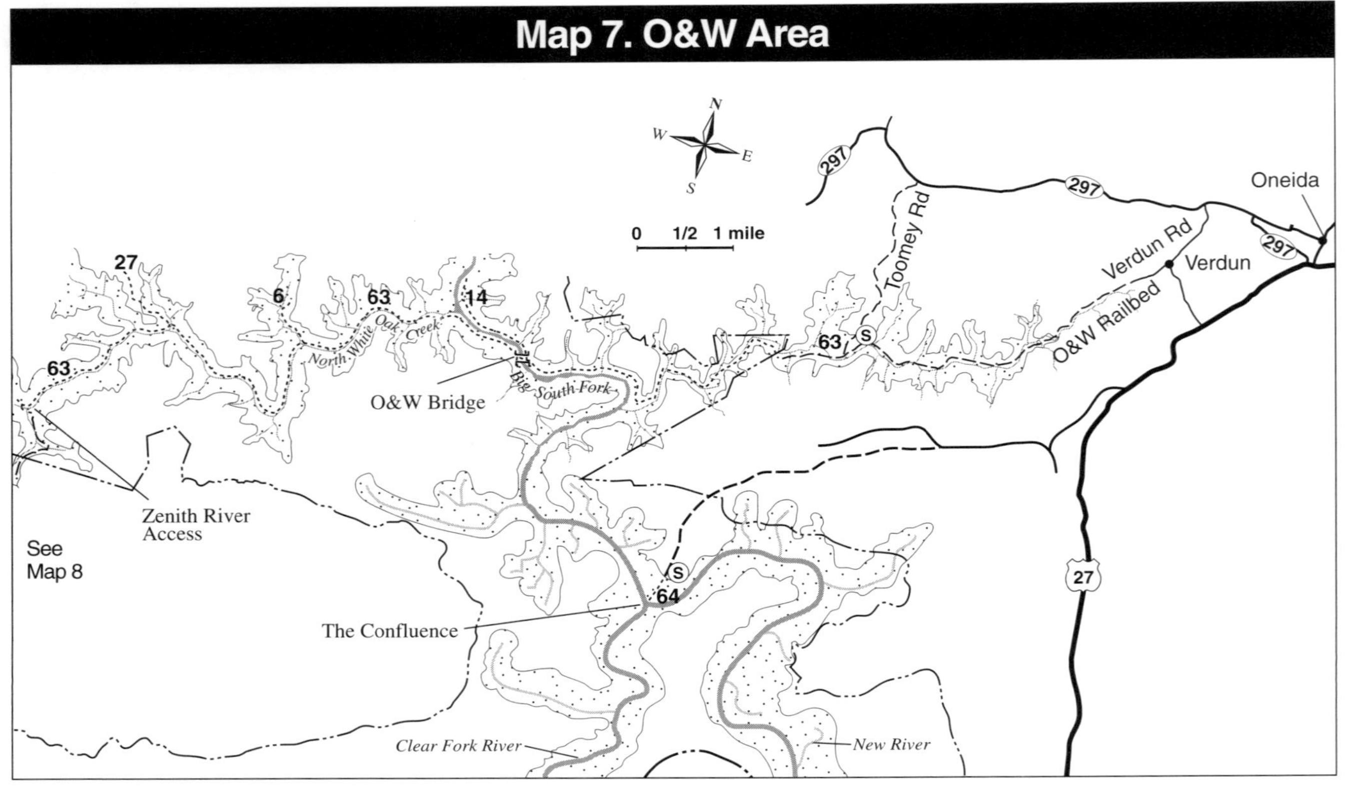

148

The Oneida & Western (O&W) Railroad operated during the first half of the 1900s, hauling coal and lumber out of the Big South Fork Gorge to Oneida, where the material was loaded on the Southern Railway line and shipped out of the region. The O&W extended to Jamestown on the west side of the park. The rail line stopped operating in 1954 and the rails were pulled up.

Today the O&W Railbed can be accessed via connecting roads from TN 297, which runs through the Tennessee portion of the park. The railbed offers a clear path for some 15 miles, reaching almost to the national area's southern boundary near Mount Helen Road.

Also in this vicinity, the New River and the Clear Fork River join at a confluence to create the Big South Fork of the Cumberland River.

63 | O&W RAILBED Ω

Distance: 12.1 miles one-way
Difficulty: Strenuous
Elevation change: 300 ft
Cautions: Creek fords, mudholes, at this writing still open to ATVs
Connections: John Muir Trail ⅍, Coyle Branch Trail Ω, Gernt Trail Ω

Attractions: The O&W Railbed runs along Pine Creek into the Big South Fork Gorge to cross the river on the old O&W Bridge and continue up North White Oak Creek. The railroad bed makes a great mountain bike ride that fords streams, skirts mudholes, and passes old bridge abutments left from the rail line.

Trailhead: The best place to begin the ride along the old O&W railbed is at the former site of Toomey, one of the camps along the route of the railroad. Head east from the park on TN 297; at 0.6 mile east from the corner at the Terry and Terry Store, turn south onto Toomey Road, a gravel road. This road descends to join the O&W Railbed in 2.5 miles; the last part is steep as it drops into the gorge and can be a bit rough. At the junction there's a little room to park. You can also reach the site of Toomey along the railbed from the small community of Verdun. At 1.7 miles west of Oneida on TN 297, turn south on Verdun Road. In another 0.6 mile turn right on the railbed, here a paved road. It becomes a gravel road in a mile as you head down along Pine Creek. Cross two bridges over Pine Creek and one over a tributary stream and reach the junction with the Toomey Road at 4.2 miles. For now, the route is a county road down to the river, but over the years the road has become rough with exposed rock and potholes. Passenger cars will have trouble making the drive unless it has been repaired.

Description: From the junction with the Toomey Road, head west along the old railbed. Cross a high wooden bridge over Pine Creek; because the planking runs vertically, it's best to walk your bike across so you don't get a tire caught in the space between boards. At 0.5 mile, pass through a narrow section where the rail line cuts through rock to leave walls on both sides. At 0.7 mile, cross the boundary into the BSFNRRA.

After penetrating several more narrow passages, the railbed crosses another wooden bridge over the creek at 1.7 miles. Pass through another narrows and at 2.9 miles enter another rock passageway with tall rock walls on both sides. Emerging, bear right as the railbed follows the Big South Fork downstream. At 3.0 miles, a road to the left blocked by a gate leads down toward the mouth of Pine Creek.

On the O&W Railbed

At 3.9 miles, with the river on your left, a hollow to the right with layered stone contains a wet-weather waterfall. You'll reach the O&W Bridge at 4.5 miles. Stairs on the left lead down to the river's edge. Just before the bridge, the JMT comes in on the right from Leatherwood Ford.

Walk your bike or horse across the 200-foot railroad bridge, erected in 1914–15. On the other side, the JMT turns down to the left for another half mile to Devils Den, a rock shelter; the trail currently ends there, but eventually will be constructed south to Honey Creek. Continue along the railbed as it parallels the river downstream. At 4.8 miles, a cascading stream on the left passes through a culvert under the railbed.

At 5.4 miles, pass through another narrows as the railbed curves left to follow North White

Oak Creek upstream. At 5.8 miles, the railbed runs straight out to a bridge abutment where a rail bridge once spanned the creek. Turn down left on a rocky path that leads to the creek's edge. Ford the creek here. This can be a difficult crossing if there is much water in the creek; enter only at low water. Regain the railbed on the other side.

A side path left at 6.0 miles leads down to the creek. Continue along the railbed with the creek on your left and occasional rock walls on the right. You'll encounter an occasional long mudhole that spans nearly the entire width of the road. At 8.0 miles is a junction with the Coyle Branch Trail that follows the old Coyle Branch Road up to the right; the road is blocked by posts. Continue straight to a ford of Coyle Branch where there was once a rail bridge; you can see the abutments here and at other stream crossings.

Head down along Coyle Branch, then curve right to continue up North White Oak Creek. At 9.4 miles, cross a washed-out area in the railbed. A side road to the left at 9.9 miles leads down to a campsite and swimming hole in the creek.

Turn up to ford Groom Branch at 10.5 miles and then turn back down; there was once a rail bridge over this side creek. At 10.7 miles is a junction with the Gernt Trail that follows the old Gernt Road up to the right; the road is blocked by posts.

Continue on the railbed. At 10.9 miles, pass a beautiful campsite on the left with a huge block of stone sitting beside the creek. Soon after, there's a fork where the old railbed turns down to the left. The road heads straight up the Laurel Fork of North White Oak Creek for a couple of miles, perhaps a spur off the old railroad.

Head down the left fork; on your left are old bridge supports on both sides where the rail line crossed the creek. Just downstream to the left, Laurel Fork joins North White Oak Creek. You must ford Laurel Fork; attempt this ford only at low water. Then turn up left to regain the railbed.

At 12.1 miles, turn down to the left to a diagonal ford across the North White Oak Creek to the Zenith River Access and the Zenith Road, or continue to 12.4 miles to another turn down to the left and a ford across the creek. (The railbed continues but eventually becomes overgrown.) On the other side, at the far crossing, bear left downstream along the creek; a road to the right leads to a campsite on a side creek. Stay with the road, and at 12.7 miles, ford Camp Branch above where it joins North White Oak Creek. On the other side, connect with the Zenith Road at the same location as the first ford. Zenith was another loading station along the O&W; concrete foundations lie in the woods between this end of the road and the creek.

To emerge from the gorge, turn up Zenith Road and make a steep climb. At 14.5 miles, after crossing Camp Branch, which flows under the road in a culvert, and following the south fork of the branch upstream, emerge on the paved Mount Helen Road. To the right it's 5.2 miles out to TN 52, 7.1 miles west of Rugby, or you can turn left to reach the Honey Creek area of the park in 5.0 miles and the Burnt Mill Bridge River Access beyond.

64 | CONFLUENCE TRAIL 🚶‍♂️🚶

Distance: 0.5 mile one-way
Difficulty: Easy
Elevation loss: 200 ft
Cautions: Steep descent
Connections: None

Attractions: The Clear Fork River and the New River converge to create the Big South Fork of the Cumberland River that flows through the heart of the recreation area. At the river's rocky edge, waters from the two

tributaries join to the left and flow to the right down the main channel of the river.

Trailhead: At 2.5 miles south of Oneida on US 27, turn west on Niggs Creek Road toward the airport. Cross a bridge over the Norfolk–Southern Rail Line and immediately turn left on Hellenwood Detour Road. At 3.5 miles turn right on Airport Road, and then at 4.7 miles stay straight on a gravel road as the paved road curves to the right. The gravel road passes behind the Scott County Memorial Airport. At 7.5 miles keep left at a fork. Cross the boundary into the park at 7.9 miles, pass the Dewey–Phillips Family Cemetery on the right at 8.7 miles, and reach the end of the road at a turn-around and parking at 8.8 miles.

Description: Walk the gated road to the right, which descends into the river gorge. The road curves right in a steep descent at 0.4 miles and runs down to the rocky shore at 0.5 mile. The confluence lies to the left.

The Confluence

Map 8. Burnt Mill Bridge, Rugby, and Colditz Cove

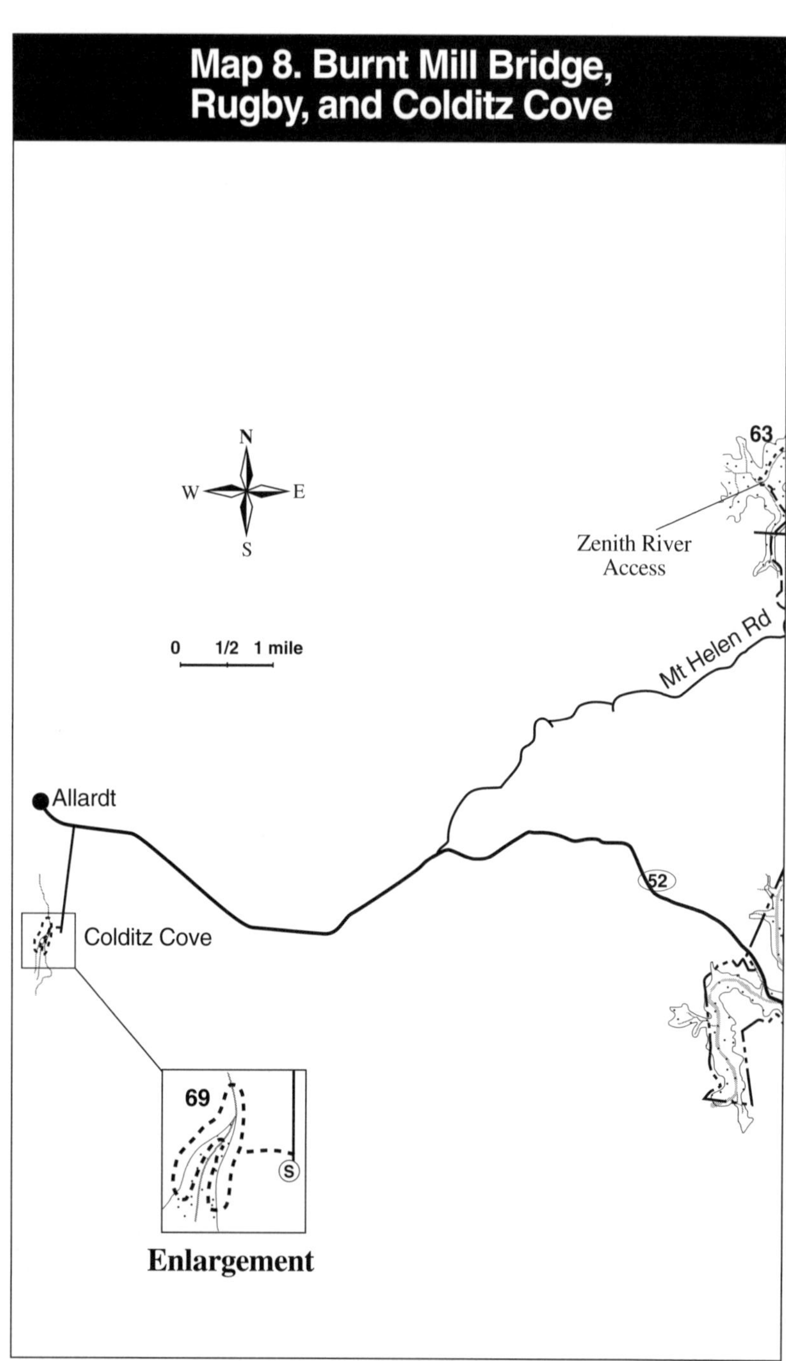

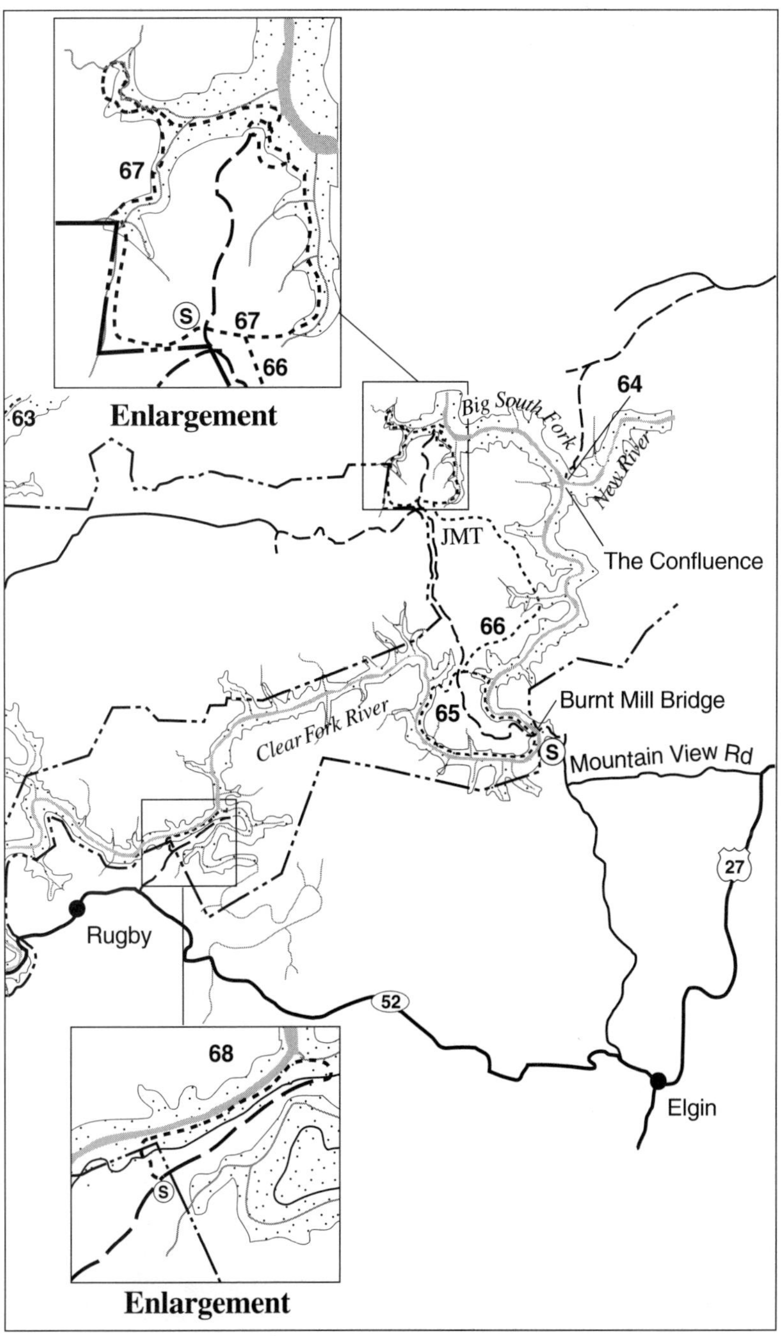

67
67
66
63
Enlargement
64
Big South Fork
New River
The Confluence
JMT
66
65
Burnt Mill Bridge
Clear Fork River
Mountain View Rd
S
27
Rugby
52
Elgin
68
S
Enlargement

BURNT MILL BRIDGE, RUGBY, AND COLDITZ COVE

Hikes out of the Burnt Mill Bridge area follow the Clear Fork River and penetrate the Honey Creek watershed, which contains cascading streams, waterfalls, and rock shelters. Historic Rugby on TN 52 on the southern border of the recreation area was originally an English colony founded in the late 1800s; trails from there lead to a swimming hole on the Clear Fork River and to the confluence of White Oak Creek. Outside the recreation area, nearby Colditz Cove State Natural Area offers a hiking trail descending into a small gorge to pass behind an impressive waterfall.

On US 27, 10 miles south of Oneida and 4.6 miles north of Elgin, turn west on Mountain View Road to head toward the Burnt Mill Bridge River Access. At 1.6 miles, turn right, then left, and at 3.9 miles at a four-way intersection, turn right again on a small side road. (You can also reach this point from TN 52; a half mile west of Elgin, turn north on West Robbins

Burnt Mill Bridge

Road and go 3.4 miles to the four-way intersection and keep straight ahead.) Bear left in another 0.5 mile on a gravel road, and then in another 0.4 mile, cross Burnt Mill Bridge to the west side of the Clear Fork River. Parking is on the left. The Burnt Mill Ford that people used here before the bridge was built got its name from the burning of a nearby grist mill on the river's east side. Do not drive across this old bridge in a large vehicle, such as a bus or a large RV. To avoid the bridge crossing, you can get to this trailhead from the west by turning north on Mount Helen Road off TN 52 7.1 miles west of Rugby. At 5.0 miles along this road, stay left at a fork; the road becomes gravel at 8.0 miles. Pass the turnoff on the left for Honey Creek at 10 miles and then reach the Burnt Mill Bridge at 14.0 miles.

To get to Rugby, continue south on US 27 from Mountain View Road. In the community of Elgin, turn west on TN 52 and drive 7 miles to the historic site. Several of the buildings in the town are open to the public; stop in the visitor center, housed in the old schoolhouse. There's lodging at Newbury House and Pioneer Cottage. Colditz Cove lies 11 miles west of Rugby off TN 52; turn left on Crooked Creek Hunting Lodge Road for 1 mile to the state natural area.

65 | BURNT MILL BRIDGE LOOP 쩄

Distance: 4.3 miles
Difficulty: Moderate
Elevation change: 200 ft
Cautions: Stairs
Connections: John Muir Trail 쩄

Attractions: This loop parallels the Clear Fork River. The cool forest and places for taking a dip in the river make this a good trail to hike in summer. Spring and early summer, wildflowers scatter across the lowlands beside the river: hepatica, trout lily, trillium, toothwort.

Trailhead: Start at the Burnt Mill Bridge parking area.

Description: Walk across the road from trailhead parking to where the trail leads into the woods to parallel Clear Fork River downstream. Watch for side paths that give access to the river.

Cross a boardwalk over a wet area and begin following a rock wall on your left. At 0.1 mile the trail climbs through rocks. A low rock overhang stands on the left and soon the trail passes under another overhang. Return to creek level amid hemlocks and rhododendron. The trail crosses a small stream and then climbs slightly and drops back to the edge of the river by a wooden stairway at 0.4 mile. Along the river's edge, the floodplain is littered with debris from floods and down trees. The trail then passes under another overhang at 0.9 mile and at the corner turns left up a creek, away from the river.

At 1.0 mile, cross the creekbed on two footbridges only 10 yards apart and continue up this side drainage. At 1.1 miles the trail crosses the creek on a third footbridge and swings right to join an old roadbed; turn left and ascend steeply.

The trail turns left off the road but simply swings in a broad curve to the right to rejoin the road. At 1.4 miles is a junction with the JMT to the right that connects with the Honey Creek Loop in 5.0 miles. Plans call for the JMT to be constructed south from the O&W Bridge to connect with this section of trail.

Bear left to continue the loop, then cross the road up from Burnt Mill Bridge. Back into the woods, a footbridge crosses a small drainage at 1.7 miles, and the trail curves right to ascend over a rise and begin a descent back toward the Clear Fork River. The trail switchbacks right at 2.0 miles and then left as it descends into the Clear Fork Gorge. The path drops along a ravine with a small falls at a rock lip in the drainage and with rock walls up to the right. Near the river at 2.1 miles, bear left downstream.

Again with the river on your right, descending through low drops and rapids, follow a rock bluff on your left. The trail crosses the slope above the river before dropping to the sandy shore at 2.5 miles. Along this section, watch for several places to walk out on rocks that stand at the river's edge and places where you can easily go wading.

Pass through a campsite at the river's edge with a broad slab of rock to the left. At 2.6 miles, the trail enters a hemlock woods that offers another fine camping site. Do not camp at these locations during flood seasons because the water occasionally reaches these areas.

The trail passes by large blocks of stone sitting between the path and the river, fallen from the rim ages ago. Step over small streams cutting across the trail. At 3.1 miles, the trail passes under a tall overhang and later drops into a large camping site with easy access to wading in the creek.

Through another camping site, the trail joins the end of an old road running along the creek at 3.3 miles. Cross a drainage and the road soon forks; stay to the right along the creek. The trail passes between a low rock bluff on the left and a house-size boulder on the right while the deep river drifts silently by.

After passing under another overhang, the old road turns down toward the river while the trail stays straight at 4.0 miles. Cross another old roadway down to the river and soon after rejoin the old road along the river.

At 4.1 miles, veer right off the old roadway but soon rejoin the road. At a fork with a path straight ahead, turn up left along the road that climbs steeply, but immediately turn off the road to the right on a footpath. Cross a footbridge over a drainage and reach the end of the parking area at the trailhead and close the loop at 4.3 miles.

You can take one last dip under the Burnt Mill Bridge; this is a popular swimming hole and also a favored put-in for river runners.

66 | LOWER JOHN MUIR TRAIL 🚶🚶

Distance: 5.0 miles one-way *(Beaver Falls 2.4 miles one-way)*
Difficulty: Moderate, strenuous to falls
Elevation change: 800 ft
Cautions: Steep ascents, creek crossing
Connections: Burnt Mill Bridge Loop 🚶🚶, Honey Creek Loop 🚶🚶

Attractions: This segment of the JMT connects Burnt Mill Bridge with Honey Creek, passing Beaver Falls on a tributary of the Clear Fork River.

Trailhead: From Burnt Mill Bridge, continue northwest on the road, now Honey Creek Road, 1.6 miles to where the Burnt Mill Bridge Loop crosses the road. Park here beside the road and walk 50 yards east to the junction with the JMT.

Description: The JMT leads north, bearing right to cross a drainage at 0.1 mile and moving up and down along the rolling surface of the plateau, paralleling the Clear Fork River in the gorge below.

The trail swings left into a tributary hollow and at 0.4 mile angles across a boardwalk and then a short footbridge to traverse a wet area at the head of the drainage before returning to parallel the river. Cross the trace of an old roadbed and then swing left into another hollow. The trail crosses two drainages as it curves right across the head of the hollow and reemerges along the river gorge.

Repeat this pattern of swinging left into side drainages and coming back out to parallel the Clear Fork River upstream as you continue north. At

Beaver Falls

2.1 miles, the trail swings left into a deep side drainage and descends to the edge of a broad, shallow creek at 2.4 miles. Beaver Falls is a quarter mile downstream. Unfortunately, at this writing there is no trail to the waterfall. To get to it, ford the creek and turn downstream. Climb around deadfalls, make your way through tangled brush, and descend a steep slope to the head of the falls with a precipitous drop into a narrow gorge. Only experienced hikers should attempt this route. It's a pretty spot where the stream meanders down a long stretch of bare rock to plunge over a rock ledge 20 feet into a deep green pool.

Back on the main trail, ascend from the ford of the creek. The trail swings to the right; you can hear Beaver Falls below, but there is no view. At 2.7 miles, ascend to an old road where it curves to the right; stay straight on the roadbed.

The trail ascends along the old road, emerging to a couple of posts that once marked the end of vehicle access at 3.1 miles; vehicles are no longer allowed this far in. Stay on the road. Ascend steeply and pass through posts blocking access to a four-way junction at 4.1 miles. Stay straight through the intersection until at 4.6 miles the trail turns right off the road (straight ahead the road reaches a junction with Honey Creek Road).

On a path now, parallel the Honey Creek Road and pass into a pine forest. At 4.9 miles, the trail reaches a junction with an old roadbed covered in pine needles. Turn right and walk up to a junction with the Honey Creek Loop at 5.0 miles; the overgrown roadbed continues straight. Turn left to emerge at the Honey Creek Loop Trailhead in another 0.1 mile.

67 | HONEY CREEK LOOP 👣

Distance: 5.2 miles
Difficulty: Strenuous
Elevation change: 460 ft
Cautions: Stream crossings impassable in high water, caged ladders, boulder passages, steep slopes
Connections: John Muir Trail 👣, Honey Creek Overlook Trail 👣

Attractions: This fascinating loop has rock shelters, gorge overlooks, waterfalls, streams, and boulder passages, and may be the most exciting trail in the recreation area.

Trailhead: From the Burnt Mill Bridge, continue up the road, passing the access to the JMT where the Burnt Mill Bridge Loop crosses the road. At 3.4 miles take a right fork 0.1 mile to a wide area where you can park on the left. The trail begins just ahead on the right side of the road. (This gravel road continues 0.8 mile to the Honey Creek Overlook of the Big South Fork.)

Description: The trail climbs a few steps from the road and swings left around a rock outcrop to ascend the hill through a pine woods. At 0.1 mile, cross an old roadbed at a junction with the JMT, which follows the road to the right, connecting with the Burnt Mill Bridge Loop in 5.0 miles. Across the top of the ridge, cross a couple of faint roadways through the woods and at 0.2 mile connect with a more obvious road and turn right. Soon the trail turns off the road to the right and winds down to cross another old roadway at 0.4 mile and begin a steep descent.

Descend to a small stream at 0.6 mile and cross a footbridge over a tributary at 0.9 mile. As the stream drops more steeply into a hemlock and rhododendron cove, the trail curves left up steps to swing by a rock wall at 1.1 miles. The swirls in the rock are iron deposits that erode more slowly than the encasing stone. The trail switchbacks right to descend back to creek level at a small waterfall.

At 1.2 miles, the trail turns left up the slope to ascend over a low rock overhang. Descending, you'll reach the bottom of 10-foot Moonshine Falls. The trail crosses the stream at the foot of the waterfall and turns downstream to cross again at 1.3 miles. Descend through switchbacks, a narrow wooden bridge, and a slippery slope back to the main creek. Turn downstream.

The trail follows a massive rock wall to a large beech tree. Turn left up the steep slope to a junction at 1.4 miles. The Honey Creek Overlook Trail to the left leads up ladders, switchbacks, and steps to the top of the bluff, where it swings right along the rim, crossing a small creek, to the overlook that's at the end of the access road. On the other side, the trail descends through ladders and steps to return to the main trail. Because you can drive to the overlook, stay on the trail below.

Walk along the rock bluff, which leans over the trail. The roar from the river echoes off the wall. Beyond is Hideout Falls, a tall, slender waterfall created by the small stream you'd cross on the overlook trail. Reach the junction with the other end of the overlook trail at 1.6 miles. Turn right down a steep slope and curve left to walk above the river.

The trail then curves left up the Honey Creek drainage. At 1.9 miles, curve right and descend steeply to Honey Creek. Turn left along the creek. Then bear right through boulders into the creekbed. Scramble across the top of a boulder and curve left to get out of the creek. At 2.2 miles, the trail crosses the creek and then turns downstream to a low rock overhang where the trail turns right to go around and head up the slope. The trail ascends to pass a large boulder with a hemlock growing on it and a good campsite.

The trail now works its way into the drainage for the North Fork of Honey Creek. Pass through a rock squeeze; turn left. At 2.3 miles is a junction with the Indian Rockhouse Loop to the right. Straight and curving up the slope to the left is a 100-foot shortcut to the main trail. If you have had

Boulder House Falls

trouble crossing the creek already, the side loop will be impassable and you should take this shortcut. But in times of low water, turn right.

You'll soon reach the North Fork. Enter the creek and make your way upstream, occasionally climbing over boulders. Along the way, enter a narrow gorge. At 2.4 miles, Indian Rockhouse opens in the bluff on the left. Then head down the right side of the creek in a rhododendron thicket, curve left to cross the creek, and pass another rock shelter. The trail then reenters the stream. At 2.5 miles, head up the slope to the left. The trail switchbacks a couple of times and passes a low rock shelter and then switches left above the rock wall. Parallel the cliff through a pine wood.

The trail reaches a junction at 2.8 miles with the other end of the shortcut. Stay straight. Switchback in a descent to Boulder House Falls at 3.1 miles, where a stream spills down among giant leaning boulders. Ford the creek. The trail then turns right to pass through a rock maze and come out above the waterfall. The trail curves left to cross the creek and climb steeply up the slope. At 3.2 miles, pass a rock shelter and reach a junction with a right side trail to Tree-Top Rock; it's 100 feet to the large block of stone with a hemlock growing on top.

The main trail curves left and descends steeply to a stream; to the right is a small half-waterfall, half-cascade. Downstream to the left, cross the creek and climb steeply up the opposite slope; watch for a right turn at 3.3 miles. After passing under an overhang, the trail turns right down stone steps to another creek crossing above the small waterfall. Bear left upstream to enter a narrow gorge.

The trail turns away from the creek and ascends the slope. At the top, walk onto an expanse of bare rock with patches of reindeer moss at 3.5 miles. Turn left and reenter the woods. The trail curves right to head upstream high above Honey Creek. At 3.6 miles, you'll be above Honey Creek Falls.

Curve down left to a creek crossing on a footbridge at 3.7 miles. Then walk downstream on the other side. After passing the top of the falls again, the trail curves away from the creek to a left side trail to the waterfall at 3.9 miles. Taking this side trail, scramble through the drainage of a small tributary 50 yards to a view of 20-foot Honey Creek Falls plunging into a deep green pool embedded in a rock grotto.

Continue up the main trail, which crosses the small tributary. Pass a large pool on the right. Continue ascending. The trail then turns right to cross the stream at 4.0 miles; this turn is easy to miss because there is also a path continuing straight that is a shortcut back to the road. The trail swings right to pass above the pool.

Ascend the ridge, cross an old road, and descend into the drainage for another tributary of Honey Creek. At 4.4 miles, turn left and walk upstream through thickets of rhododendron and laurel. At 4.6 miles the trail ascends away from the creek, crosses two branches of an old road, and continues to ascend gradually. Cross a stream twice and head up the slope to cross an old road and return to the trailhead at 5.2 miles.

68 | GENTLEMENS SWIMMING HOLE / MEETING OF THE WATERS TRAILS 🏃🏃

Distance: 2.0-mile loop *(Swimming Hole 0.4 mile one-way)*
Difficulty: Moderate
Elevation change: 240 ft
Cautions: Creek crossings, rocky and steep in places, mudholes on return portion
Connections: None

Attractions: Rugby, founded in 1880, is an important historic attraction of the region. On your visit, you can walk this trail into the BSFNRRA to the swimming hole on the Clear Fork River and to the confluence of White Oak Creek.

The last English colony in the United States, Rugby was founded by English writer Thomas Hughes as a home for second sons of English gentry. When Hughes visited the colony in 1880, he awoke the first morning to the sounds of young men gathering. "In a few minutes," he wrote, "several appeared in flannel shirts and trousers, bound for one of the two rivers which run close by.... They had heard of a pool 10 feet deep ... and a most delicious place it is, surrounded by great rocks, lying in a copse of rhododendrons, azaleas, and magnolias." The pool the young men were bound for was the Gentlemens Swimming Hole.

Trailhead: Rugby is 7 miles west of Elgin and 18 miles east of Jamestown on TN 52. A new bridge over the Clear Fork River and a bypass around Rugby for TN 52 have been constructed, so watch for TN 52 veering around Rugby and take old TN 52 into the historic town. East of the center of the community, turn north on the Donnington Road, a gravel road that leads to the Laurel Dale Cemetery. Along this road and along the trail, numbered posts mark points of interest; brochures are available at the Rugby Visitor Center or at the Bandy Creek Visitor Center. At the end of the road, you'll find the cemetery and, to the left, parking for the Rugby Trailhead.

Description: Follow the trail from the cemetery. The path descends through a mixed hardwood and pine forest. You'll continue to see numbered posts corresponding with the brochure that interprets the surrounding forest. The trail descends to cross into the BSFNRRA, winding down to a creek at 0.2 mile, which you can step across. The trail then turns right and descends several stone steps while following the creek as it cascades down into a cove of rhododendron and hemlock.

The main trail curves to the right while still descending. The creek drops over a ledge in a two-step waterfall. Step over the creek again below this

Christ Church at Rugby

waterfall. The trail then curves around a rock bluff. At 0.4 mile is a junction with a side trail that leads down to the Gentlemens Swimming Hole. Straight ahead, the trail leads on to the Meeting of the Waters.

The side path is a short walk down to the shore of the river and a deep pool in the river channel. To the right along the river bank, a long rock juts into the water; it's easy to picture the young men of Rugby leaping into the river from the end of the rock. Take care if you go swimming; search the water for submerged rocks before diving. Do not enter the stream at high water.

On the main trail, continue north through thick rhododendron. The trail for the next mile travels along the strip of land between the rock bluff to your right and the river's edge on the left, occasionally nearing the rock wall. You'll see rock overhangs in the wall and huge blocks of stone that have fallen into the river. In wet weather, water drips from the overhangs and runs down the rock wall. In winter, watch for falling icicles.

At 1.1 miles is the confluence of White Oak Creek with the Clear Fork River. The trail curves right and drops to bare rock at the edge of White Oak Creek, with the Meeting of the Waters just to the left. The path continues up White Oak Creek, squeezing between the stream and the rock bluff; if the water is up, you'll have to wade. The trail then ascends, steeply in places with steps; watch for slippery ice in winter. As you near the top of the White Oak Creek Gorge, the forest opens at a junction with an old road. Turn right and continue ascending to a junction with another road at 1.2 miles. Turn right again. Walking along the road, you'll encounter several mudholes if it has rained recently; at 1.6 miles, pass large storage tanks on the right with a natural gas pipe sticking out of the ground. The road returns to the trailhead at 2.0 miles.

69 | COLDITZ COVE LOOP 👫

Distance: 1.5 miles
Difficulty: Moderate
Elevation change: 100 ft
Cautions: Steep descent, boulder passages
Connections: none

Attractions: Colditz Cove is a Tennessee State Natural Area near the southern border of the BSFNRRA. Because this is one of the loveliest spots on the Cumberland Plateau, you should combine this hike with your visit to Rugby. Big Branch drops 60 feet into Colditz Cove to form Northrup Falls.

Colditz Cove is practically within the community of Allardt, originally a German colony founded about the same time as Rugby. Although the English colony was not a great financial success, the Germans who came from Michigan and directly from Germany to settle the town established a good financial base combining farming, lumbering, and coal mining.

The architecture of the town is not as elaborate as that of Rugby, which is why Rugby is better known. But you can still find the small white building in the center of town that is the Gernt Office, where the descendants of Bruno Gernt, who founded the community along with M. H. Allardt, still manage the family's holdings. The town was named for Allardt, who died just as the settlement began to form. East of the

Northrup Falls

Gernt Office stands the abandoned Colditz Store, which operated until 1962. Rudolph and Arnold Colditz donated Colditz Cove to the state of Tennessee. The hiking trail through the natural area was constructed by volunteers with the Cumberland Mountain Chapter of the Tennessee Trails Association.

East from the center of Allardt, off TN 52 on a gravel road, you can see the old Bruno Gernt House, a large gray farmhouse with brick-red trim that is on the National Historic Register. The house is open to the public as a bed and breakfast.

Trailhead: Colditz Cove is off TN 52 11 miles west of Rugby and just east of the Allardt town center. Turn south on the Crooked Creek Hunting Lodge Road. In 1.0 mile along this road, turn right into the parking area.

Description: Walk around the gate and down an old road. As you walk through scrub forest, you'll probably wonder whether this is going to be a waste of time. But suddenly the forest turns to a lush, green wonderland. Even in winter, the cove is green because of the profusion of hemlocks and rhododendron.

Just before the edge of the cove and a precarious view of the top of Northrup Falls on Big Branch, you'll encounter the loop part of the trail at 0.3 mile. The waterfall ahead is named for a family that once lived here. Turn left to walk the loop clockwise.

The trail passes along the bluff to a good view of the falls. Cross a bridge over a small drainage and at 0.5 mile turn right to drop into the cove in a short descent with switchbacks. The trail then doubles back along the base of the rock wall, moving over rocks and ducking behind a small waterfall formed by the stream you crossed above. Then enter a long rock shelter that sweeps around to Northrup Falls. Pass over boulders to the back of the rock shelter to stay on the trail.

The trail passes behind the falls at 0.7 mile; you may get wet if there is enough water to kick up a good mist. Then pass along the rock wall on the other side with seeps and trickles of water in wet weather; watch for a spout of water coming out of the rock wall after a recent rain. Begin the gradual ascent out of the cove, turning right at 0.8 mile, to return to the top of the plateau. The trail then circles back, crossing a bridge over Big Branch, to the beginning of the loop at 1.3 miles. Then walk the old road back to the parking area at 1.5 miles.

Map 9. Slavens Branch

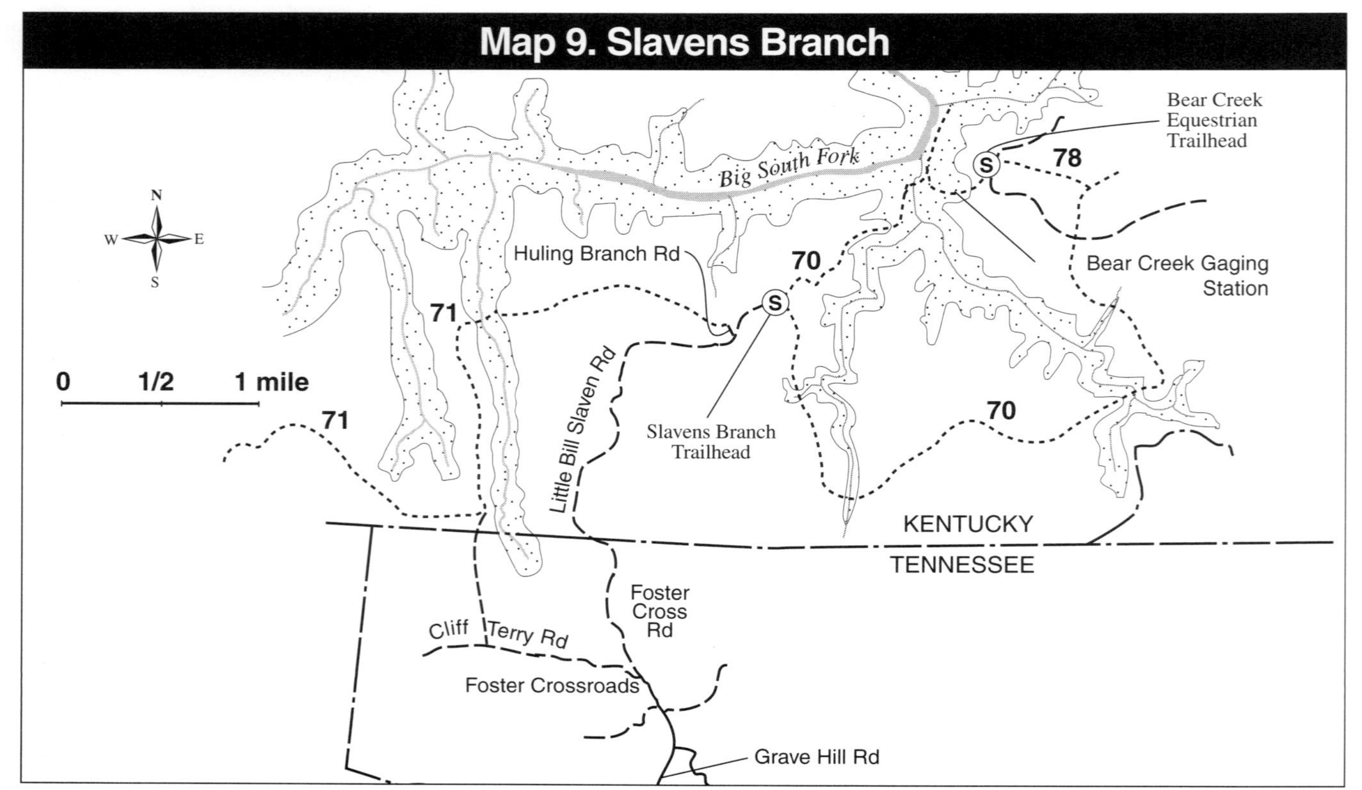

The Slavens Branch Trailhead provides access to a remote region in the Kentucky portion of the recreation area. Trails lead into deep, narrow tributary gorges and along the Big South Fork.

Turn west off US 27 on Litton Road in Oneida, 0.9 mile north of the junction of US 27 and TN 297. In 0.2 mile, bear left on Grave Hill Road, and then at 0.5 mile keep right to stay on Grave Hill. At 2.1 miles keep left and arrive at Foster Crossroads at 7.4 miles. (If you're coming from the park on TN 297, at 3.8 miles east of the right turn of TN 297 at the Terry and Terry Store, turn north on Williams Creek Road. At 4.5 miles turn right to connect with the Grave Hill Road at 5.9 miles. Turn left another 5.0 miles to Foster Crossroads.) At the Foster Cross Road Baptist Church, the road continues straight as the gravel Cliff Terry Road. Turn right at the church to take the gravel Foster Cross Road 1.0 mile down to cross the Kentucky state line and also the boundary of the BSFNRRA onto Little Bill Slaven Road. At 2.2 miles, pass the Huling Branch Road on the left that gives access to the Cub Branch Trail. Just beyond, another road on the left leads to the Dolen/Musgrove Cemetery. At 2.8 miles, turn right into parking for the Slavens Branch Trailhead. The road continues another 0.5 mile before the end of vehicle access.

70 | COTTON PATCH LOOP ∩

Distance: 10.7 miles
Difficulty: Moderate; strenuous descent and ascent at Bear Creek Gorge
Elevation change: 600 ft
Cautions: Creek fords, steep descents and ascents
Connections: Cub Branch Trail ∩, Bear Creek Loop ∩

Attractions: This horse trail loops through a remote section of the park, dropping into narrow gorges as it crosses Bear Creek and its tributary streams.

Trailhead: Start at the Slavens Branch Trailhead.

Directions: From the trailhead, ride or walk down Little Bill Slaven Road 0.1 mile to the beginning of the Cotton Patch Loop on the right. You'll return up the road to close the loop at this junction. To travel the loop counter-clockwise, turn right onto a broad path through the woods that is an old roadbed.

Bear Creek Gorge

At 0.5 mile, the road turns down right to a bar gate preventing further vehicle access. Go around the gate and descend on a steep, winding trail into a small gorge. At the bottom, ford the shallow stream of Slavens Branch at 0.8 mile and ascend the other side, reaching the level plateau top again at 1.1 miles.

After a passage across the plateau, begin a descent again at 2.6 miles. Descend through an S-curve and wind down into a gorge to creek level with a low overhang on the right at 2.8 miles. Ford left across Line Fork, shallow but rocky, and switch left to ascend steeply from the creek. Climbing through a small cove, reach the plateau again at 3.2 miles.

At 3.4 miles, the trail emerges onto an old road. Turn left and follow the roadway as it ascends gently, reaching a high point at Cottonpatch Knob at 4.1 miles. The roadway then descends, passing the end of vehicle access at 4.4 miles, marked by a sign on a tree.

The roadway fades into the horse trail, which turns left at 5.3 miles into a very steep descent into the narrow gorge of Bear Creek; walk horses and mountain bikes. Bottom out at creek level and turn to the right to parallel the stream, with the rock walls of the gorge standing on the other side. The path reaches the creek's edge at 5.7 miles. Ford the creek, which is deeper than the tributaries you have crossed so far.

Ascend from the creek, passing up a ridiculously steep ascent. You can barely walk up the slope, so do not try to ride. After a short ascent, turn right along a rock wall to a left turn up the bluff in another very steep ascent, bearing right and then left again to climb between blocks of rimrock to reach the top of the plateau at 6.0 miles.

Across the plateau once again, descend into a small cove at 6.2 miles where a roadway, blocked by fallen trees, leads off to the right. At this intersection, you can hear a waterfall in the nearby stream. You can bushwhack down several yards to where Dardy Branch spills over a lip of stone into a small gorge.

The trail ascends out of the cove and then traverses the plateau. At 6.7 miles, descend once again, winding steeply down to a crossing of Tappley Branch at 6.9 miles. Up from the creek, bear left to a crossing of a tributary stream in a culvert. Ascending steeply to gain the top of the plateau, the trail joins the end of an old roadway. The end of vehicle access is marked by a sign on a tree facing the other direction. Pass into an open area that was once a farm and house site and at 7.4 miles reach the gravel road that passes through the Bear Creek Scenic Area. Cross the road and ascend, reaching a junction with the Bear Creek Loop at 7.6 miles.

Turn left along a trail where the Cotton Patch Loop and the Bear Creek Loop coincide. At 7.8 miles, a roadway to the right leads into an open field to pass over a knoll and descend to the Bear Creek Scenic Area. Stay straight. Emerge to cross the Bear Creek Scenic Area road and enter the Bear Creek Equestrian Trailhead at 8.1 miles. Turn left to pass through the parking area and reenter the woods to drop to a junction with the Bear

Creek Gaging Station Road. Turn right down the road, which descends steeply into the Big South Fork Gorge. Bottom out near the river at 8.6 miles where you'll see an old gauging station near the confluence of Bear Creek that measured water flow in the river. The Bear Creek Loop turns to the right to head toward the Bear Creek Horse Camp. Turn left to continue on the Cotton Patch Loop.

The trail turns up Bear Creek, dips to cross a side channel, and reaches a ford of Bear Creek at 8.8 miles; this is the deepest ford on this loop, but most times of the year it's not a problem. The trail ascends from the creek to pass an old roadway to the right, now blocked by down trees, that will be the route of a proposed Huling Branch Loop.

Continue up the road in a steep ascent. Pass rimrock as you ascend out of the Bear Creek Gorge, eventually reaching the end of the Little Bill Slaven Road at a gate at 10.2 miles. The trail now follows the road, ascending to close the loop at 10.6 miles. It's another 0.1 mile up the road to the Slavens Branch Trailhead.

71 | CUB BRANCH TRAIL ∩

Distance: 2.5 miles one-way
Difficulty: Moderate
Elevation change: 500 ft
Cautions: Creek fords
Connections: Cotton Patch Loop ∩, Pilot/Wines Loop ∩

Attractions: This trail will join the horse trails in Kentucky with the trails in Tennessee, connecting the Slavens Branch Trailhead with the Pilot/Wines Loop out of the Station Camp East Trailhead. At this writing, only the northern part of the trail is complete.

Trailhead: Start at the Slavens Branch Trailhead, which is also the beginning of the Cotton Patch Loop. When completed, the Cub Branch Trail will begin on the other side of the road from the trailhead; it will bear left to parallel the road and reach a junction with the Huling Branch Road. For now, to access the trail, travel back down the road 0.6 mile to the Huling Branch Road on the right.

Description: Head up the Huling Branch Road. An old roadway on the right will be the likely route for the Cub Branch Trail connecting from the trailhead. Soon begin descending on the old roadway, now graveled as a horse trail. Pass around a bar gate that prevents vehicle access and continue down the road.

The trail descends between boulders as it drops steeply into the gorge of Huling Branch and curves left below the rim rock. At 0.3 mile, make another steep descent. Curve right through a tributary drainage and then a second stream drainage as the trail drops farther into the gorge with rock bluffs up to the left.

At 1.0 mile the trail bottoms out at a junction with an old road. Turn right and soon turn left off the road to a ford of Huling Branch, usually a shallow crossing. Ascend from the creek, climbing back out of the gorge, until at 1.6 miles the trail reaches a junction with an old road. Turn left to complete the ascent and continue along the more level plateau top.

An old roadway to the left is blocked to vehicle access at 1.8 miles. Then a road to the right at 2.0 miles leads 0.8 mile to the Duncan Cemetery, two unmarked gravestones on the left side of the road. Stay straight past the turn for the cemetery as the main road heads out a narrow ridge. At 2.5 miles, the Cub Branch Trail will turn down to the right where the trace of an old road leads off this main road. From here the trail will descend along Cub Branch to turn left and ford the creek. After climbing to regain the top of the plateau and continuing southwest, the trail will cross the state line into Tennessee at around 5 miles and join an old roadway. At a junction, the road continues straight to emerge from the park as the Rob Watson Road, which leads to Foster Crossroads. The trail will turn right at the junction on another old road.

At about 7.0 miles, the old road ends where the trail will continue as a broad path. Descend steeply into the gorge of the Big South Fork and turn upriver. Eventually, the trail reaches Williams Creek and a ford across to a connection with the Pilot/Wines Loop at 9 miles. To the right this loop fords Grassy Fork and ascends out of the gorge to reach the Station Camp East Trailhead in 6.6 miles. To the left, this loop also climbs out of the gorge past Pilot Rock and reaches the Station Camp East Trailhead in 8.2 miles.

From the junction where the Cub Branch Trail will turn down to the right after the Duncan Cemetery Road, you can continue straight out the main road. This dirt road becomes gravel in another 0.6 mile and passes clearings and traces of roads left and right, eventually reaching a junction with the Cliff Terry Road out of Foster Crossroads at 1.2 miles. From here, you can return the way you came, or you can turn left up Cliff Terry Road for 0.7 mile to Foster Crossroads and turn left down Foster Cross Road, reentering the recreation area in another 1.0 mile and returning to the beginning of the Huling Branch Road in an additional 1.2 miles. The Slaven Branch Trail is then another 0.6 mile down the road. Total loop distance from the trailhead is 7.8 miles.

Map 10. Blue Heron, Bear Creek, and Yamacraw Bridge

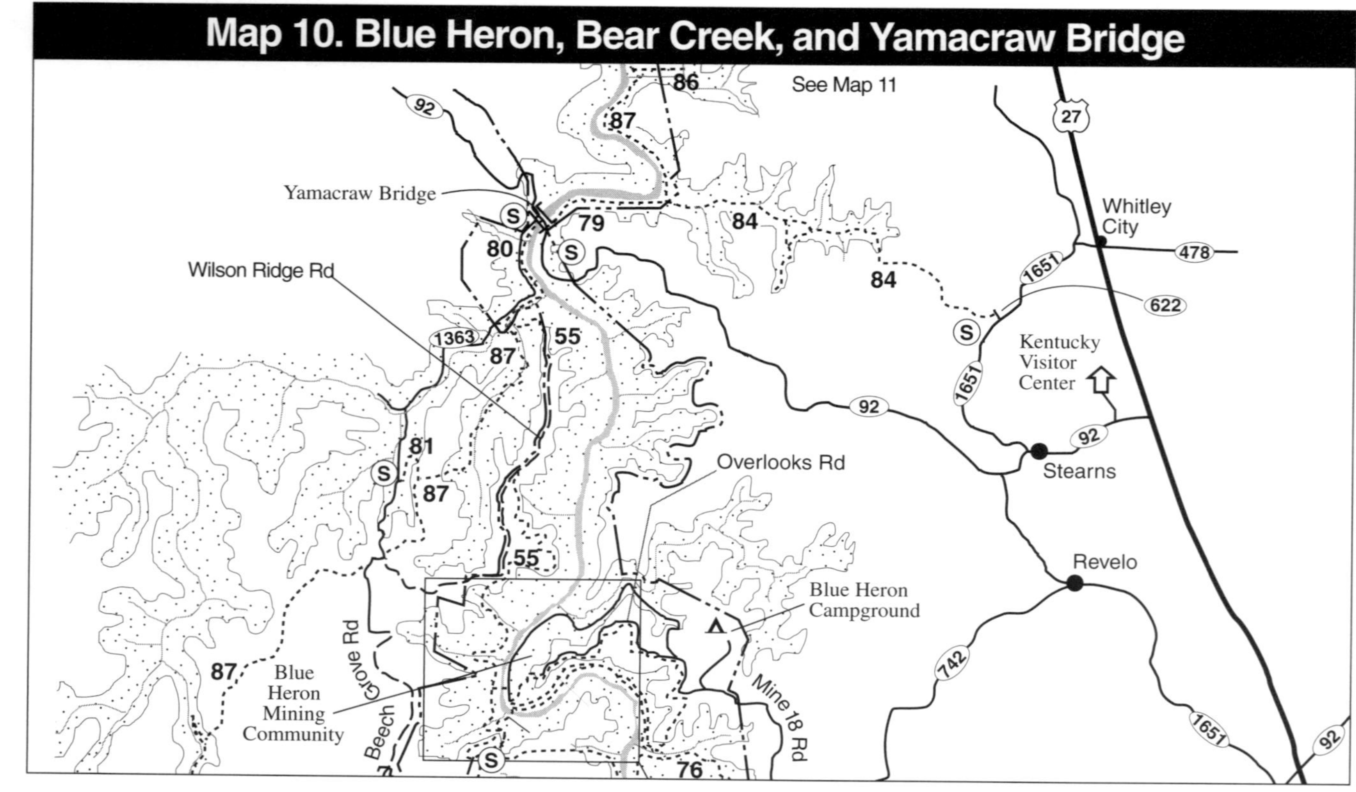

32
32
Dick Gap Rd
Bald Knob Rd
55
76
76
Bear Creek Horse Camp
See Map 5
Ledbetter Place Trailhead
78
82
Big South Fork
77
Bear Creek Scenic Area
1470
27
55
70
70
Bear Creek Gaging Station Rd
N
W   E
S
0   1/2   1 mile
74
72
Dick Gap Overlook
75
73
32
83
Enlargement

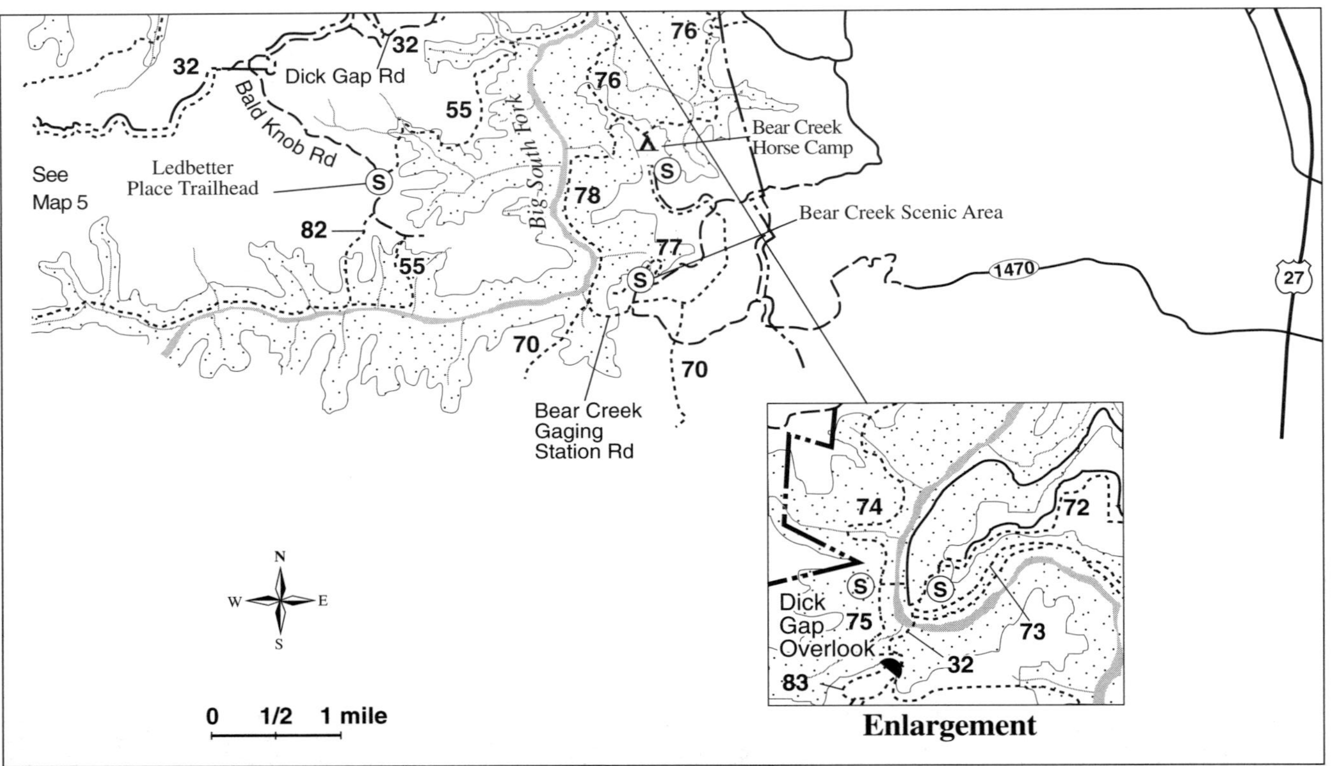

175

The Kentucky portion of the recreation area is most easily accessed at the recreated Blue Heron Mining Community, part of the Stearns Coal and Lumber Company, which operated in the area during the first half of the 1900s. Trails loop through a maze of boulders called Cracks-in-the-Rock and lead to Devils Jump, a large rapids in the Big South Fork River.

On the way to Blue Heron, you can also visit the Bear Creek Scenic Area, which contains an overlook of the Big South Fork and one of the recreation area's large arches. To the north, the Yamacraw Bridge crossing of the river offers access to the Sheltowee Trace.

Heading north on US 27 from Tennessee or south on US 27 in Kentucky, turn west on KY 92 toward Stearns. Pass the Big South Fork Kentucky Visitor Center to the right. In the former company town for the Stearns Coal and Lumber Company, you can pick up the Big South Fork Scenic Railway for a train ride to Blue Heron. In Stearns, you can continue west on KY 92 to descend into the river gorge to the Yamacraw Bridge crossing. To drive to Blue Heron, bear left on KY 1651 in Stearns. In 1.1 miles, in Revelo, turn right on KY 742. At the left turnoff for the Bear Creek Scenic Area, the road becomes the Mine 18 Road. Pass the Blue Heron Campground on the right and the Overlooks Road on the left, which leads to the Devils Jump and Blue Heron Overlooks. Mine 18 Road descends into the Big South Gorge to pass on the right a gravel road that leads to the Barthell Mining Camp, a historic reconstruction outside the park boundaries; there is an admission fee. Continue to the Blue Heron Mining Community, 8.2 miles from Revelo.

72 | BLUE HERON LOOP 🚶🚶

Distance: 6.6 miles (*Cracks-in-the-Rock 0.6 mile one-way; Devils Jump 0.4 mile one-way in reverse direction*)
Difficulty: Moderate
Elevation change: 450 ft
Cautions: Boulder passages, steep stairs
Connections: Kentucky Trail 🚶🚶, Devils Jump and Blue Heron Overlooks 🚶🚶, Laurel Branch Trail ∩, Long Trail ∩

Attractions: From the historic Blue Heron Mining Community, this trail offers overlooks, rock formations, and river rapids. Blue Heron was a

Blue Heron tipple

coal-mining camp built by the Stearns Company in the early 1900s. The community has been resurrected as a historic exhibit, with frame structures showing the locations of the houses and buildings that were gathered around the old tipple, a huge structure with equipment used to separate chunks of coal by size.

Trailhead: At the Blue Heron Mining Community, begin the hike near the snack bar at the far end of the parking area; stairs lead up to a walkway.

Description: From the top of the stairs, turn left up the walkway. Pass the tram bridge that leads over the tipple and the river to the Kentucky Trail on the river's west side. Stay straight; at 0.2 mile the Blue Heron Loop turns right to leave the community. After a couple of ascending switchbacks and footbridges, the trail curves up stone steps to Cracks-in-the-Rock at 0.6 mile. You'll find stairs sandwiched between rock monoliths. Over the stairs, turn left to exit. Curve around the rocks and ascend a flight of stairs up a rock crack; turn left.

The trail turns right at 0.7 mile, where an unofficial path to the left leads out to a rock shelf offering a view of the Blue Heron tipple and bridge. Climbing gradually from this side path, you'll reach a junction at 0.9 mile with a side trail left that leads up to the Blue Heron Overlook off the Overlooks Road. Keep right. At 1.2 miles, ascend to the Devils Jump Overlook parking area. Follow the paved path down toward the overlook until the trail turns left.

At 2.0 miles a path leads out to Overlooks Road and additional trail access. You'll occasionally skirt Overlooks Road, and then swing right to parallel Mine 18 Road. Stairs lead up to the road at 3.2 miles. Turn right, staying on this side of the guardrail to reenter the forest.

You'll reach a junction with an old road at 3.9 miles. Left it's 100 yards out to the highway across from the road into the campground. Turn right and follow the old road down the ridge. The trail drops through boulders and skirts rock shelves as it descends. Watch your head at a low overhang. Descend stairs that drop to a junction with the Laurel Branch Trail at 4.8 miles (which leads left to the Lee Hollow Loop). Turn right. There's an immediate fork; stay left with the Blue Heron Loop while the Laurel Branch Trail takes the right fork following the old tramroad that ran along the river for hauling coal from the mines to the Blue Heron tipple.

Follow the river north through former coal mine areas. At 5.7 miles, rejoin the Laurel Branch Trail on the tramroad. Turn left and soon pass a small waterfall.

At 5.9 miles the trail turns left off the tramroad down steep steps to cross a reclaimed mine area. Descend toward the river and swing right into the woods on the lower side of a settling pond, following an old road. At 6.2 miles, the trail turns left off the road. Soon a side trail leads down to Devils Jump, a rapids in a narrow part of the river. Use caution near the water's edge; boulders can be slick and the currents are strong. This rapids is so dangerous that daredevil lumbermen riding rafts of logs downriver jumped from the rafts to let them go through on their own.

The trail emerges at the Blue Heron Mining Community at 6.6 miles. River access leads down to the left for canoes and rafts and for horse riders that ford from the west side after riding the Long Trail; this is also the beginning of the Laurel Branch Trail that turns up right. Walk into the parking area straight ahead. Stairs to the right lead up to the upper-level parking where you began the hike.

13 | LAUREL BRANCH TRAIL ∩

Distance: 1.9 miles one-way
Difficulty: Easy
Elevation change: Mostly level
Cautions: Stream ford
Connections: Long Trail ∩, Blue Heron Loop 𝕩, Lee Hollow Loop ∩

Attractions: This ride or hike along an old tramroad links the Blue Heron Mining Community with the Lee Hollow Loop. A side trip offers a walk down to Devils Jump Rapids in the Big South Fork River.

Trailhead: From the Blue Heron Mining Community, proceed to the far end of the lower parking area. A ramp leads down to the river access and the ford for the Long Trail. The Blue Heron Loop heads straight ahead from the parking area and the Laurel Branch Trail turns up to the left.

Description: After a short, steep climb, you'll reach the grass-covered old tramroad. To the left are a picnic shelter and snack shop. Turn right. At 0.1 mile, hitching rails stand on the left. At 0.3 mile, another tramroad comes in from the left; this one leads from the upper part of the old mining

Devils Jump Rapids

operations. At 0.5 mile, pass a trail down to the right that leads 100 yards to connect with the Blue Heron Loop. You can walk down this hiking trail to the river to see the Devils Jump Rapids in 0.3 mile.

The trail continues along the old tramroad; you'll see remains of mining operations along the way. At 0.6 mile the horse trail joins the Blue Heron Loop while both use the tramroad. At 0.9 mile the hiking trail turns off to the right; continue straight. At 1.7 miles, curve left up the cove of Laurel Branch and at 1.8 miles reach another junction with the Blue Heron Loop. Continue straight to a ford of Laurel Branch and bear right up to a junction at 1.9 miles with the Lee Hollow Loop. From here you can ride the loop either way to get to the horse camp at the Bear Creek Scenic Area.

74 | OLD TRAMROAD 🚶

Distance: 2.3 miles one-way
Difficulty: Moderate
Elevation gain: 100 ft
Cautions: Marshy areas, stream crossing, boulder passages
Connections: Kentucky Trail 🚶

Attractions: This trail follows the roadbed of an old electric tram once used to haul coal to the Blue Heron tipple. Small electric engines pulled tramcars from the west side of the Big South Fork over the high bridge that still spans the river. The trams, flat open cars, were loaded with coal that was dumped into the tipple for separating; the coal fell into waiting railroad cars underneath. The tram bridge is now a footbridge that connects with the Kentucky Trail on the river's west side.

Trailhead: Start at the Blue Heron Mining Community.

Description: Take the tram bridge across the river. On the other side, turn right to follow the old tramroad that runs up and down the west side of the river.

At 0.1 mile, cross a boardwalk and a bridge to where the trail forks; stay right. At 0.3 mile, upright posts that carried the electric lines for the tram system stand on the left. Switchbacks take you up to a junction with the upper roadbed; turn right. This part of the trail is overgrown in summer and marshy in rainy seasons.

At 1.2 miles, turn right off the road to descend to a crossing of Devils Creek; most times you'll be able to rockhop. The trail then climbs to rejoin the old tramroad. At 1.8 miles, you'll see evidence of mining: pits in the side of the hill to your left, spoil down the slope to your right, and coal underfoot. More tram utility poles stand beside the trail. At 2.0 miles the trail curves left as it once more parallels the Big South Fork. Watch for a tiny cinder-block building in a mining area. At 2.3 miles, two concrete piers on the right anchored some sort of mining structure. You can turn around to return to Blue Heron; the Kentucky Trail continues north for several more miles.

75 | CATAWBA OVERLOOK AND BIG SPRING FALLS 🚶🚶

Distance: 3.6 miles one-way (Catawba Overlook 1.6 miles one-way)
Difficulty: Moderate
Elevation change: 400 ft
Cautions: Stream crossings, steep stairs, mudholes, poison ivy
Connections: Kentucky Trail 🚶🚶, Long Trail ∩

Attractions: This trail climbs to a scenic view of the river from Catawba Overlook, passes Dick Gap Falls, and reaches a waterfall in Big Spring Hollow. The 60-foot Big Spring Falls spills halfway down to splash on a rock ledge before making its second drop into a pool at the base.

Trailhead: At the Blue Heron Mining Community, cross the river on the tram bridge to west side of the river.

Description: Turn left from this end of the tipple bridge to walk the Kentucky Trail south, following the old tram road that ran along the west side of the river. A boardwalk crosses a marshy area, but you may still have to slog through other parts of the trail if there has been a recent rain. Watch for abandoned tramcars tipped over to the left of the trail. Also watch for a few of the utility

Big Spring Falls

posts that still stand beside the tramroad; they held the wires carrying electricity for the tramline.

Cross a plank bridge and at 0.2 mile reach a fork in the trail. The left fork has been closed for some years because of slides. The trail continuing along the old tramroad is designated for repair, and once it has been reopened, the two forks will create the Catawba Overlook Loop.

For the time being, take the upper trail to the right to cross a short footbridge. Join an old roadbed and then bear left to Three West Hollow at 0.4 mile. Cross the creek on a footbridge and switchback left. The trail climbs from the creek and crosses a footbridge over a wet-weather stream at 0.5 mile. There's a great rock bluff on your right at 0.6 mile. Watch for wildflowers in spring: purple phacelia, stonecrop, violets, foamflower. Continue walking along the rock bluff through a forest of mixed hardwoods, cross another footbridge, and at 1.0 mile climb steep wooden stairs over a rock shelf lined with rhododendron.

Cross another footbridge, and at 1.1 miles the trail briefly joins the Long Trail. To your left, the horse trail descends a steep rocky slope to cross the lower part of the Catawba Overlook Loop and reach the river ford across to Blue Heron. Just beyond this junction, the hiking trail turns left off the horse trail; you can follow the horse trail up to the right for 0.2 mile to reach the end of the Dick Gap Road and walk 0.3 mile out to the Dick Gap Overlook of Blue Heron.

Turning left on the hiking trail, cross a footbridge to head toward the bluff's edge at 1.6 miles and the Catawba Overlook, named for the Catawba rhododendron that blooms rose-purple in May. A short side trail takes you down to your left to a point of rock looking out over the river gorge. To the left the tram bridge spans the river, and below to the right, Devils Jump roils the water's surface.

From Catawba Overlook, follow the trail south; in late summer the path becomes a little overgrown. In places it's thick with poison ivy. The trail drops into a cove. At 1.9 miles, cross a stream on a boardwalk. Ascend from the stream and join an old roadbed, but then bear left off the road.

At 2.1 miles, use a set of wooden stairs to climb over a hemlock lying across the trail. Soon after, descend stairs over a bluff and bear left to join an old road that leads to Dick Gap Falls at 2.3 miles. The slender waterfall is off trail to the left.

The trail bears right past the falls; at 2.4 miles join an old roadbed and switchback left. You'll hear a small stream to the right and then descend stone steps to cross the stream. To the left, this side stream joins the stream that runs from Dick Gap Falls.

As you continue down the old roadbed, the main stream cascades down a small gorge. Descend to a junction at 2.6 miles with the old tramroad where the bottom part of the Catawba Overlook Loop will connect. Turn right on the tramroad along the Big South Fork.

As the trail turns up a side gorge, watch for a slag slope at 3.2 miles and then a vent hole for a mine up to your right. At 3.3 miles, the trail crosses Big Spring Creek. Some old foundations lie on the left on the far side of the creek. Switchback left and right and, at 3.4 miles, left again, where a side trail to the right leads 0.2 mile to Big Spring Falls. Heading toward the waterfall, first ascend a few stone steps and later cross a boardwalk over a marshy area at the dripline of a rock overhang; watch out for sprinkling water and, in winter, falling icicles. The path then crosses a small stream and ascends stone steps on its way to the falls.

The Kentucky Trail continues southwest from Big Spring Falls to the Ledbetter Place Trailhead in another 3.6 miles.

76 LEE HOLLOW LOOP Ω

Distance: 5.6 miles
Difficulty: Moderate
Elevation change: 450 ft
Cautions: Creek fords, steep descent
Connections: Laurel Branch Trail Ω

Attractions: This loop ride connects the Bear Creek Horse Camp with the Blue Heron Mining Community while passing along the Big South Fork River and turning up the cove of Laurel Branch.

Trailhead: Heading toward the Blue Heron Mining Community on KY 742, watch for the Bear Creek Scenic Area sign 3.2 miles from Revelo. Turn left. The road becomes gravel in 1.9 miles and then a one-lane road. At 2.0 miles, stay straight through an intersection to continue toward the scenic area. At 2.5 miles, at a junction, turn right to reach the Bear Creek Horse Camp at 3.1 miles. There's parking on the right just before the camp entrance. From the parking area, pick up the Perimeter Trail on the right side of the entrance (from here, you can also access the Bear Creek Loop on the other side of the road). The Perimeter Trail circles the camp to the back, where you'll find the trailhead.

Description: Pass around a gate and head into the woods on an old roadbed at the back of the camp. At 0.2 mile is a junction with the loop. Keep straight to hike or ride the loop clockwise. The trail leads out along a ridge above the Big South Fork.

At 0.7 mile, pass a side road that drops off to the left, which is part of the Bear Creek Loop that descends the slope to the river and leads south to Bear Creek. Continue straight from this junction.

Bear right and begin a descent off the ridge. At 1.4 miles the descent is steep. Notice the interesting rock bluff to the right.

The trail levels off with the cove of Blair Creek to the right, but then it begins another descent. At 1.8 miles, the trail switchbacks right to a level above the river; now head downstream along the Big South Fork. At 2.0 miles, the trail curves right up a cove in large hemlocks and hardwoods to make a steep descent to ford Blair Creek, brown with mine drainage. From the creek, make a long ascent to continue north with the river.

At 2.5 miles, curve right up the cove of Laurel Branch and begin a descent toward the creek. Pass a rock monolith on the left with "Laurel Branch, September 28, 1944" in fading paint on its side. Just beyond is a junction with the Laurel Branch Trail at 2.7 miles. (The trail fords Laurel Branch to the left and leads along an old tramroad to the Blue Heron Mining Community.) Keep straight.

Begin a long ascent, crossing a few small streams as you climb the slope. At 3.0 miles, an overgrown roadway lies to the left. At 3.5 miles, the trail passes a post and at 3.7 miles reaches a gate at the park boundary. The Lee Hollow Loop continues on the road to the right. The road beyond the gate leads out to the Mine 18 Road in another 0.3 mile.

At the park boundary, turn right to stay on the Lee Hollow Loop. At 4.2 miles, notice a rock shelter up to the left. A steep downhill leads to a ford of the upper end of Blair Creek at 4.5 miles. Up from the stream, ride through a rock passageway and along a rock wall. Down to the right, cross another branch of Blair Creek and then make a long uphill climb, passing an overhang at a reprieve in the middle of the climb. Ride over the ridge and down into Lee Hollow, then make another long uphill climb and pass along the level plateau top to close the loop at 5.4 miles. Turn left to return to the horse camp at 5.6 miles.

77 | SPLIT BOW ARCH LOOP 🚶🚶

Distance: 0.7 mile
Difficulty: Easy
Elevation change: 100 ft
Cautions: Rock steps, boulder passageway, wooden stairs
Connections: Bear Creek Overlook 🚶🚶

Attractions: This loop takes you through a slender arch in one of the most picturesque settings in the park. Split Bow Arch was created by the widening of a joint; this crack in the rock eroded enough to separate a rock wedge from the bluff. Water collecting in the crack eventually opened a hole in the rock. Over time, this erosion widened the hole to leave a delicate expanse of rock overhead. A small stream passes through the opening of the arch.

Trailhead: On KY 742, watch for the Bear Creek Scenic Area sign 3.2 miles

Split Bow Arch

from Revelo. Turn left. The road becomes gravel in 1.9 miles and then a one-lane road. At 2.0 miles, stay straight through an intersection. At 2.5 miles is a junction where you can turn right to reach the Bear Creek Horse Camp at 3.1 miles. At this junction, turn left. The Bear Creek Loop crosses the road. Then pass a narrow gravel road up to the left that is gated at a distance in the woods. In 1.0 mile from the junction is an overlook to the right where you can walk out to see the top of Split Bow Arch. Pass through a wet area with some deep puddles (go slowly) and at 1.1 miles reach trailhead parking on the right. At 0.2 mile beyond this parking, there's also parking for the Bear Creek Loop. From the scenic area parking, you can walk 0.3 mile on a one-way trail straight ahead to the Bear Creek Overlook for a panoramic view of the Big South Fork. The Split Bow Arch Loop leads into the woods on the right.

Description: The trail winds down steps made with waterbars and steps carved into the sandstone rimrock. Turn right and reach a junction at 0.2 mile with the loop part of the trail. Stay straight to hike counterclockwise. The trail ascends to a rock wall and into a narrow passageway at 0.3 mile. You'll come to Split Bow Arch, created by a hole in the rock wall on your left.

Descend a wooden stairway to pass through the arch to the base. Turn right to cross the shallow stream flowing from the arch and continue the loop around to your left.

The trail descends steps to again cross the arch stream on a plank walkway at 0.4 mile and then ascends steps through hemlock and hardwood to complete the loop at 0.5 mile. At the junction, turn right to return to the parking area.

78 BEAR CREEK LOOP ∩

Distance: 6.1 miles
Difficulty: Moderate
Elevation change: 590 ft
Cautions: Creek fords, rocky sections
Connections: Cotton Patch Loop ∩, Lee Hollow Loop ∩

Attractions: This loop takes you down to the junction of Bear Creek with the Big South Fork River after traveling along the river and ascends to the back of the Bear Creek Horse Camp before looping back across the plateau to the trailhead.

Trailhead: On KY 742, watch for the Bear Creek Scenic Area sign 3.2 miles from Revelo. Turn left. The road becomes gravel in 1.9 miles and then a one-lane road. At 2.0 miles, stay straight through an intersection, and at a junction at 2.5 miles turn left to reach the scenic area at 3.6 miles. Continue on the gravel road past the Bear Creek Scenic Area another 0.2 mile to a parking area beside the Bear Creek Gaging Station Road. The main road continues out to US 27 as KY 1470 at 7.0 miles from the Bear Creek Scenic Area; this provides a shorter route if you are coming from the south.

Description: At the far left end of the parking area, the Bear Creek Loop descends past the end of an old rock wall and connects with the Bear Creek Gaging Station Road, a gravel road that descends from the main road, where it's gated. Turn right to descend steeply toward the river.

At 0.2 mile, a small stream flowing from the right passes under the trail in a culvert and continues down on the left side of the road. Bottom out at 0.5 mile beside the river, with the confluence of Bear Creek just to the left. At a junction here, the Bear Creek Loop continues to the right. (The Cotton Patch Loop turns to the left to head upstream along Bear Creek to ford this tributary of the river and then continue up to the Slavens Branch Trailhead in 2.1 miles.) At the junction, old gauging station towers that measured the water flow stand beside the river.

Turn right on the Bear Creek Loop, which now parallels the river on your left. Pass through a gate and at 0.7 mile reach a U.S. Geological Survey gauging station where a cable spans the river to carry a person on a metal frame over the river to drop water-flow measuring devices into the current. The trail follows an old roadway along the river that's now a broad gravel trail.

Along the trail a small stream flows across the roadway; soon after, bear right up the Salt Branch tributary to a ford at 0.9 mile. The trail ascends steeply from the stream to top a ridge and descend back to the river. Watch for a large block of sandstone on the right that has slid down from the gorge rim.

At 1.5 miles, the trail turns right, away from the river, in a steep, rocky ascent. With the trail moving straight up the slope directly away from the river, the footing has eroded and the trail washes toward the river.

Curving left to continue along the river, you can glimpse the bare rimrock of the gorge up to your right through the trees. The trail moves up and down, crossing low ridges and dipping into drainages in the hollows between. At 1.9 miles, bear right in a steep ascent that begins the climb out of the gorge. The trail follows a stream in a deep hollow to your left that drops over a spillway at 2.2 miles. Soon after, turn down left to ford the stream.

The trail ascends steeply from the ford, but soon makes a small descent to cross a culvert. Up to the right, you'll see a rock overhang at the gorge rim where a small stream trickles off the bluff.

At 2.7 miles, ascend to the top of the plateau and continue up to a junction with the Lee Hollow Loop at 2.8 miles. Turn right as the Bear Creek Loop coincides with the Lee Hollow Loop. At 3.3 miles is another junction with the Lee Hollow Loop turning off to the left. Stay right to reach the

Bear Creek Horse Camp at 3.5 miles. At this back end of the camp, turn right on the Perimeter Trail that circles the camp. In another 0.2 mile, you'll reach the front of the camp beside the entrance station, with the continuation of the Bear Creek Loop to the right.

Paralleling the gravel road into the camp, the trail descends along an old fence row; watch for terraced rock on your left. The trail crosses a small stream in the bottom of the hollow and then climbs back to a level with the road. Pass beside the road before turning away to the right.

The trail descends, passing the road junction where you entered the Bear Creek area, which you might see through the trees. Then turn up left to cross the gravel road at 4.5 miles. The road swings through a drainage as it travels through the woods. You may notice a pond down to your right. Pass through another drainage and ascend, crossing a gravel road at 5.1 miles; this is the gated road off the main road into the Bear Creek Scenic Area.

Walk out a knoll along the top of the plateau; the trail curves right where an old roadway to the left continues out to descend the other side of the knoll. An old sign here calls it Knobby Ave.

At 5.6 miles is a junction with the Cotton Patch Loop to the left. Turn right to stay on the Bear Creek Loop, with the Cotton Patch Loop coinciding. At 5.8 miles, you'll see an old roadway to the right that ascends to top a knoll and run down to parking for the Bear Creek Scenic Area. Stay straight. Walk between walls of debris from ice storms: broken and bent trees and piles of brush. At 6.1 miles, emerge onto the road and cross back into the parking area where you began this hike or ride.

79 | YAMACRAW BRIDGE TO NEGRO CREEK 🚶🚶

Distance: 3.0 miles one-way *(Princess Falls 1.3 miles one-way)*
Difficulty: Moderate
Elevation change: 60 ft
Cautions: Mudholes, creek crossings
Connections: Yamacraw Loop 🚶🚶, Lick Creek Trail 🚶🚶, Negro Creek Trail 🚶🚶, Sheltowee Trace 🚶🚶

Attractions: This pleasant walk along the east side of the Big South Fork north from Yamacraw Bridge leads past a side trail to Princess Falls. The name Yamacraw comes from Native Americans who lived in the region and were thought to be part of the Yamacraw tribe of South Carolina.

Trailhead: In Stearns, stay on KY 92 headed west from the junction with KY 1651. Descend into the Big South Fork Gorge, enter the BSFNRRA, and reach the Yamacraw Bridge over the river at 6.5 miles from US 27. Just before the bridge, turn right into the Yamacraw Day Use Area. Park at the trail sign. There's extra parking to the left under the bridge. The Sheltowee Trace National Recreation Trail passes through here. If you were hiking south on the trace, you'd cross the river on the bridge and then turn south along the west bank of the river. For this hike, follow the trace north along the east side of the river.

Description: The trail enters the woods to the right. At 0.1 mile, the trail crosses a small streambed on a stone footbridge and reaches a junction with the Yamacraw Loop turning off to the left; the junction is not signed. (This 0.4-mile day loop drops down to the river and circles back to the parking area.) Continue straight, passing through a mixed hardwood forest with occasional hemlocks and large beech trees.

Princess Falls

The trail drops to join an old road along the river at 0.4 mile. You'll encounter occasional long mudholes as the trail follows the road for most of the way. At 0.8 mile the trail drops to a stream crossing with a small waterfall up to the right. At 1.0 mile, a stream passes between boulders before washing across the trail. As you ascend from the small creek, Lick Creek on your left meanders to join the Big South Fork. Pass over a rise that has a good campsite and descend to an area cut with roads. Bear right and follow Lick Creek upstream.

At 1.2 miles is a junction. The main trail turns down to the left to a bridge crossing of Lick Creek. An old road leads to the right uphill. The trail in the middle is the Lick Creek Trail; a 0.1-mile walk up this trail gets you to Princess Falls, where the creek spills over a shelf into a deep pool.

Continuing on the Sheltowee Trace, turn down to cross Lick Creek on the sturdy footbridge and turn left downstream. At 1.3 miles, the trail curves right to once more follow the Big South Fork downstream. At 1.5 miles the road turns down to the river, but the trail stays straight. At 1.6 miles the trail curves right up a small stream to cross it on stepping stones.

At 1.8 miles, walk through the floodplain of the river, occasionally dropping into low areas and passing stands of cane. At 2.5 miles the trail drops to a drainage branch and crosses on stepping stones.

The trail veers away from the river to the right to go up Negro Creek at 2.7 miles. Watch for a switchback left that leads down to a creek crossing at 2.8 miles; the path straight ahead leads to an alternative crossing. If you were to take the first crossing, you'd drop onto boulders in the creek and then climb over a large boulder that divides the waters and then jump across to another boulder; the jump here is not recommended. Try the alternative crossing, which is a ford. If the creek is in flood, you may not have any choice; be careful if you take the jump on the first crossing. On a day hike, this may be a good place to turn around.

Switchback up from the crossing and bear left to rejoin the river headed downstream. The trail reaches a junction at 3.0 miles below a leaning rock with the Negro Creek Trail coming in from the right.

80 K&T Bridge 👣

Distance: 0.6 miles one-way
Difficulty: Moderate
Elevation change: Mostly level
Cautions: Stream crossing
Connections: Sheltowee Trace 👣

Attractions: South from Yamacraw Bridge, you can take a short walk on the Sheltowee Trace to the Kentucky and Tennessee (K&T) Bridge. The Stearns Coal and Lumber Company operated the K&T Railroad to haul coal and lumber from its camps along Rock Creek across the river and up to the central operations in Stearns. When the bridge was built in 1907, it was the largest concrete railroad bridge in the South, 575 feet long with five arches.

Trailhead: In Stearns, stay on KY 92 headed west from the junction with KY 1651. Descend into the Big South Fork Gorge, enter the BSFNRRA, and reach the Yamacraw Bridge over the river at 6.5 miles from US 27. Pass the Yamacraw Day Use Area and continue across the Yamacraw Bridge. The Sheltowee Trace crosses the Big South Fork on this bridge to the west side of the river. On the other side, turn left on KY 1363 and take an immediate left on a dirt road that descends in a sharp curve left under the bridge to the river access, where you can park. Walk back up the road to the curve; here the Sheltowee Trace leads off the road to the south.

Description: The trail heads into the woods to parallel KY 1363. Bear left down stone steps to the river bank. Take care if the water is up. At 0.2 mile, dip through a drainage where the water flows from a passage under the

K&T Bridge

highway. The trail crosses another drainage with a large culvert and then bears right up to the trace of an old road that comes down from the highway. Turn left back toward the river and continue upstream. At 0.6 mile is the old K&T Railroad Bridge that spans the Big South Fork.

81 | KOGER ARCH TRAIL

Distance: 0.3 mile one-way
Difficulty: Easy
Elevation gain: 220 ft
Cautions: Creek crossing
Connections: None at this writing

Attractions: This short walk leads to an impressive arch in the Daniel Boone National Forest. The mass of suspended stone, a clearance of 18 feet

Koger Arch

and a span of 91 feet, apparently was once a rock shelter, but the back part has caved in to separate the arch from the slope.

Trailhead: In Stearns, stay on KY 92 headed west from the junction with KY 1651. Descend into the Big South Fork Gorge, enter the BSFNRRA, and reach the Yamacraw Bridge over the river at 6.5 miles from US 27. On the west side of Yamacraw Bridge, turn left onto KY 1363. At 0.7 mile, watch for the top of the old K&T Railroad Bridge on your left. At 2.3 miles, turn left onto the Beech Grove Road and cross a bridge over Rock Creek. After the bridge, the road surface consists of broken pavement and gravel. Watch for the trail on the left at 3.1 miles as you ascend the ridge; there's room for one vehicle to park. Another half mile up the road is where the Sheltowee Trace emerges at a junction with Wilson Ridge Road.

Description: Steps take you down to cross a shallow branch of Koger Fork. The trail then bears left up a ravine, makes a sharp left, and ascends, paralleling the road below on your left.

As you round the corner of a rock wall on your right at 0.3 mile, the arch appears. The Koger Arch Trail continues through the arch and up steps toward the Sheltowee Trace. At this writing, the route is closed because of storm damage; there are no immediate plans to clear the trail above the arch. Once it is open again, you'll switchback several times to gain the top of the bluff and then emerge onto a dirt road at 0.5 mile. A few paces to the right, you'll connect with the Sheltowee Trace. To head north on the trace toward Rock Creek, turn left off the road to descend through the woods. To head south and emerge on Beech Grove Road, follow the dirt road straight for a mile.

82 | OIL WELL BRANCH ROAD ∩

Distance: 1.3 miles one-way
Difficulty: Strenuous
Elevation loss: 460 ft
Cautions: Undeveloped old road
Connections: Kentucky Trail 👣

Attractions: This old road has been proposed as part of an Oil Well Branch Loop. The route provides the shortest access to the site of the Beaty Oil Well. The well was drilled in 1818 by Marcus Huling and Andrew Zimmerman, who were searching for salt on land owned by Martin Beaty, but they struck oil instead. Only experienced outdoorspeople should attempt this undeveloped route.

Trailhead: From the Yamacraw Bridge crossing of the Big South Fork on KY 92, on the west side of the river, turn south on KY 1363. At 2.3 miles, turn left on Beech Grove/Devils Creek Road, which crosses Rock Creek on a concrete bridge; you'll see a sign for Bald Knob and Wilson Ridge. After the bridge, the road consists of gravel and broken pavement and passes the Koger Arch Trail on the left at 3.1 miles. Over Wilson Ridge, where the Sheltowee Trace emerges from the left and the gravel Wilson Ridge Road turns to the left, continue on Beech Grove Road to pass through the community of Beech Grove, dip through a cove, and head up the plateau. After ascending steeply, top Bald Knob, pass a turn on the left to the Dick Gap Overlook, and reach the Bald Knob Road to the left at 7.2 miles; turn left. At 1.4 miles down Bald Knob Road, you'll find parking for the Ledbetter Place Trailhead, which is an intermediate trailhead for the Kentucky Trail; that trail turns off the road to the left just before the trailhead.

The first commercial oil well in the United States

Description: Continue down the gravel Bald Knob Road, which on this section is also the Kentucky Trail. At 0.2 mile, turn right on a dirt road that is Oil Well Branch Road. Just up this road, the Hill Cemetery sits on the right.

The roadway continues through the woods. Pass a low rock overhang on the right at 0.2 mile. This undeveloped road narrows as vegetation and fallen trees crowd the trail, but passage is occasionally cleared of blowdowns. An earthen berm in the roadbed at 0.5 mile prevents further vehicle access.

At 0.7 mile, the road forks. The route straight ahead is overgrown and blocked by fallen trees. Turn down left to begin a descent into the gorge of the Big South Fork on an eroded, rocky roadbed. You'll see rimrock up to the right as you descend along the drainage of a tributary stream of the river. You can hear the river at 1.1 miles, and soon after the road curves right to parallel the river. At 1.3 miles, the trail turns off the road to the left; the roadbed straight ahead that once led to the Kentucky Trail is now overgrown. The trail winds down a few yards to a newer junction with the Kentucky Trail.

From this junction you can walk 0.2 mile to the right to get to the Beaty Oil Well (horses and mountain bikes are not allowed on the Kentucky Trail). Pass the old roadbed up to the right and reach a ford of Oil Well Branch. Ascending onto a rise, watch for a path to the left to the site of the well in the floodplain between the trail and the river. A sign in the woods marks the site. Beyond the sign is the oil well, a pipe sticking out of the ground. (The proposed Oil Well Branch Loop will continue south on the Kentucky Trail and turn up Lone Cliff Branch Road to circle back to the Ledbetter Place Trailhead.)

From the junction of Oil Well Branch Road with the Kentucky Trail, you can also turn north on the Kentucky Trail to walk out of the gorge and connect with the Bald Knob Road in 1.2 miles and return to the Ledbetter Place Trailhead in 0.6 mile up the road to the left. Horses and mountain bikes must return the way they came.

83 | DICK GAP OVERLOOK TRAIL 🚶

Distance: 0.3 mile one-way
Difficulty: Easy
Elevation change: Level
Cautions: None
Connections: Long Trail ∩

Attractions: This short trail leads out to Dick Gap Overlook, which offers an expansive view of the Big South Fork Gorge. You'll see the Blue Heron Mining Community to the left, with the tram bridge spanning the river from the old tipple on the east side; to the right, Devils Jump Rapids obstructs the river flow.

Trailhead: From the west side of the Yamacraw Bridge on KY 92, turn south on KY 1363; after 2.5 miles, turn left on Beech Grove/Devils Creek Road. Across a bridge over Rock Creek, the road becomes gravel and broken pavement. The road passes over Wilson Ridge, travels through the Beech Grove Community, and climbs the plateau, becoming Laurel Ridge Road. At 4.0 miles from the beginning of Beech Grove Road, pass the Beech Grove Baptist Church on the left; just beyond, turn left on the Waters Cemetery Road. The Long Trail, which has come on Laurel Ridge Road from the other direction, here turns down Waters Cemetery Road. In a half mile, turn left on Dick Gap Road; the Long Trail turns here also, but in half a mile turns to the right into the woods. Continue on to reach the end of the road and parking in another half mile; an old roadway continues to the right to connect with the Long Trail. Down to the left from the parking area is the trail to the overlook.

Description: The wide sand and gravel path drops from the parking area to skirt a rock bluff on the left as the trail curves right. The trail then curves left and right to reach the overlook on the rim of the river gorge.

84 | LICK CREEK TRAIL 👫

Distance: 4.3 miles one-way (*Lick Creek Falls 2.8 miles one-way; Princess Falls 4.2 miles one-way*)
Difficulty: Moderate
Elevation loss: 460 ft
Cautions: Creek fords
Connections: Sheltowee Trace 👫

Attractions: You'll pass two of the best waterfalls in the area plus a wet-weather waterfall in a deep rock alcove on this Daniel Boone National Forest trail.

Trailhead: On US 27 north of Stearns, on the southern end of Whitley City, turn west on KY 478. In 0.3 mile, join KY 1651; turn left. At 1.2 miles, turn right on FDR 622 and in a few hundred feet you'll see the trailhead at a gated dirt road on the left. You can also reach this point by driving KY 1651 north from Stearns 1.6 miles to a left turn on FDR 622. At the trailhead, there's room for a couple of vehicles to park without blocking the road.

Description: Walk up the road, following the white diamond blazes; cross the boundary into the Daniel Boone National Forest. At 0.2 mile the road passes under a powerline. As you continue, you'll see traces of old roads left and right, but stay with the main road straight.

At 0.8 mile the road curves left, and soon after, the trail turns right on a side road, which heads out along a ridge. At 1.0 mile the side road becomes a footpath; at 1.1 miles, begin a descent into Lick Creek Gorge. Stone steps, several switchbacks, and two metal stairways assist in the descent below the rock bluff. Pass an overhang on the right and a tall rock bluff to pass under another overhang; at 1.3 miles, turn right into a deep rock alcove encircling massive boulders that have fallen from the rock wall. A wet-weather waterfall spills from overhead as you follow the alcove around, passing under suspended rock.

Continue your descent into coves of hemlock and rhododendron to cross a small tributary at 1.6 miles and soon after reach Lick Creek on your right; the trail now follows the creek downstream, often in the floodplain. Cross a couple of tributary drainages and then parallel a long, low overhang on your left to reach a junction at 2.2 miles with the trail up to Lick Creek Falls to your left; the Lick Creek Trail, continuing straight, fords

Lick Creek Falls

Lick Creek. Turn left to get to the waterfall.

As you ascend the side trail, cross a cascading tributary of Lick Creek and continue up to a junction at 2.5 miles. The path to the right is another way back down to the Lick Creek Trail; stay straight to get to the waterfall. As you continue ascending, parallel a tributary of Lick Creek below to your right, which is the stream the waterfall is on. At 2.6 miles, the trail bears right to cross a small stream. At 2.7 miles, you'll reach a tall rock wall on the left and pass into a massive rock alcove and overhang. Lick Creek Falls pours over the lip in the center of the alcove and drops 60 feet to the rocks and a pool below.

Walk back along the path from the waterfall to the fork, where you can stay left to rejoin the main trail a little farther down from where you left it. Descend to ford Lick Creek and rejoin the main trail at 3.2 miles; turn left.

At 3.6 miles, ford Lick Creek again. During high water, these fords are impassable. At 4.0 miles, the trail runs through rocks along the creek. Soon after, diagonally cross an old road leading down to the creek and then rockhop a tributary stream. Skirt the creek once again and reach a point above Princess Falls on Lick Creek at 4.2 miles. Here the water spills over a long rock shelf that cuts diagonally across the creek. The waterfall is named for Princess Cornblossom, the daughter of Chief Doublehead. The Cherokees did not use such honorifics as *Princess,* so the title probably was attached to her name by the white settlers of the region. Beyond the waterfall, a side path right drops to the pool below the falls. Continuing on the trail, enter the BSFNRRA and connect with the Sheltowee Trace at 4.3 miles.

Map 11. Yahoo Falls

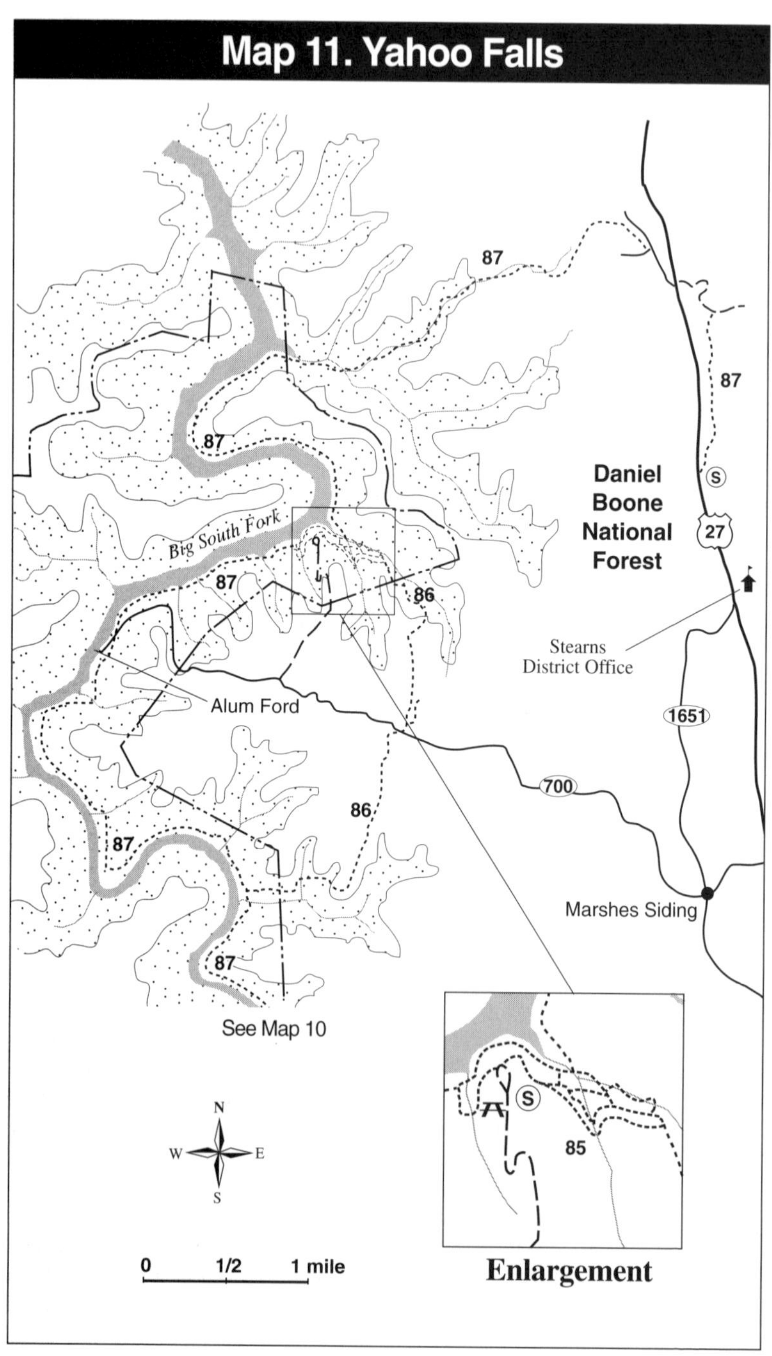

The Yahoo Falls Scenic Area contains an intricate network of trails that leads to Roaring Rocks Cataract and Yahoo Falls, the tallest waterfall in Kentucky. Yahoo Arch and Markers Arch stand on national forest land bordering the recreation area. The Sheltowee Trace passes through this northern end of the park to head south into Tennessee.

Just north of Whitley City on US 27, turn west on KY 700. Travel on KY 700 through Marshes Siding as you cross KY 1651; enter the BSFNRRA and at 4.0 miles turn right on a gravel road. If you were to keep going straight, you'd arrive at the Alum Ford River Access on the Big South Fork River. After making the turn, it's 1.5 miles down to the Yahoo Falls Scenic Area. At the one-way loop in the scenic area, stay to the right and drive to the backside of the picnic area to the trailhead on the right.

85 | YAHOO FALLS TRAILS 🚶🚶

Distance: Topside Loop 0.8 mile; Cascade Loop 0.2 mile; Cliffside Loop 1.1 miles
Difficulty: Moderate
Elevation change: 250 ft
Cautions: High cliffs, steep stairs, stream crossings
Connections: Yahoo Arch Trail 🚶🚶, Sheltowee Trace 🚶🚶

Attractions: This group of trails leads to a massive rock shelter with a slender waterfall dropping off the edge 113 feet, the tallest waterfall in the BSFNRRA and the tallest in Kentucky.

Trailhead: Start at the Yahoo Falls Scenic Area Trailhead.

Description: Enter the woods to walk the Topside Loop. The trail is blazed with a yellow arrow, but you'll also see a green arrow because this is also the return route for the Cliffside Loop. You'll soon see a side trail on the left that leads 50 yards down to an overlook of the confluence of Yahoo Creek with the Big South Fork. The river at this location is also the upper reaches of Lake Cumberland, created by Wolf Creek Dam far downstream on the Cumberland River.

At 0.1 mile, the Cliffside Trail comes in on the left. Stay straight. Walk along an old roadbed until at 0.2 mile the trail bears down to the left. The trail soon switchbacks left below a couple of primitive restrooms and then right to a side path to the left that leads to an overlook of Yahoo Falls, where a small creek spills over a rock lip into a large plunge basin.

The main trail soon passes the top of the falls on the left and moves upstream along this tributary of Yahoo Creek. At 0.3 mile, turn left to make a shallow ford of the creek and walk up to an overlook on the other side of the waterfall. The trail takes you by one more overlook before reaching a junction at 0.4 mile with the Yahoo Arch Trail (which leads 0.8 mile to Yahoo Arch).

The Topside Loop turns downhill to the left and descends through switchbacks to a junction below a rock wall with the Cascade Loop. This 0.2-mile side loop, blazed blue, passes by the Roaring Rocks Cataract, where Yahoo Creek shifts through boulders as it drops steeply downstream; on this side loop, cross the creek several times and enter the creek to pass through two boulders and reach a junction with the Cliffside Loop. Turning left up the Cliffside Loop, you'd then turn left up a connector that returns you to the Topside Loop. From the first junction with the Cascade Loop, follow the rock wall along the Topside Loop to reach this lower junction with the Cascade Loop at 0.5 mile.

Yahoo Falls

Continue from this junction, and the trail leads under the massive overhang that supports Yahoo Falls. The trail circles behind the falls through this amphitheater to the other side. Steps lead down to the small plunge pool. In the freezing cold of winter, a mound of radiant blue-green ice forms beneath the falls.

Continuing on the trail, you'll reach a side trail to the right at 0.6 mile where the Cliffside Loop joins the Topside Loop. A little farther, another short side trail leads right to connect with the Cliffside Loop. You'll then come to a metal structure of platforms and stairs that ascends the laurel-covered rock bluff to close the loop at 0.7 mile. Turn right to return to the parking area at 0.8 mile.

From this same trailhead, you can walk the Cliffside Loop. Instead of entering the woods to the right, walk down the road about 50 yards and watch where the trail turns down steps to the right. The way is blazed with a green arrow. You'll see another overlook of the river. The trail bears left to circle the picnic area. At 0.2 mile, curve right where a path leads left up to the road. The trail then crosses a small stream on a stone footbridge. At 0.3 mile, descend stone stairs to a long flight of steep metal stairs that takes you below a rock cliff. The trail then leads through several switchbacks as it descends to a junction with the Sheltowee Trace at 0.4 mile.

The Cliffside Loop now follows the Sheltowee Trace to the north. First cross a bridge over the same small stream you crossed earlier and later turn up Yahoo Creek and pass a short connector to the Topside Loop at 0.7 mile. Then cross a bridge over Yahoo Creek and reach a junction at 0.8 mile where the Sheltowee Trace turns left. The Cliffside Loop turns right.

Cross Yahoo Creek again, this time on stepping stones near the junction of the Yahoo Falls tributary with Yahoo Creek. The trail now passes between the two creeks. You'll soon reach a junction where the Cascade Loop comes in from the left to join the Cliffside Loop. At 0.9 mile is a second junction where a connector turns left to ascend to a junction with the Topside Loop. Turn right. The trail leads across a bridge below the waterfall and then joins the Topside Loop. Turn right, passing the other end of the connector you passed earlier, and climb the metal and stone stairs back to the top of the cliff. Then turn right to return to the trailhead and parking area at 1.1 miles.

86 | YAHOO ARCH, NEGRO CREEK, AND SHELTOWEE TRACE TRAILS 🚶🚶

Distance: 9.9-mile loop *(Yahoo Arch 1.2 miles one-way)*
Difficulty: Moderate
Elevation change: 550 ft
Cautions: Mudholes, overgrown sections, steep descent
Connections: Cliffside and Topside Loops 🚶🚶, Markers Arch Trail 🚶🚶

Attractions: This hike takes you past Yahoo Arch and Markers Arch and then loops around to join the Sheltowee Trace along the Big South Fork. The trace then heads downstream to return to the scenic area.

Trailhead: Start at the Yahoo Falls Scenic Area Trailhead.

Directions: Follow the Topside Loop for 0.4 mile past the junction with the Cliffside Loop to the junction with the Yahoo Arch Trail and turn right. At 0.6 mile, cross a small side creek on stepping stones and ascend stone

Markers Arch

stairs, following Yahoo Creek upstream. Along the way, cross the un-marked boundary of the BSFNRRA and enter the Daniel Boone National Forest, following a white diamond blaze.

The trail crosses another small side stream at 0.8 mile and ascends the ridge with several switchbacks. You'll reach a tall rock wall before coming at 1.1 miles to a rock overhang dripping ribbons of water at your feet. At the far end stands Yahoo Arch, an impressive span of 80 feet with an opening 10 feet high. Stone steps take you to the arch.

The trail does not pass through the arch but turns left to circle the north end. Switchbacks take you above the arch and then along a rock wall to a right turn up stone steps at 1.3 miles. Make a couple more switchbacks and then a gentle ascent through a drier mixed pine and hardwood forest to a junction with an old roadbed at 1.4 miles. Turn left. At 2.2 miles you'll reach KY 700; just before the highway, a half-mile side trail left leads to Markers Arch, a 60-foot span.

At the highway, turn right a few paces up the road and then turn left on gravel FDR 6003. You can walk down this road to pick up the trail later on, but the trail actually turns right off the road in just 20 yards and swings around to rejoin the gravel road at 2.5 miles. From there, walk down the road to where the powerline cuts across and turn right.

The trail now drops down stairs carved into the rock. At 2.7 miles, stone steps help you over a small creek; bear left downstream. At 3.3 miles, the trail ascends over a grassy knoll where there's good camping. The trail gradually curves right where the creek you have been paralleling joins Negro Creek in the valley below. The trail now follows Negro Creek downstream, although the trail is so high up the slope that you can't see the stream.

The trail becomes rocky. Steps are cut in a dead tree across the trail at 3.8 miles. Begin moving downhill, in some places quite steeply. At 4.5 miles the trail hits a faint roadway. Turn left a few paces and then turn right off the road. The trail drops steeply to a stream crossing at 4.6 miles and turns left down this tributary. Along the way, reenter the BSFNRRA at an unmarked boundary.

The trail crosses an old road at 4.7 miles and then curves left to drop down to the old road; turn right but then stay left at a fork. The trail crosses another old road and then is back to a footpath.

Descend to a junction at 5.2 miles with the Sheltowee Trace. To the left, the trace leads toward the Yamacraw Bridge. Turn right to complete this loop hike while following the Big South Fork to the north.

The trail passes among huge boulders and then crosses a small stream at 5.3 miles; you'll see a short waterfall to the right. The trail then curves right to cross Cotton Patch Creek where large boulders form a bridge.

Back at the river, the trail descends the slope to cross a wet-weather stream and then a footbridge over a drainage. At 6.1 miles is a side trail to the Cotton Patch Shelter. The shelter is in disrepair, but if you want to spend the night here, you'll need to haul water from Cotton Patch Creek. Back on the main trail, pass an old stone chimney that marks a former house site.

At 7.4 miles, turn up to cross another drainage on stepping stones and at 8.0 miles reach the Alum Ford River Access, which has picnicking and primitive camping. Walk down the gravel road to a junction with KY 700 at 8.2 miles, with a boat ramp to the left. The trail crosses the road on a diagonal; walk up the road several yards to where the trail reenters the woods.

The trail descends from the road and stays level. At 8.4 miles, cross a rutted road. Stay to the right at a fork. Cross three streams spilling over ledges and cascades. Passing below a tall rock bluff, the trail reaches a junction with the Cliffside Loop at 9.5 miles. Turn right; several switchbacks take you up the bluff to stone and metal stairs that get you on top. Return to the parking area and trailhead at 9.9 miles.

87 | SHELTOWEE TRACE

Distance: 46.8 miles one-way
Difficulty: Moderate
Elevation change: 700 ft
Cautions: Creek fords, mudholes, steep ascents and descents
Connections: Yahoo Falls Trails, Negro Creek Trail, Lick Creek Trail, Kentucky Trail, Long Trail, Mark Branch Trail, Gobblers Arch Trail, John Muir Trail, Rock Creek Loop, Rock Creek Trail

Attractions: The 257-mile Sheltowee Trace National Recreation Trail travels north to south through Daniel Boone National Forest in Kentucky. Toward its end, the trace passes through the northern part of the BSFNRRA and then generally parallels the northeastern boundary to reenter the park at the Tennessee state line and end at Pickett State Rustic Park and Forest.

While traveling through the remote woods of Kentucky in February 1778, Daniel Boone was captured by a band of Shawnees, who took him to one of their towns along the Ohio River. Boone escaped 4 months later, but during his stay, Chief Black Fish befriended him and gave Boone the name *Sheltowee*, meaning "Big Turtle." The Sheltowee Trace, named in Boone's honor, has an occasional blaze in the shape of a turtle, but most often a white diamond blaze.

Trailhead: The easiest access for the trail section that enters the Big South Fork is on US 27 2.7 miles north from KY 700 in Whitley City, on the east side of the highway; pass the Stearns District Office of the national forest along the way. The trace can also be accessed at Yahoo Falls, Alum Ford, Yamacraw Bridge, and Peters Mountain Trailhead and in the national forest at the Hemlock Grove picnic area and Great Meadows Campground on FDR 137.

Description: From the trailhead on US 27, you can turn right to hike the trace northeast 20.4 miles to Cumberland Falls State Park. But to head toward the Big South Fork, go straight, away from the highway, to pass under a powerline and enter the woods and bear left. Emerge onto a gravel road at 0.7 mile. Turn left. Pass some houses and at 1.0 mile reach a church and a sawmill on US 27. Cross the highway onto a paved road that curves right over railroad tracks. At 1.3 miles, at a side road to the left, the trail ascends into the woods. At 1.4 miles, the trail dips to join an old road bearing left. Cross under a powerline and join another dirt road.

At 1.6 miles, the trail turns left off the road onto a path. Descend into a hollow and reach a gravel road at 1.9 miles. A few paces to the right the trail reenters the woods. Pass under a powerline and reach a switchback right down through rocks at 2.2 miles to enter Big Creek Gorge. At 2.3 miles the trail swings through a rock shelter, with the North Fork of Big Creek streaming off the lip in wet weather. The trail circles along the rock bluff and then descends to cross a small stream at 2.4 miles at a low overhang. Descend to rockhop the North Fork at 2.5 miles. The trail now follows the creek downstream, crossing it nine times before emerging onto a gravel road at 3.2 miles. Turn right on the road and then left back into the woods.

At 3.4 miles, climb up a bank to an old road. Turn left to a hunting cabin on a private inholding within the national forest; do not trespass. The road makes a sharp curve left here, but the trail stays straight onto a side road in front of the cabin. Stay with this side road and watch for a turn left off the road and descend stone steps to a ford of Big Creek at 3.6 miles; cross only at low water.

Ascend from the creek and cross the boundary of the national forest into the BSFNRRA. As you near the confluence with the Big South Fork, the lower part of Big Creek is flooded with the waters of Lake Cumberland. At 3.9 miles, the trail curves left as it turns upstream along the Big South Fork.

At 5.8 miles, massive rock walls stand to your left as you enter the Yahoo Falls area. Then follow Yahoo Creek upstream. The trail crosses a tiered boardwalk over a drainage. At 6.2 miles is a junction with the Cliffside Loop to the left that leads up to Yahoo Falls. Bear right to cross Yahoo Creek on a bridge and ascend stone steps and reach another junction at 6.3 miles; a connector trail to the left leads to the Topside Loop. The trace continues down Yahoo Creek to soon curve left and once more parallel the Big South Fork upstream.

After crossing a bridge over a tumbling stream, you'll reach another junction with the Cliffside Loop at 6.6 miles. From here the Sheltowee Trace continues south along the Big South Fork. At 8.1 miles, cross KY 700 at the Alum Ford River Access and reach a junction with the Negro Creek Trail at 10.9 miles. At 11.1 miles, ford Negro Creek and at 12.7 miles cross Lick Creek on a bridge to reach a junction with the Lick Creek Trail to the left. Arrive at Yamacraw Bridge on KY 92 at 13.9 miles. (See Trails 79 and 86 for details.)

Walk up to the highway and cross the bridge over the river. Turn left on KY 1363, then turn off the paved road on the gravel road that leads down to the river access; in just a few yards, the trail leads into the woods where the road switchbacks left. Then parallel KY 1363 along the river to the old K&T Railroad Bridge at 14.5 miles.

Just past the bridge is the confluence of Rock Creek with the river. The trail follows Rock Creek upstream. Pass traces of coal mining: cables, slag piles, and, if you can see through the trees to the right, a large concrete support structure. At a junction at 14.8 miles, turn left to descend to a ford of Rock Creek; watch for deep mud along the bank. If the water is up, do not ford; instead, take an alternative route to the right at the junction. Walk

Old support structure from coal mine operations

up to the old railbed of the K&T and turn right to walk past the old support structure and out to KY 1363. Then walk left on the paved road to a left turn on Beech Grove/Devils Creek Road and walk the road up the mountain, where it eventually becomes Laurel Ridge Road.

If you can make the ford at Rock Creek, you'll have left the BSFNRRA and reentered Daniel Boone National Forest. On the other side, follow an old railbed along Grassy Fork Creek. The trail reaches a junction at 14.9 miles with the northern end of the Kentucky Trail to the left.

At this writing, the next section of the Sheltowee Trace is closed because of heavy storm damage; in 1998 a tornado felled trees in a broad section, virtually obliterating the trail. The Forest Service intends to reopen the trace, but it may take a few years before the down timber is harvested and the trail repaired. If the trail has not been reopened by the time you come this way, the best route south is to turn left on the Kentucky Trail and hike it all the way to the Peters Mountain Trailhead in 26.2 miles. Or you can take the alternative that avoids the ford of Rock Creek and walk the backcountry roads all the way to Peters Mountain Trailhead.

If the trail has been repaired, stay straight. At 15.1 miles, pass some old foundations remaining from the coal-mining days; the mines opened on the slopes above and the coal was hauled out on the narrow-gauge train that ran along the railbed the trail is following. At 15.3 miles, ford Grassy Fork at the site of a bridge where the rail line once crossed the creek; you'll see rockwork that supported the span. Ford the creek above a small cascade and enter a narrow rock passageway that the train must have barely cleared and continue on to ford the creek four times.

Ascend to a junction with a road at 16.9 miles. Across the road and to the right is the end of the Koger Arch Trail. The Sheltowee Trace turns left to follow the road out to the Beech Grove Road at 17.9 miles at the junction with the Wilson Ridge Road. If you have been walking the roads to avoid the ford of Rock Creek, join the Sheltowee Trace here.

Now walk up the paved road. At 18.1 miles, the trace leaves the road to the right, ascending into the woods (stay on the road if the trail is still closed here). The trail ascends steeply to the top of the ridge. Continue along the ridgeline, with views of the Rock Creek and Big South Fork Gorges.

The trail eventually descends and at 21.4 miles fords Trace Branch. Ascend to the gravel Laurel Ridge Road at 23.3 miles, which is actually the continuation of Beech Grove Road. If you have been walking the road to bypass the storm damage section, rejoin the actual route of the Sheltowee Trace here. Hike up the gravel road (turning right on the road if you have been walking the trail); this is also part of Long Trail, which travels from Middle Creek to Blue Heron. Long-range plans call for rerouting the trace off the road and onto a trail within the recreation area; watch for this change.

At 24.4 miles, the road passes a fenced cabin. At 24.7 miles, where a side road goes straight, the road curves right into a steep descent to a crossing of a fork of Puncheoncamp Branch at 24.9 miles. Then make a steep ascent to get back to the top of the plateau.

At 26.2 miles a road to the right leads past a cabin in the woods. Pass the Blevins–Kidd Cemetery on the right; an old shack stands behind the cemetery. The road then curves right at 26.3 miles, where a side road leads past a clearing to the left. This Cat Ridge Road leads down toward the river to connect with the Kentucky Trail.

At 27.5 miles is a junction with the Laurel Hill Road to the left that is the route for Laurel Hill Trail. If you took the Kentucky Trail because the Sheltowee Trace is still closed through this section, emerge here on Laurel Ridge Road. Continue south on the road. Make a steep ascent and then level off in a more open area.

At 29.0 miles is a junction with FDR 6101. Turn left to reach a junction of roads at 29.2 miles. Up to your left lies the Peters Mountain Trailhead. Straight ahead is FDR 569, also called Peters Mountain Road. To the right is FDR 139, which leads toward the Bell Farm Horse Camp. The Sheltowee Trace heads to the right on a path into the woods. This section may still be closed from storm damage; if so, continue straight down Peters Mountain Road to the Mark Branch Trail and follow it to a junction with the Sheltowee Trace. If the trace has been reopened south of Peters Mountain Trailhead, take the path into the woods at the junction of roads.

Soon the trail descends into a cove and crisscrosses Mark Branch at 29.8 miles. Rockhop a side stream and cross Mark Branch again to reach the top of Mark Branch Falls. The trail swings right and switchbacks left in a descent into the plunge basin. At 30.3 miles, pass behind the 50-foot waterfall.

The trail soon crosses the creek below the waterfall and continues down the cove. From here, the trail fords Mark Branch 11 times. At 31.4 miles is a junction with the Mark Branch Trail. Continue straight and cross Mark Branch four more times. The trail emerges into an open area at a junction at 31.8 miles. The trace turns left here, but you can also follow a side path straight ahead to a ford of Rock Creek in 0.1 mile to get to the Forest Service's Hemlock Grove Picnic Area on FDR 137. From here, the Sheltowee Trace is open; the forest here was not as affected by the 1998 storm.

Turning left, you'll reach a junction at 31.9 miles with the Gobblers Arch Trail (which takes off to the left to form a loop with the Mark Branch Trail). Continue straight to parallel Rock Creek upstream and at 33.9 miles pass a path down to the right to a ford across to the Forest Service's Great Meadows Campground. At 36.4 miles is a junction with a path to the right. (This path fords Rock Creek to FDR 137; just to the right up that road is the end of the Parker Mountain Trail.) Continue straight from this junction.

The trace crosses a boardwalk over Massey Branch at 36.5 miles. Ascend to cross a small drainage on a footbridge and reach a junction at 36.8 miles with the JMT. Continue straight. The JMT and the Sheltowee Trace now coincide; this is also the Rock Creek Loop.

At 40.2 miles is a junction with the Rock Creek Loop turning up left and the JMT/Sheltowee Trace turning right to ford Rock Creek. On the other side, turn left upstream to cross into Pickett State Forest. A concrete piling perched on a rock on the other side of the creek once supported a logging railroad bridge.

Connect with the Rock Creek Trail at 40.4 miles. You can continue straight on the Rock Creek Trail, passing a junction with the Tunnel Trail and fording the creek three times to reach TN 154 at 40.3 miles. Another option is to turn left on the Rock Creek Trail; ford the creek to the other side and make a steep ascent to connect with the Hidden Passage Trail at 41.9 miles. Turn left and continue on to emerge at the trailhead for the Hidden Passage Trail on TN 154 at 46.8 miles.

Map 12. Pickett State Park and Forest

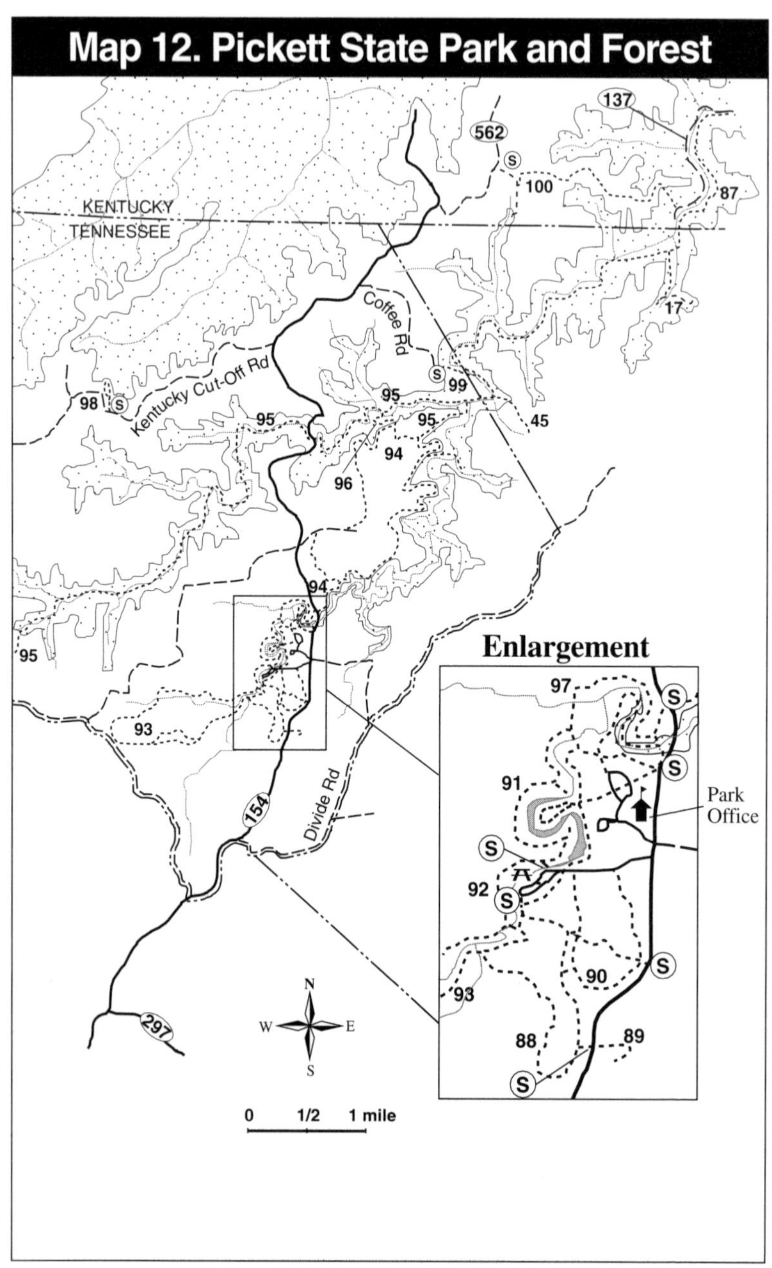

PICKETT STATE PARK AND FOREST

Tennessee's Pickett State Park and Forest, with arches and rock shelters, lies adjacent to the Big South Fork's Middle Creek area. With the same geology and similar topography to the BSFNRRA, the state park should be included in your visit to the area. North on TN 154 from Divide Road (the turn into the Middle Creek area), pass through Pickett State Forest and at 0.8 mile enter Pickett State Rustic Park.

88 | HAZARD CAVE TRAIL 🥾

Distance: 2.5-mile loop (*Hazard Cave 0.2 mile one-way*)
Difficulty: Moderate
Elevation change: 200 ft
Cautions: Steep concrete stairs, creek crossings
Connections: Indian Rockhouse Trail 🥾, Ridge Trail Loop 🥾, Lake View Trail 🥾, Natural Bridge Trail Loop 🥾

Attractions: This trail swings by Hazard Cave, a large rock shelter where erosion has opened a hole above the opening so that the entrance is an arch; walk to the back of the shelter and look toward the entrance to see the crack of light above the opening.

Trailhead: Enter Pickett State Rustic Park. In another 0.2 mile, the parking and trailhead for Hazard Cave lie on the left. (The Indian Rockhouse Trail begins across the road.)

Description: Descend gravel-filled steps and concrete steps to access the Hazard Cave Trail, which has a white blaze. Turn left for the shortest access to Hazard Cave. Descend another long flight of concrete steps and curve left to a footbridge across a drainage at the base of a long rock wall. The trail follows the wall to Hazard Cave, a large rock shelter with a sand floor at 0.2 mile.

At the far end of the shelter, the trail ascends from the opening and swings left to another exposed part of the bluff. The trail curves right and drops to a crossing of a small creek at 0.5 mile. Follow a long downhill to another creek crossing. At 0.9 mile, the trail drops into a cove; cross a creek at a small waterfall, stepping down the 2-foot ledge. Drop steeply to cross the creek again. At 1.2 miles is a junction with the green-blazed Ridge Trail. Turn right.

Hazard Cave

Soon after, you'll reach a junction where the Ridge Trail turns left across a bridge over Thompson Creek. Turn right. This section is also blazed green because this is the access to the Ridge Trail from the picnic area; it's also part of the Lake View Trail, blazed gray. At 1.4 miles is another junction. The path straight ahead leads into the picnic area (where a side path, blazed white, leads right to the Recreation Lodge). Turn right at this junction; this route also has a brown blaze because this is a connector to the Natural Bridge Trail.

The trail now ascends. At 1.6 miles, pass two paths left to the Natural

Bridge Trail. At 1.9 miles, pass a third connector to the Natural Bridge Trail. Stay straight. The trail soon tops the ridge. At 2.4 miles, a path left leads up to the trailhead. The trail straight ahead is the completion of the loop to your beginning point below the first set of stairs. Turn left to get back to the parking area.

89 | INDIAN ROCKHOUSE TRAIL 🚶🚶

Distance: 0.2 mile one-way
Difficulty: Easy
Elevation loss: 100 ft
Cautions: None
Connections: Hazard Cave Trail 🚶🚶

Attractions: The trail ends at a sweeping rock overhang that may be the largest in the Big South Fork region.

Trailhead: Enter Pickett State Rustic Park. In another 0.2 mile, the parking and trailhead for Hazard Cave lie on the left. The Indian Rockhouse Trail begins on the other side of the highway.

Description: Cross the highway to the Indian Rockhouse Trail, which drops gradually 0.1 mile to an overlook where you'll see the rock shelter below and to the right. Continue from there as the trail descends and then circles right into the rock shelter. Although the trail ends, you can enjoy a walk through the massive 250-degree circular structure. A small pool at the center is fed by water falling 60 feet from the rim above.

Indian Rockhouse

90 | NATURAL BRIDGE TRAIL 🚶🚶

Distance: 0.7-mile loop
Difficulty: Easy
Elevation change: 100 ft
Cautions: Steep stairway
Connections: Hazard Cave Trail 🚶🚶

Attractions: You'll pass two natural arches—one large, one small—on this stroll through the woods. The larger, Natural Bridge, sometimes called Highway 154 Natural Bridge, is an exceptionally thin arch, with a span of 86 feet and a clearance of 23 feet.

Trailhead: Enter Pickett State Park and pass the Hazard Cave Trailhead. In another 0.3 mile into the park, there's parking for the Natural Bridge on the left.

Description: From the parking area, step down to a junction, which is the loop trail left and right. Turn right to get to the Natural Bridge. The trail curves down stone steps to the top of the arch. A side trail to the right leads across the top of the arch and heads into the woods to connect with the road into the picnic area in half a mile. Turn left to descend steep rock steps and then curve right to get to the bottom of the arch.

Walk under the arch to where the trail turns left to head straight out through a forest of hardwood and laurel. The trail is blazed brown. At 0.1 mile, cross a footbridge over a wet-weather drainage and continue down and turn left to again cross the drainage on a footbridge at 0.2 mile. The trail ascends the hollow and switchbacks right up a slope to reach a junction at 0.3 mile. Straight ahead, the trail leads 0.2 mile to another junction where the left fork connects

Natural Bridge

to the Hazard Cave Trail in 0.2 mile and the right fork heads down to the picnic area.

To complete the Natural Bridge Trail, turn left at the first junction. Continue an ascent of the slope until, at 0.4 mile, another connector leads right 0.1 mile up to the Hazard Cave Trail. Continue straight. The trail curves left at a rock wall, where you'll find another natural arch. This smaller opening penetrates the ridge. The trail then curves right around the point of the ridge and swings left at the head of a deep hollow.

At 0.6 mile the trail narrows, with a rock wall on the right and a dropoff into the hollow on the left. Then skirt the highway and walk along the top of a bluff to complete the loop at 0.7 mile above Natural Bridge. Turn right up to the parking area.

91 | LAKE TRAIL / ISLAND TRAIL 𝕩

Distance: 3.0-mile loop
Difficulty: Easy
Elevation change: 100 ft
Cautions: Swinging bridge
Connections: Lake View Trail 𝕩, Bluff Trail 𝕩, Ladder Trail 𝕩

Attractions: This hike around the park lake passes by an arch that spans the lake waters backed up by Thompson Creek Dam. The bridge is an incised meander where Thompson Creek folded back on itself to eventually wear a hole through the ridge. The bridge was eventually left high and dry as the creek continued to erode, cutting its valley deeper. At one time a narrow-gauge railway, used to haul lumber out of the area, paralleled Thompson Creek and passed under the natural bridge. The construction of the Thompson Creek Dam brought the water back to a level with the bridge opening. Today you can rent boats and float under the bridge.

Trailhead: At 1.0 mile into Pickett State Park on TN 154, you'll see the office/visitor center and two roads to the left. Take the first road into the picnic area (the second road leads to cabins and the campground). Begin your walk at the swinging bridge that crosses Pickett Lake.

Description: Cross the bridge to a shelter overlooking Pickett Lake. To the left lies the Lake View Trail to the south. Turn right; the Lake Trail with a red blaze climbs rock stairs and then follows the bluff above the lake's swimming and boating area.

At 0.2 mile, the trail turns left, with a side path continuing straight to a grudging overlook of the Pickett Lake Natural Bridge; you'll get better views later. After turning left, you'll encounter a junction with a side trail to the left (which connects with the Lake View Trail behind the shelter

Pickett Lake Natural Bridge

above the swinging bridge). Stay straight ahead to keep on the main trail. At 0.7 mile, you'll find a rest shelter to the right.

At 1.0 mile a short side trail leads down to the Thompson Creek Dam, which creates Pickett Lake. The Civilian Conservation Corps built the dam in the 1930s. From the top of the dam, you'll get the best view of Pickett Lake Natural Bridge stretching across an arm of the lake.

Continue on the Lake Trail. At 1.5 miles, the Bluff Trail leads left to TN 154. Bear right, passing down to a footbridge over Thompson Creek below the dam. A slight climb from the creek takes you through hemlock and rhododendron to a junction with the Ladder Trail (which also leads out to TN 154). Pass a side path to another rest shelter.

At 2.0 miles, the Island Trail leads to the right over the top of Pickett Lake Natural Bridge, where you can see the Thompson Creek Dam below. The half-mile Island Trail loops around the peninsula, passes another rest shelter, and returns over the natural bridge to this junction at 2.5 miles. Here, a short path to the left leads up to the park campground.

Continuing on the Lake Trail, pass behind the park chalets and drop to cross a small wet-weather stream, then ascend past another shelter at 2.8 miles. Follow the blazes up to the left through the cabins to emerge onto the cabin road. Turn right along a fence to a gap where the trail turns down stone steps and crosses a gravel service road behind the boating area. Bear left upstream along a small creek to a right turn over a footbridge. The trail leads on to the Recreation Lodge and the picnic area at 3.0 miles where you began the hike.

92 | LAKE VIEW TRAIL 🚶🚶

Distance: 0.7 mile one-way
Difficulty: Easy
Elevation change: 50 ft
Cautions: Steep stairs
Connections: Lake Trail 🚶🚶, Ridge Trail 🚶🚶, Hazard Cave Trail 🚶🚶

Attractions: This trail follows a bluff above Pickett Lake for views of the lake waters. With Thompson Creek backed up by the dam to create the lake, you'll see deep emerald-green pools.

Trailhead: At 1.0 mile into Pickett State Park on TN 154, you'll see the office/visitor center and two roads to the left. Take the first road into the picnic area. Cross the swinging bridge over the lake.

Description: On the other side of the bridge, ascend steps to get above the rest shelter and turn left to hike the Lake View Trail. The Lake Trail leads to the right.

Heading south on the Lake View Trail, walk along a bluff above Pickett Lake across from the picnic area. The trail bears right through the forest to cross a stream at 0.3 mile on a footbridge. Turn downstream, passing a small waterfall in the creek. The trail reaches the lake again and continues upstream.

At 0.4 mile, swing right around a shelter where you can stop for a rest on a bench. At 0.5 mile is a junction with the Ridge Trail to the right. Stay straight to cross Thompson Creek on a bridge and reach a junction with the Ridge Trail and Hazard Cave Trail to the right. Turn left and stay straight past a connector to the Natural Bridge Trail to get back to the picnic area at 0.7 mile.

93 | RIDGE TRAIL 👥

Distance: 3.0-mile loop *(under-bluff / over-bluff loop 1.8 miles)*
Difficulty: Moderate
Elevation change: 150 ft
Cautions: Creek ford
Connections: Hazard Cave Trail 👥, Natural Bridge Trail 👥, Lake View Trail 👥

Attractions: This walk into Pickett State Forest passes rock shelters and rock bluffs; an under-bluff/over-bluff loop offers a shorter walk.

Trailhead: At 1.0 mile into Pickett State Park on TN 154, you'll see the office/visitor center and two roads to the left. Take the first road into the picnic area. At the far end of the picnic area, 0.5 mile from the turnoff on TN 154, is the trailhead. This trailhead is an access point for several trails in the park, so you'll see white, gray, brown, and green blazes. For the Ridge Trail, follow the green blaze.

Description: Head straight into the woods. Almost immediately, a trail to the left leads to the Recreation Lodge you passed on the road into the picnic area. Stay straight.

You'll soon come to a trail to the left that is part of both the Natural Bridge and the Hazard Cave Trails. Again stay straight. The trail descends gradually to cross a small stream on a footbridge and reach a junction with the loop part of the Ridge Trail. To the right a bridge crosses Thompson Creek and also gives access to the Lake View Trail. Keep left to hike the Ridge Trail clockwise. Ascend to another junction where the Hazard Cave Trail comes in from the left. Stay right and cross the park boundary into the contiguous Pickett State Forest.

From this junction, descend to an inclined bridge that spans Thompson Creek where Natural Bridge Creek joins it on your right at 0.3 mile. The trail then passes through the bottomland of rhododendron, laurel, and small hemlocks between the two creeks. Ascend into a drier forest of laurel and pine, cross a region of thin soil and exposed rock with reindeer moss, and follow a ridge up to a junction at 0.6 mile. From here you can keep to the left to hike over the bluff or to the right to walk under the bluff; walking under the bluff is more interesting, so stay to the right.

The trail drops below the bluff line. Pass several overhangs in a rock wall on your left; at 0.7 mile the trail passes under a small rock shelter. Finally, ascend to a junction with the over-bluff route at 0.9 mile. If you are out for a shorter hike, you can use this under-bluff/over-bluff loop to return to the trailhead for a walk of 1.8 miles.

To complete the Ridge Trail, continue straight in a hardwood forest atop the ridge. Ascend to pass through an understory of young pines at 1.2 miles. The trail curves right to encounter a rock bluff. Bear left to pass along the bluff and then turn right to climb to the top. You'll see an old road to the left, but stay right to walk along the edge of the bluff. At 1.4 miles the trail begins a descent from the bluff and then curves right to head back toward the park. The trail bottoms out in a hollow and sinkhole area at 1.7 miles. Ascend slightly into a more moist area and reach a ford of Natural Bridge Creek at 1.8 miles. If the water is up, you'll have to wade.

From the ford, the trail follows a small tributary upstream. The trail curves right and left to reach the bluff above Natural Bridge Creek. The trail curves left to pass through a couple of hollows and once more reach the bluff above the creek; you'll see bare rock at the bluff edge on your right at 2.4 miles.

The trail swings through another hollow and crosses the boundary from the state forest back into the state park and drops to a junction with the Lake View Trail at 2.8 miles. Turn right. Cross the bridge over Thompson Creek and close the loop at 2.9 miles. Turn left to walk back to the trailhead at 3.0 miles.

94 | HIDDEN PASSAGE TRAIL 🚶🚶

Distance: 10.0-mile loop *(side trip to Double Falls 1.0 mile one-way)*
Difficulty: Moderate
Elevation change: 100 ft
Cautions: High bluffs, stream crossings
Connections: Rock Creek Trail 🚶🚶, Sheltowee Trace 🚶🚶, John Muir Trail 🚶🚶, Tunnel Trail 🚶🚶

Attractions: Small arches, waterfalls, numerous rock shelters, and the Hidden Passage make this one of the most interesting trails in Pickett State

Hidden Passage (photo by Sondra Jamieson)

Park and Forest. The hidden passage is the way through a jumble of boulders under a low overhang along the trail, which also passes Crystal Falls and a side trail to Double Falls. Camping is permitted on this trail; register at the park office.

Trailhead: Head north from the park office on TN 154. In 0.3 mile you'll see the Hidden Passage Trailhead on the right. There's room for two vehicles to park.

Description: As you walk into the woods to begin the Hidden Passage Trail, you'll find the way marked with green blazes and occasionally the shape of a white turtle. The turtle signifies that this is also part of the Sheltowee Trace National Recreation Trail, which travels south from Kentucky through the northwest portion of the BSFNRRA to end at Pickett State Rustic Park. This part of the Hidden Passage Trail is also one alternative ending of the JMT.

The trail passes through woods of pine, mixed hardwood, and laurel. In spring you'll notice birdfoot violets, yellow star grass, and bluets. Climbing fern decorate the shrubs as Thompson Creek flows downstream on your right, creating a gorge that grows deeper as you continue on the trail.

Follow a side creek upstream and cross at a spillway. The hollow of the stream contains hemlock and rhododendron. This stretch of trail is typical of the Hidden Passage Trail, meandering across the top of the plateau in predominantly pine and mixed hardwoods and periodically dropping into coves where the hemlock and rhododendron predominate.

At 0.5 mile is the junction with the loop part of the trail; you can walk left or right, but the best approach is to walk right, hiking counterclockwise. You'll soon encounter a small arch created by a short column of rock supporting an overhang. Turn right and descend to a large overhang where the passageway through rocks is somewhat hidden, from which the trail gets its name.

At 0.7 mile, a short side trail takes you down to the foot of Crystal Falls. This tributary spills down two steps into a green pool of water before making its way toward Thompson Creek.

Back on the main trail, climb up stone steps and cross the stream just above Crystal Falls. Watch your step. The trail parallels the gorge for a time and then turns away from the rim. The loop periodically swerves from the edge of the gorge but later returns.

At 1.3 miles, the trail reaches a bare rock overlook of the gorge and then turns away from the gorge edge. Cross a jeep road at 1.5 miles. Then at 1.8 miles the trail swings right while a side trail to the left leads to a low rock shelter. From here the trail passes many rock shelters and overhangs, some quite large and long. Many of these have benches inside, built by the Civilian Conservation Corps in the 1930s when the park was being developed out of Stearns Coal and Lumber Company land donated to create the park and forest.

At 2.1 miles, dip into a long rock hollow sheltered by thick rhododendron and with a wet-weather waterfall in the center. When you emerge, watch for a huge hemlock balanced at an angle on your left. At 2.4 miles the trail passes under a powerline.

At 2.8 miles is a narrow section of trail with a rock bluff on the left and Thompson Creek Gorge on the right. Around a point, pass a long rock overhang and then a long rock wall. At 3.2 miles, the trail crosses a stream on a stone walkway. Then at 4.0 miles there's a large rock shelter that sweeps around in a 180-degree curve; a small waterfall spills from the lip of rock overhead. After another rock overhang, at 4.2 miles, is the 1-mile side trail to Double Falls, which is on a tributary of Thompson Creek.

This side trail, marked with a white blaze, drops from the bluff to Thompson Creek at 0.7 mile. Keep following the trail and you'll reach a fork where you can turn down to the creek across from the confluence of a tributary. To get to Double Falls, stay left. The trail descends to the creek, which you must wade across unless the weather has been dry. The trail then curves right to follow the tributary upstream to a rock alcove that contains the picturesque two-step waterfall, each drop about 10 feet.

From the junction with the side trail to Double Falls, switchback up and walk along the bluff to Thompson Overlook at 4.4 miles, where you'll have views of the gorge. You'll find the end of a road that has come from the Group Camp in the park; vehicles are not allowed past the Group Camp. You can shorten your walk by taking this road left.

At 5.0 miles, cross a stream on a bridge and come to a junction with the Rock Creek Trail marked by a brown blaze. Both the Sheltowee Trace and the JMT leave the Hidden Passage Trail at this point, following the Rock Creek Trail to the right.

After this junction, the trail switchbacks up, crosses a jeep road, and switchbacks down

Crystal Falls

into a hollow to a junction with the 1-mile Tunnel Trail marked with a blue blaze at 5.4 miles. This side trail leads to an abandoned railroad tunnel and to a junction with the Rock Creek Trail.

From the Tunnel Trail junction, switchback up and walk along the bluff of Rock Creek Gorge. The trail bears away from the gorge, crosses a jeep road, and passes under a powerline at 6.2 miles, circling back to the left. At 7.5 miles, emerge onto the road running from the Group Camp to Thompson Overlook to the left. Turn right and walk down the dirt road to the Group Camp; bear left around the compound until at 8.5 miles the trail turns left off the road to reenter the woods. Walk along the top of a circular rock wall and at the far end pass over a small arch.

The trail descends to a rock shelter and at 9.1 miles crosses a stream at the top of a small falls. The trail ascends, crosses an old road, and drops to the junction at 9.5 miles where you first encountered the loop. It's then a half mile back to the trailhead.

95 ROCK CREEK TRAIL 🚶🚶

Distance: 8.4 miles one-way
Difficulty: Moderate
Elevation loss: 250 ft
Cautions: Dropoffs, steep downhill, numerous creek fords
Connections: Hidden Passage Trail 🚶🚶, Rock Creek Loop 🚶🚶,
Tunnel Trail 🚶🚶, John Muir Trail 🚶🚶, Sheltowee Trace 🚶🚶

Attractions: This trail descends to Rock Creek, which has a mostly rock bottom for which it is named. Total hiking distance from the trailhead with access on the Hidden Passage Trail is 13.4 miles. The Rock Creek Trail can be combined with the Hidden Passage and Tunnel Trails for a round-trip hike of 15 miles from the trailhead. Good camping sites lie beside Rock Creek; register at the park office.

Trailhead: North from the park office on TN 154, turn into the Hidden Passage Trail parking area on the right at 0.3 mile. Then hike the Hidden Passage Trail 5.0 miles to a junction with the Rock Creek Trail on the right.

Description: Turn east off the Hidden Passage Trail, half a mile north of Thompson Overlook, onto the Rock Creek Trail, which has a brown blaze. Both the JMT and the Sheltowee Trace coincide with the Rock Creek Trail.

The trail skirts the northern edge of a hollow containing a small creek. You'll hear a waterfall in the grotto below, except during the dry season. At 0.5 mile you'll reach the gorge of Thompson Creek and curve left to follow the bluff high above the creek with steep dropoffs to the right. Along the way, a few stone steps take you to a higher level.

At 0.8 mile, the trail joins a faint road and turns right to follow the old roadbed down a ridge into the gorge. The trail turns left off the roadbed at 1.1 miles in a steep descent to a more level area above the creek and then another steep descent to Thompson Creek; the descent includes a step down a rock shelf that's slippery in wet weather. The trail then leads left down Thompson Creek in hemlock and rhododendron. At 1.4 miles, Thompson Creek flows into Rock Creek.

The trail turns upstream along Rock Creek to a ford at 1.5 miles. On the other side is a junction with the JMT/Sheltowee Trace to the right (the Rock Creek Loop lies 0.2 mile to the right). Turn left to complete the Rock Creek Trail, headed upstream. This part of the Rock Creek Trail is an alternative for completing the John Muir and Sheltowee Trace Trails into the state park and forest. The trail follows an old lumbering railbed remaining from when the Stearns Coal and Lumber Company operated in the region. At times, the trail goes along the creek edge. At 1.8 miles the trail is almost in the creek, and it may be covered in high water, in which case you must find a place to climb around or wade in the creek.

Pass along a rock bluff to a junction with the Tunnel Trail at 2.5 miles. The Rock Creek Trail turns right at this junction and the Tunnel Trail heads steeply down to a creek ford and then up the other bank to an abandoned railroad tunnel carved into the rock ridge (passing through the tunnel is not recommended). The Tunnel Trail, which does not pass through the tunnel but turns right to pass up and over it, can be used to loop back to the Hidden Passage Trail. This makes a good 5-mile loop hike from the beginning of the Rock Creek Trail, a total of 15 miles round-trip from the trailhead.

From the junction with the Tunnel Trail, continue on the Rock Creek Trail by turning right along a rock wall with the creek below on the left. Drop steeply into a ravine with a small waterfall in an alcove to the right. At 2.6 miles the trail drops steeply again to ford a small tributary of Rock Creek, and later another tributary stream runs under the trail in a culvert. At 2.7 miles is a junction with the path to the left that passes through the tunnel; a bridge takes you over Rock Creek to the mouth of the tunnel.

Stay right at the junction to continue on the trail, following the old railbed again. Ford Rock Creek at 2.8 miles. At 3.0 miles, step over a trickle of water that runs across the trail; it forms a small waterfall to your left. Ford the creek again at 3.2 miles and walk up a washed-out area where the trail turns left. The trail then curves right to stay on the old railbed; pass a road to the right and then reach another ford of Rock Creek at 3.3 miles.

The trail leads up to a gravel road; turn right on the road to a parking area and a road that leads left up to TN 154 at 3.4 miles. Here is secondary access for the trail that is north of the beginning of the Hidden Passage Trail; pass the Group Camp on the right along the way. On TN 154, turn north to walk across the road bridge over Rock Creek and then turn left off the road back into the woods, now following a double blaze of blue and white.

At 3.5 miles, ford Rock Creek, the first of 29 crossings in the next 4 miles of this section of trail, along with several crossings of small side streams. At low water, you can rockhop most crossings; at times of high water, the trail is impassable, so you should not attempt this section.

This Rock Creek Trail/JMT alternative continues to follow the old railbed along Rock Creek; it often runs along an artificial ridge on which the narrow-gauge railroad ran.

After crossing 11 at 5.2 miles, you'll come to some metal pieces left from the railroad operation. At crossing 18 at 6.1 miles, you'll see a rail lying beside the trail. After crossing 22 at 6.8 miles, notice that the creek flows under massive boulders, creating a passageway. Make crossing 25 at 7.3 miles on a swinging bridge. At crossing 28 at 7.6 miles, you'll see the remains of a wooden bridge just downstream; there would have been bridges at all the crossings when the railroad was operating. Make crossing 29 at 7.7 miles on a wooden bridge. Afterward, the trail turns up left to leave Rock Creek.

Ascend through a drier forest and emerge on Boundary Road at 8.4 miles. You can access this trail from the west end on Boundary Road, a gravel road marked by a stone pillar off TN 154 south of the park entrance and south of Divide Road; at 3.7 miles along this road, which follows the boundary of Pickett State Forest, you'll find the trailhead on the right.

96 | TUNNEL TRAIL 🚶🚶

Distance: 1.0 mile one-way
Difficulty: Moderate
Elevation loss: 225 ft
Cautions: Creek ford
Connections: Hidden Passage Trail 🚶🚶, Rock Creek Trail 🚶🚶

Attractions: This short connecting trail passes by a couple of small arches and takes you to an old railroad tunnel. Total hiking distance from the trailhead is 6.4 miles one-way.

Trailhead: North from the park office on TN 154, turn into the Hidden Passage Trail parking on the right at 0.3 mile. Then hike the Hidden Passage Trail 5.4 miles to a junction with the Tunnel Trail on the right.

Description: The Tunnel Trail, with a blue blaze, descends north from the Hidden Passage Trail. The trail curves left in its descent to pass over a ridge and switchback right. The trail then curves left, eventually passing around the point of a ridge to arrive at a rock wall and a wooden bench at 0.1 mile. Facing the rock wall, you will see a small arch up to the left.

The trail then follows the wall, gradually descending and passing a small rock shelter. At 0.2 mile is a

Railroad tunnel

Small, intricate arch beside Tunnel Trail

rock overhang with another bench. A small arch there has four openings. The trail begins descending again at 0.3 mile.

Toward the end of your descent, pass over the old railroad tunnel and circle right and down to stand in front of the tunnel at 0.9 mile. The tunnel was carved through the rock for a rail line (passing through the tunnel is not recommended). The Tunnel Trail turns left away from the tunnel and drops steeply to a ford of Rock Creek and then ascends the opposite bank to a junction with the Rock Creek Trail at 1.0 mile. The Tunnel, Rock Creek, and Hidden Passage Trails form a 5-mile loop hike, 15 miles from the Hidden Passage Trailhead.

97 | LADDER TRAIL / BLUFF TRAIL 👥

Distance: 1.8-mile loop
Difficulty: Moderate
Elevation change: 130 ft
Cautions: Ladders, creek ford
Connections: Hidden Passage Trail 👥, Lake Trail 👥

Attractions: Rock overhangs and ledges adorn Thompson Creek. The Ladder Trail uses ladders to descend into the small Thompson Creek Gorge and climb back out.

Trailhead: Head north from the park office on TN 154. In 0.3 mile you'll see the Hidden Passage Trailhead on the right. There's room for two vehicles to park.

Description: From the parking area, walk south back down the road and cross Thompson Creek on the highway bridge. At 0.1 mile, turn right on the Ladder Trail. Just up the road, you'll see another access to the Ladder Trail, but take this first trail.

Follow the brown blaze of the Ladder Trail on a bluff above Thompson Creek. A rock wall lines the trail on the left. At 0.2 mile, the trail drops below a tall rock bluff to emerge on a shelf over the creek. Climb down a metal ladder to get to creek level; the stream flows under the ladder. At the bottom, continue for several yards to a ford back across the creek. Climb a wooden ladder to get back on the rock shelf.

The trail continues along the rock wall, passing a wooden bench below an overhang and then another. Pass beyond the rock wall for a walk in the woods to a four-way junction at 0.6 mile. The trail to the left is the connector that leads out to TN 154 just up the road from where you began the Ladder Trail; use the connector if the water is up in Thompson Creek. The middle trail leads 0.1 mile up to the campground at site 13. To continue on the loop hike, take the right trail that leads down to a junction with the Lake Trail at 0.7 mile. Then turn right to cross a bridge over Thompson Creek.

At 0.8 mile is the junction with the Bluff Trail. Turn right. The yellow-blazed Bluff Trail follows the bluff above Thompson Creek downstream. Cross footbridges over side streams, pass rock overhangs, rest on benches along the way. At 1.3 miles, the trail crosses a small footbridge that spans water running off the rock wall. Turn steeply up to the left. The trail soon forks; stay to the right. The left fork is an old route that is now abandoned; above, you'll see where it comes back to the present trail. Then the trail stays fairly level through the woods to emerge on TN 154 at 1.8 miles. You'll see to the right just down the road the Hidden Passage Trailhead where the loop hike began.

98

KENTUCKY VIEW 🚶🚶

Distance: 0.2-mile loop
Difficulty: Easy
Elevation change: 60 ft
Cautions: Dropoffs
Connections: None

Attractions: This short walk offers a grand view north into Kentucky.

Trailhead: North from the park headquarters along TN 154, turn left at

3.5 miles on the gravel Kentucky Cut-Off Road. Watch for parking and the trailhead on the right in another 2.0 miles.

Description: Walk up the trail into the woods. In 100 yards is a junction that is the loop part of the trail. Turn right to walk the loop counterclockwise.

The trail skirts the edge of a bluff to reach the point of the ridge and a view north at 0.1 mile. You'll have a sweeping view down Flint Fork Cove into Kentucky.

Continue on the loop to circle back to the junction; watch for massive rock walls in the cove to your right. Then retrace your steps back to the trailhead.

99 | COFFEE TRAIL 🚶🚶

Distance: 0.5 mile one-way
Difficulty: Moderate
Elevation loss: 300 ft
Cautions: Steep descent, creek ford
Connections: Rock Creek Loop 🚶🚶, Sheltowee Trace 🚶🚶, John Muir Trail 🚶🚶

Attractions: This trail provides short access to the Rock Creek Loop in the BSFNRRA.

Trailhead: At 4.6 miles north of the state park visitor center on TN 154, turn right on Coffee Road, a dirt road that may be passable to passenger cars in dry weather. If the road is muddy, park wherever you can and walk the road 1.2 miles to Coffee Overlook. The trees have grown up at the overlook so that you do not have much of a view, but you can see the bluffs above Rock Creek through the trees. The trail begins to the right, blazed orange.

Description: The trail descends from the road to a house-sized boulder sitting on the point of the ridge. Turn right here to descend steeply and curve left toward Rock Creek. At 0.3 mile, the trail levels off and then descends again to the floodplain of the creek; turn right to cross a small side creek above its confluence with Rock Creek. Then cross the boundary into the BSFNRRA. The trail follows a low ridge along Rock Creek, part of the old Stearns lumbering rail line that once operated in this gorge.

The trail soon turns left off the old railbed to a ford of Rock Creek and, on the other side, a junction with the Rock Creek Loop. This is also the Sheltowee Trace and the JMT; all three trails coincide here.

Kentucky View

100 | BUFFALO ARCH / PARKER MOUNTAIN TRAIL 👣

Distance: 2.0 miles one-way *(Buffalo Arch 0.4 mile one-way)*
Difficulty: Moderate
Elevation loss: 100 ft
Cautions: Stairs down a bluff
Connections: Sheltowee Trace 👣

Attractions: On Daniel Boone National Forest land north of Pickett State Rustic Park, this route connects with Rock Creek and the Sheltowee Trace after a side trip to Buffalo Arch. The huge arch, with a clearance of 19 feet and a span of 82 feet, is actually at the end of a ridge. The ridgeline descends across the back of the arch into the small valley created by the Right Fork of Pennington Branch, so the arch looks like a flying buttress holding up the hillside.

Trailhead: From the Pickett State Park office, drive north on TN 154 5.1 miles to the Kentucky State line. In another 0.3 mile, turn right on the gravel FDR 562 and enter Daniel Boone National Forest, which abuts the BSFNRRA on the north. In another 0.8 mile, turn right on FDR 6305, a dirt road that's not marked. Because of the roughness of the road from here on, you may not want to proceed without four-wheel drive, although it should be passable in dry weather; if you park here, do not block the road. Walk down the dirt road, which makes a sharp downhill curve to the right. Stay with the dirt road until at 0.3 mile you reach the Parker Mountain Trailhead on the left.

Description: Before walking the Parker Mountain Trail, keep straight on the road to Buffalo Arch. Soon an overgrown side

Buffalo Arch

road leads to the left; keep straight. At 0.3 mile is a turnaround in the road, although the road actually keeps going. The Buffalo Arch Trail heads into the woods on the right. The trail descends left into a cove, crosses a small creek over a metal culvert, and ends under the arch at 0.4 mile.

Retrace your steps back to the beginning of the Parker Mountain Trail and head up the path. At 0.2 mile from the trailhead, the path parallels an old logged area to the left, and you'll soon cross a road. Soon after, the trail crosses the trace of another road. At 0.8 mile, skirt the logging road to cross a side road and stay on the path into the woods; watch for white diamond blazes to stay on the trail. Soon after, the trail veers left.

Begin a gradual descent at 1.3 miles. The trail swings right to a switchback left and then reaches a set of stairs at 1.5 miles that descends a low bluff. Drop into a hollow where a small wet-weather waterfall spills down the rock wall. At the bottom of the stairs, turn right. The trail then curves left to a flight of stone steps that drop among large boulders and rock walls to curve right again.

At 1.6 miles, swing under a low overhang on the left. The trail crosses a small stream emerging from rocks and then another emerging from under a huge boulder. Circle right to cross the second drainage again and descend to a gravel road at 2.0 miles. This is FDR 137 that parallels Rock Creek below. You can walk to the left to reach the Great Meadows Campground in 2.8 miles. Or you can walk to the right for 0.1 mile to where the road swings down to a ford of Rock Creek and connects with the Sheltowee Trace on the other side.

To drive to this end of the Parker Mountain Trail, continue north on FDR 562 from the turnoff for the Parker Mountain Trail for 7.0 miles to the beginning of FDR 137. Or if you are coming from the north on KY 1363 from the Yamacraw Bridge, when the pavement ends, bear right on the gravel FDR 564 to the junction of FDR 562 and 137. Then head down FDR 137 for 7.0 miles past the Hemlock Grove Picnic Area and the Great Meadows Campground to the junction with the Parker Mountain Trail.

SELECTED REFERENCES

Des Jean, Tom. "Prehistory: Introduction and Conceptual Framework." Unpublished paper, National Park Service, Big South Fork National River and Recreation Area, n.d.

Howell, Benita J. *A Survey of Folklife Along the Big South Fork of the Cumberland River.* Knoxville: University of Tennessee Press, 1981.

Humphrey, Steve E. "The History of the No Business and Station Camp Communities." Unpublished manuscript, National Park Service, Big South Fork National River and Recreation Area, 1981.

Manning, Russ. *Exploring the Big South Fork, A Handbook to the National River and Recreation Area.* Norris, Tennessee: Mountain Laurel Place, 1994.

————. *The Historic Cumberland Plateau, An Explorer's Guide.* 2d edition. Knoxville: University of Tennessee Press, 1999.

National Park Service. *Roads and Trails Management Plan Draft.* Big South Fork National River and Recreation Area, 1995.

Stanley, Steven M. *Earth and Life Through Time.* New York: W. H. Freeman, 1986.

Thomas, J. Patrick. *Lore & Legend, History Magazine,* Vol. 1 No. 1, 1989. Devoted to the history of the Stearns Coal & Lumber Company.

U.S. Army Corps of Engineers. *Big South Fork General Design Memorandum* and *Final Environmental Impact Statement.* Nashville: 1976.

Land Managers

Big South Fork National River and Recreation Area
4564 Leatherwood Road
Oneida, TN 37841
www.nps.gov/biso
931-879-3625 (Bandy Creek Visitor Center)
606-376-5073 (Kentucky Visitor Center)
606-376-3787 (Blue Heron Mining Community)
931-879-4869 (Bandy Creek Campground and Group Camps)
423-569-9778 (Park Headquarters)
800-365-2267 (camping reservations) or http://reservations.nps.gov

Pickett State Rustic Park
Rock Creek Route, Box 174
Jamestown, TN 38556
931-879-5821

Stearns Ranger District
Daniel Boone National Forest
P.O. Box 429
Whitley City, KY 42653
606-376-5323

Attractions and Activities

Bandy Creek Stables
1845 Old Sunbright Road
Jamestown, TN 38556
931-879-4013

Big South Fork Scenic Railway
P.O. Box 368
Stearns, KY 42647
800-462-5664

Big South Fork Horse Camps
P.O. Box 4411
Oneida, TN 37841
423-569-3321

Historic Rugby, Inc.
P.O. Box 8
Rugby, TN 37733
423-628-2430

Lodging

Charit Creek Lodge
250 Apple Valley Road
Sevierville, TN 37862
865-429-5704

EMERGENCY SERVICES

Fentress County Ambulance
931-879-8147

Fentress County General Hospital
West Central Avenue
Jamestown, TN
931-879-8171

Fentress County Sheriff
931-879-8142

McCreary County Ambulance
606-376-5062

McCreary County Sheriff
606-376-2322

Scott County Ambulance
423-569-6000

Scott County Hospital
Highway US 27
Oneida, TN
423-569-8521

Scott County Sheriff
423-663-2245

CHAMBERS OF COMMERCE

Fentress County Chamber of Commerce
P.O. Box 1294
Jamestown, TN 38556
www.jamestowntn.org
931-879-9948

McCreary County Tourism Commission
P.O. Box 72
Whitley City, KY 42653
606-376-3008

Scott County Chamber of Commerce
P.O. Box 4442
Oneida, TN 37841
800-645-6905

Russ Manning began his career as a science writer, but for the past ten years has devoted his attention to travel and outdoor subjects. He has authored several books about the Southeast, including *75 Hikes in Virginia's Shenandoah National Park; 100 Hikes in the Great Smoky Mountains National Park;* and *40 Hikes in Tennessee's South Cumberland.* He has also written over 200 articles for such magazines as *Outside, Backpacker, The Tennessee Conservationist, Appalachia,* and *Environmental Ethics.*

THE MOUNTAINEERS, founded in 1906, is a nonprofit outdoor activity and conservation club, whose mission is "to explore, study, preserve, and enjoy the natural beauty of the outdoors . . . . " Based in Seattle, Washington, the club is now the third-largest such organization in the United States, with 15,000 members and five branches throughout Washington State.

The Mountaineers sponsors both classes and year-round outdoor activities in the Pacific Northwest, which include hiking, mountain climbing, ski-touring, snowshoeing, bicycling, camping, kayaking and canoeing, nature study, sailing, and adventure travel. The club's conservation division supports environmental causes through educational activities, sponsoring legislation, and presenting informational programs. All club activities are led by skilled, experienced volunteers, who are dedicated to promoting safe and responsible enjoyment and preservation of the outdoors.

If you would like to participate in these organized outdoor activities or the club's programs, consider a membership in The Mountaineers. For information and an application, write or call The Mountaineers, Club Headquarters, 300 Third Avenue West, Seattle, Washington 98119; (206) 284-6310.

The Mountaineers Books, an active, nonprofit publishing program of the club, produces guidebooks, instructional texts, historical works, natural history guides, and works on environmental conservation. All books produced by The Mountaineers are aimed at fulfilling the club's mission.

Send or call for our catalog of more than 300 outdoor titles:

 The Mountaineers Books
1001 SW Klickitat Way, Suite 201
Seattle, WA 98134
1-800-553-4453
mbooks@mountaineers.org
www.mountaineersbooks.org

Other titles you may enjoy from The Mountaineers:

40 HIKES IN™ TENNESSEE'S SOUTH CUMBERLAND, 3rd Edition,
Russ Manning
Full of trails in this remote and beautiful region between Knoxville and Nashville. Guide contains sections on history, plants and animals, and geology.

100 HIKES IN™ THE GREAT SMOKY MOUNTAINS NATIONAL PARK, 2nd Edition, *Russ Manning*
Escape the crowds with the best backcountry trail advice for the Smoky Mountains. This completely updated and expanded guide offers more than 30 new hikes, making it the most complete guidebook to the region.

100 HIKES IN™ SERIES: These are our fully detailed, best-selling hiking guides with complete descriptions, maps, and photos. Chock-full of trail data, safety tips, and wilderness etiquette.
100 HIKES IN™ WASHINGTON'S ALPINE LAKES, 2nd Edition
100 HIKES IN™ WASHINGTON'S GLACIER PEAK REGION: THE
    NORTH CASCADES, 3rd Edition
100 HIKES IN™ WASHINGTON'S NORTH CASCADES NATIONAL
    PARK REGION, 2nd Edition
100 HIKES IN™ WASHINGTON'S SOUTH CASCADES AND
    OLYMPICS, 3rd Edition
100 HIKES IN™ THE ALPS, 2nd Edition
100 HIKES IN™ ARIZONA
100 HIKES IN™ NORTHERN CALIFORNIA
100 HIKES IN™ CALIFORNIA'S CENTRAL SIERRA AND COAST RANGE
100 HIKES IN™ THE INLAND NORTHWEST
100 HIKES IN™ OREGON

A HIKER'S COMPANION: 12,000 Miles Of Trail-Tested Wisdom,
Cindy Ross & Todd Gladfelter
An entertainingly written real-life guide to surviving and thriving in the outdoors. Gathers the best trail secrets, tips, and techniques into one easy reference for hikers and backpackers of all abilities.

STAYING FOUND: The Complete Map & Compass Handbook, 2nd Edition, *June Fleming*
An easy-to-use, unified map-and-compass system including instruction on route planning and winter navigation.

GPS MADE EASY: Using Global Positioning Systems in the Outdoors, 2nd Edition, *Lawrence Letham*
Never get lost in the outdoors again! This revised edition includes extensive new material on using GPS with maps and in rough terrain.